The TV
and Movie Business

Also by Harvey Rachlin

The Encyclopedia of the Music Business
The Songwriter's Handbook
The Money Encyclopedia (editor)
Love Grams
The Kennedys A Chronological History:
  1823–Present
The Songwriter's and Musician's Guide to
  Making Great Demos

The TV and Movie Business

An Encyclopedia of

Careers,

Technologies,

and Practices

by

Harvey Rachlin

Harmony Books
a division of Crown Publishers, Inc.
New York

Published by Harmony Books, a division of Crown Publishers, Inc., 201 East 50th Street, New York, New York 10022. Member of the Crown Publishing Group.

Harmony and colophon are trademarks of Crown Publishers, Inc.

Manufactured in the United States of America

Library of Congress Cataloging-in-Publication Data

Rachlin, Harvey.
    The TV and movie business / by Harvey Rachlin.
  —1st ed.
        p.   cm.
    1. Television broadcasting—United States—Dictionaries.
    2. Motion picture industry—United States—Dictionaries.   I. Title.
    PN1992.18.R3   1991
    384.55′03—dc20   90-47133
                                                          CIP

ISBN 0-517-57578-7
10 9 8 7 6 5 4 3 2 1

First Edition

For Aggy, Max, Pearl, and Sally

The TV
and Movie Business

INTRODUCTION

Whether we're sitting in front of a TV screen or a movie screen, we are being entertained by a "product" that entire industries revolve around and that requires the services and work of a wide variety of people. Indeed, whether we're watching a sitcom or a science-fiction movie, what is produced for our viewing pleasure or information is the result of much hard work and the concerned efforts of many.

There are many types of companies, distributors, associations, unions, guilds, professionals, craftspersons, technicians, personal representatives, manufacturers, and merchants that collectively form the television and movie industries, and they work under a system that involves collective bargaining, communications law, contract law, copyright law, trademark law, government regulation, and industry technical guidelines and specifications. It's a huge business, whose complex workings are covered in the pages ahead. I'll start here with a brief exploration of how a multitude of entities and persons function and serve in one way or another to bring or enable the dissemination of creative properties to the little or big screen for the enjoyment of the public.

Television programming is created by a variety of enterprises, including studios, independent production companies, networks, cable companies, and public broadcasters. The TV networks finance prime-time series, but producers of these shows usually do not profit unless the programming is sold for syndication. Syndicators sell off-network programs (reruns) to both affiliates and independent TV stations, which produce their own programming such as news shows and public-affairs programs.

What keeps the networks and TV stations in business is advertising revenues. Commercials are paid for by manufacturers, companies, retailers, professionals, and services. Advertising agencies represent the needs and business of corporations to the broadcasting community. Both ad agencies and production companies produce

1

commercials for clients. There are research companies that determine what audiences want to see and ratings services that measure the size of audiences watching programs.

Television broadcasters consist of the networks, affiliates, independent, cable, public TV, low-power, and other kinds of stations. Both network and station personnel include executives, programmers, producers, directors, reporters, writers, researchers, salespersons, promotion and public-relations people, engineers, technicians, accountants, and business affairs people. The number and duties vary from network to network or station to station.

The use of the airwaves is regulated by laws enforced by the Federal Communications Commission. Entities cannot legally operate as television stations or occupy a space in the broadcasting frequency spectrum without a license from the FCC, and licensed stations must comply with the rules and regulations set forth by the commission. The FCC is headed by five commissioners who are appointed by the President of the United States, with the consent of the Senate.

The motion picture industry aims to satisfy the viewing tastes and desires of a very broad audience, offering a menu of films of every genre, including romance, comedy, drama, mystery, spy, adventure, horror, Western, teen, and documentary. Today, feature films cost anywhere from a few million dollars to more than $30 million to make.

Many ideas for projects circulate at studios and independent production companies, but since the financial risks involved in making a film are so high, the projects are put in development, where scripts are rewritten and where it is decided if the projects indeed merit conversion into celluloid. For the independent producer, money must also be raised.

An independent producer tries to interest a studio in financing and distributing a film he or she wants to make. The studio may put up a portion of the production costs in exchange for the right to distribute the film and share in its revenues, and the producer may obtain the remainder of the financing by borrowing and other arrangements, such as selling off television, home video, and foreign

2

rights. Without a studio commitment, the producer can try to obtain all the financing privately, make the film, and then find a distributor.

To guarantee that independent movie productions will be shot according to a predetermined schedule and budget, there are completion bond companies. If necessary, they will raise supplementary financing to finish a production when costs exceed the budget.

Films and television movies and miniseries are often based on books, magazine articles, short stories, and theatrical shows. Properties are optioned and adapted, and if good fortune holds out, they will actually be produced. Profit participants include authors, playwrights, composers, lyricists, publishers, and agents.

To achieve a sense of realism on the screen, and, frequently, to reduce the cost of labor, films are shot on location. This often requires obtaining clearances, permits, or authorizations. Serving to promote regional or local geographical areas and to help expedite obtaining permissions are state and city film commissions.

Movies play in chain and independent movie theaters. Chains book their own films and booking services assist independent theater owners. Film rental fees are divided between the distributors and the theaters. Considerable income is also derived in theaters from the sale of popcorn, soft drinks, ice cream, and candy.

Both the television and motion picture industries utilize a vast array of creative talent, craftspersons, and technicians: actors, extras, stuntpersons, singers, dancers, composers, songwriters, lyricists, arrangers, orchestrators, directors, cinematographers, camerapersons, casting directors, editors, production designers, art directors, set designers, costume designers, makeup artists, hairdressers, special-effects persons, lighting technicians, sound technicians, boom operators, prop people, shop craftsmen, grips, and gaffers. Representing above-the-line people in productions are often agents, personal managers, attorneys, and business managers.

Minimum wages (*scale*) and terms of employment are established for the people who work on movie and TV productions by unions, which negotiate with employers through collective bargaining.

Trade and professional associations guide and protect the interests of professions, crafts, and industries. These associations maintain relationships with government agencies, support beneficial legislation, run seminars and workshops, hold regular meetings and conventions, and sponsor many other types of activities.

There are sundry equipment and materials that go into shooting: cameras, film, videotape, lighting equipment, diffusion gear, sound recorders, booms, dollies, and mounting equipment. These are generic headings and there are several different brands of each.

In postproduction, film and videotapes are processed in labs, optical houses, and editing studios. Prints are made, titles are added, sounds are mixed, and much more is done to achieve a final print from which copies will be made for theatrical distribution.

Trade publications report the latest news and events of one or more areas of the entertainment industry. These are essential for industry workers to keep up with the latest developments and activities. Critics work for both trade and consumer press, and their reviews of both new films and television programs influence company executives and the public.

Because motion pictures and TV shows are creative properties, their protection against infringement by others comes under the copyright law. The statute protects "original works of authorship fixed in any tangible medium of expression, now known or later developed, from which they can be perceived, reproduced, or otherwise communicated, either directly or with the aid of a machine or device." The copyright law may protect scripts, continuities, scenarios, motion pictures, background scores, songs, sound tracks, and recordings.

Very often characters from TV shows and movies become so popular that they are saturated into the fabric of pop culture, if only temporarily. Ready to fill the public demand for products bearing the image, name, or likeness of these characters (not to mention plenishing their own coffers) are manufacturers and merchandisers. Many different products may grace the shelves of emporiums, such as pajamas and posters, lunch boxes and notebooks, perfumes and toys. Trademark and other laws prevent manufacturers and merchandisers from freely making and selling products based on characters, shows, and movies and enable the copyright owners to profit from their creations.

Endorsements are another source of income for celebrities. Stars tout products ranging from orange juice to cars, as well as services such as stock brokerage firms. Agents negotiate deals for them and even a small breed of entrepreneur called a celebrity broker has arisen who uses his or her contacts to get stars quickly and at fair prices.

Film libraries supply stock footage such as sky shots, cities, explosions, fires, and animals for theatrical motion pictures, documentaries, news programs, TV specials, and commercials. Likewise, music libraries furnish background music and sound effects for all types of productions.

Performances of music on television generate royalties for the composers, lyricists, and publishers of these works. Performing-rights organizations license musical works on behalf of authors and copyright owners to broadcasters (television and radio networks and stations) and pay the creators periodically for performances of their compositions. The organizations each have their own methodologies and formulas for determining what compositions were performed, how often, and at what rates.

Home videos are a large and growing source of revenue for studios, producers, directors, stars, and others. Movies and other programming are licensed to distributors, who supply retail stores, which in turn rent or sell the videos. They are also sold to the public through video clubs and other mail-order businesses.

Of course, this brief overview has omitted various types of companies and professionals that constitute the television and motion picture industries. But there is no limit to how inclusive a survey of the entertainment industry could be; even airlines, railways, payroll services, and insurance companies could be included. All in all, a vast array of creative and business talent goes into making the dynamic and exciting TV and motion picture industries and their related fields.

ABC. ABC is one of the three major American television **networks.**
In 1943 Edward J. Noble purchased NBC's Blue Network, a chain
of radio stations, and formed the American Broadcasting System.
Later in the decade the broadcasting chain's future was significantly
altered by a federal government anti-trust decree which forced Paramount Pictures to give up Paramount Theaters. The theater chain
merged with the American Broadcasting Company when approval
was given by the Federal Communications Commission on February 9, 1953. Leonard Goldenson became president of the resulting
corporation, American Broadcasting–Paramount Theaters. The
board of directors of AB-PT voted in 1965 to change the firm's name
to American Broadcasting Companies Inc. Two decades later, Capital Cities Communications Inc. announced that it intended to
purchase ABC for $3.52 billion, and on January 3, 1986, the deal
was completed. The holdings of Capital Cities/ABC Inc. include
television stations, AM and FM radio stations, program services for
cable television, newspapers, and consumer and trade magazines.

Historically, ABC may be distinguished from CBS and NBC by
certain elements in its programming and business activities. As the
last of the three major networks to come into existence, ABC had to
succeed without established shows, or the stars who were already
under contract to the other networks. The network turned to the
motion picture studios and made television history by convincing
them that they should produce for the small screen as well as the
large screen. For the first time, Hollywood's major studios began
producing for network television, beginning with Walt Disney in
1954 and Warner Bros. in 1955. Later, it would become common
practice for the studios to produce television programs.

ABC pioneered programming for young adult audiences. This
began in the 1950s, and when ABC became the first-place network
in the mid-1970s, several of its prime-time series were targeted for
young audiences. Some credit the network with having pioneered
the miniseries. It broadcast TV's first miniseries, *QB VII*, in 1974.
In 1977 ABC broadcast *Roots* over seven nights, and achieved record
TV ratings. Through the years ABC has also been strong in its

daytime lineup and in sports. It has broadcast more Olympics than either of the other networks.

Traditionally, ABC has had a strong station group. In 1990 the network owned and operated eight TV stations, covering 24.45 percent of U.S. households with TV sets. In contrast, NBC had seven TV stations covering 22.35 percent, and CBS owned and operated five TV stations covering 20.8 percent.

ABOVE-THE-LINE. Above-the-line is a production budgetary term that refers to the costs for the major creative contributors or elements of a motion picture. Above-the-line contributors include the producer, director, principal cast, screenwriter, director of photography, and production designer; above-the-line elements may include the price of the rights to a book, magazine article, show, or title.

See also **Below-the-Line; Budget, Motion Pictures.**

ACADEMY AWARDS. Each year prizes of merit are bestowed by the **Academy of Motion Pictures Arts and Sciences** to recognize outstanding contributions to theatrical films. These prizes are known as the Academy Awards, and they are regarded as the most prestigious accolades given for movies, both within the industry and outside it.

The Academy Awards are presented at a ceremony that is televised in the United States and more than fifty other countries around the world. The first awards ceremony, held at the Hollywood Roosevelt Hotel on May 16, 1929, to honor films of the 1927–28 year, was attended by fewer than 250 people.

The categories of awards have varied through the years. Awards are now conferred for achievements in acting, art direction, cinematography, costume design, directing, documentaries, film editing, foreign-language films, music, short films, sound, visual effects, and writing. (There may be subdivisions within these categories.) Those that are given for Best Picture, Actor, Actress, Director, Screenplay, and Song have traditionally received the most attention.

There are special awards for outstanding contributions that do not fit in the standard categories. These are the Scientific or Technical Achievement Awards (for a method or invention of special value to films), the Special Achievement Awards (for an exceptional achievement for which there is no category), the Irving G. Thalberg Memorial Award (to a producer who has consistently made high-quality motion pictures), and the Jean Hersholt Humanitarian Award (to recognize humanitarian efforts of an individual employed in the film industry). These special awards are voted upon by the Academy's Board of Governors and do not have to be given each year. The Board of Governors may also present Honorary Awards for exceptional service in the making of films or for outstanding service to the Academy when an individual's achievements do not fall within any other category.

To qualify for an award, a film must have been released in Los Angeles between January 1 and December 31 of the previous year. Only movies exhibited by means of 35-mm or larger format film are eligible, although documentaries and short films are permitted to enter 16-mm film.

The winners are chosen by active members of the Academy. The voting procedure is as follows: Members of the various branches (film editors, actors, cinematographers, etc.) nominate up to five selections within their respective fields. Individuals and films receiving the most nominations are announced in February of each year. A period follows in which the Academy screens all the nominated films for its active membership so the films may be seen by everyone under the same screening conditions. (There are five exceptions to this procedure: foreign-language film, the two documentary categories, and the two short film categories. Members who vote for films in these categories must attest that they have seen all the nominated films.) The entire active membership of the Academy then votes on the nominations to determine the winners. The Academy mails secret ballots to an independent accounting firm. Winners are not announced until the awards are presented at the actual ceremony, which has been televised since 1952. Every winner receives an **Oscar** (except the winners of the two sci-tech categories, one of which receives an Academy plaque, the other an Academy certificate, and the Thalberg award, the winner of which receives a bust of Irving G. Thalberg).

The Academy Awards may mean more to the winners than merely the respect and attention that follow the ceremony, since an award may translate into greater revenues for the individuals and motion pictures concerned. Actors' fees have been known to increase substantially after the ceremony, and for some Best Pictures, an Academy Award has meant an additional $25 million or more at the box office.

ACADEMY OF CANADIAN CINEMA AND TELEVISION.
ACCT is a nonprofit professional association of actors, craftspersons, and technicians who work in the Canadian film and television industries. Organized in 1979, the Academy seeks to recognize the creative achievements of its members and to promote the Canadian motion picture and TV industries. The Academy annually presents the Genie Awards for outstanding achievements in motion pictures, the Gemini Awards for excellence in English-language television, and the Prix Gemeaux for achievement in French-language television.

ACADEMY OF MOTION PICTURE ARTS AND SCIENCES.
AMPAS is a professional association of motion picture artists and craftspersons dedicated to furthering the arts and sciences of film. The Academy conducts many activities and programs but is best known for its annual presentation of the Academy Awards.

Regular members of the Academy belong to one of its twelve branches: actors, directors, producers, writers, music, cinematographers, executives, publicists, art directors, film editors, sound technicians, and creators of short films. To qualify for membership, one must "have achieved distinction in the arts and sciences of motion pictures." This is gauged by such criteria as having been nominated for an Academy Award or having contributed to a film of high artistic caliber. A prospective member must be sponsored by a minimum of two persons from the appropriate branch and receive the endorsement of the branch executive committee. The nomination is then submitted to the Board of Governors for approval.

The Academy of Motion Picture Arts and Sciences was organized as a nonprofit corporation in 1927. As of 1990 the Academy had more than 4,700 voting members.

ACADEMY OF TELEVISION ARTS AND SCIENCES. A professional association whose purpose is to advance the television industry. There are separate classes of active membership for actors, writers, directors, craftspersons, and others who work in TV, and there are specific eligibility criteria for each category. The Academy sponsors the **Emmy Awards**, which is televised nationally each year. In 1990 the Academy had more than five thousand members.

ACCOUNTING DEPARTMENT (Films). *See* **Production Accountant.**

ACTION-ADVENTURE SHOW. *See* **Television Programming Genres.**

ACTOR. To viewers, acting may sometimes seem natural or effortless, but it is a demanding profession that requires both talent and perseverance. On a script page there may be lines and some stage directions, but it is ultimately up to the actor (with assistance from the director) to bring a character to life, to draw out its personality to such a degree that the actor is not overacting or underacting, but expressing just the amount of energy and emotion needed to best portray the character within the context of the story. Some directors begin in other trades (such as cinematography) and have little acting experience. They depend heavily on the actors they hire to create characters and provide subtext.

Acting is to a great extent a self-styled endeavor. Indeed, some thespians have no formal training and their approach is entirely instinctual. But acting is also a skill that can be taught and for which many forms of instruction exist.

One prominent (though controversial) system of technique is Method acting, originated by the Russian actor, director, and teacher Konstantin Stanislavsky (1863–1938), and used, taught, and expanded upon in the United States by such teachers as Lee Strasberg, Robert Lewis, and Stella Adler. Method acting involves analysis of the inner life of a play's characters—what they want of one another in the scenes—the theory being that if they pursue these goals, called "actions," and do so truthfully, the emotions generated by the fulfillment or frustration of the "actions" will be more believable than the emotions non-Method actors *imagine* will fit the scenes. The Method also uses such techniques as "emotion memory" and "sense memory" to arouse emotions from the actor's past for use in the actual production.

Because of the limited number of theatrical motion pictures (about five hundred) and television programs produced each year, the competition for employment among actors is keen. The **Screen Actors Guild (SAG)** alone has more than sixty thousand members. That is why talent alone is often not enough to ensure success. The aspiring actor must intelligently and assiduously seek out opportunities and bring to them confidence, perseverance, and a good attitude.

The function of actors' unions is to negotiate minimum wages and working conditions for actors. SAG and the **American Federation of Television and Radio Artists (AFTRA)** are the two main unions for performers working in film and television. Since many actors are versatile and work in other areas, they may be affiliated with other unions, such as **Actors' Equity Association (AEA)**, for legitimate theater including Broadway, touring companies, and repertory theater; the American Guild of Variety Artists (AGVA), for comedians, singers, and dancers working in resorts, cabarets, and nightclubs; the American Guild of Musical Artists (AGMA), for narrators, vocalists, dancers, and solo instrumentalists in grand opera, recital, ballet, and concert; and the American Federation of Musicians (AFM), for instrumentalists who perform on recordings, in commercials, TV films, TV videotape, and at clubs, hotels, and other locations.

12

For actors working in television shows and motion pictures, there are many sources of potential income. What an actor (or a representative) is able to negotiate in terms of fees and percentages (above scale) depends upon such factors as reputation, track record, and box-office potential.

An actor's prominence in motion picture and television productions is generally categorized according to the following types of roles: major, minor, cameo, bit, and extra. The leading actors—stars or principals—have the major roles or those with the most lines and camera coverage. Major roles offer the opportunity for actors to achieve a richness of characterization, to take the character beyond the script. Roles subordinate to those played by the principals offer fewer lines, although they afford the actor some opportunity to bring out personality. Stars making a brief appearance are said to have a cameo. Such roles are usually only incidental to the plot but serve to bring attention to the production by interjecting a view of an immensely popular personality. A bit part is one in which an actor has a few lines or a few words to say. It is much smaller than a minor role and there is little, if any, personality to bring out. An extra is someone seen in the background who has no lines. The person is more or less a "human prop," someone to fill in the scenes, to add realism to an event. There is a union for extras, the **Screen Extras Guild (SEG)**.

Being on the set of a motion picture or television production can be tedious for actors, as there is often much waiting around while lighting and cameras are being set up. If the director is spending hours on the lighting for a close-up of a star's face, a stand-in might substitute while the star waits in a dressing room. (Out of an eight-hour day, for instance, an actor may work only perhaps sixty minutes.) Sometimes, scenes are too dangerous for a principal and a **stuntman** fills in.

Another consideration for actors is the sequence of shooting. Since films are shot out of sequence, the middle or last scenes may be shot before the first ones. An actor then has to convey the emotional state appropriate at that point in the production. A conscientious actor breaks down the various scenes, analyzes what must be accomplished in each one, and then orchestrates an approach. An actor may screen the **dailies** to evaluate the previous day's performance. Sometimes an actor may be unhappy with a particular performance and request to do it over again. Doing a scene several times—multiple takes of different shots (wide angle, medium, and close-up)—requires much energy and can be taxing on an actor.

Some actors in highly rated television series cross over successfully to feature films. They have established a following and their popularity may translate into box-office revenues. Entertainment history is mixed, however, with success and failure stories in this regard. Some television actors have never been able to rise above the stereotypes they developed and become hits in films.

One of the actor's most challenging roles may be that of a savvy businessperson. The business of acting is complex and time-consuming, and for that reason actors delegate career-related responsibilities to specialized representatives. The **personal manager** oversees day-to-day affairs and provides advice and guidance, continually promoting the actor's career; the **agent** obtains employment contacts; the **business manager** handles financial affairs; the attorney negotiates contracts; the publicist serves to promote the actor favorably in the media (*see* **Public Relations**). In the final analysis, however, the actor is the master of his or her own fate and must make sure that these people create opportunities, assure career longevity, and maximize income.

Sources of income for actors include the following types of appearances:

- *Television shows and movies.* Income from work in TV or film usually comes in the form of daily or weekly union contract rates, although some actors have personal-service contracts for substantially more than the minimum fee. Income is also earned for guest appearances on series and talk shows. For films, some stars negotiate multiple picture deals worth several million dollars over a few years. In addition to salary, some stars also receive percentages of box-office

grosses or profits, after deductions for such items as advertising and prints.
- *Videocassettes.* Some actors earn royalties from videotapes sold for home use.
- *Commercials.* There are basic (union minimum) fees or negotiated fees, plus overtime and residuals.
- *Endorsements.* Fees are earned for endorsing products or serving as a spokesperson for them.
- *Merchandising rights.* Manufacturers (and license brokers) pay fees and royalties to make and distribute products based on popular actors and characters.
- *Cable and educational television.* Cable television, pay cable services, and educational TV stations produce original programming, providing additional work opportunities for actors. Corporate training films provide employment for professional actors, but remuneration is less than for feature films.

Some actors have additional income from such areas as scriptwriting, voice-overs, music, and publishing, as well as performing in legitimate theater. There are also actors who own production companies or direct. It is not uncommon for stars of TV series to earn additional income by directing episodes of their shows.

Actors pay percentages of their earnings (commissions) to agents and personal managers. The ranges of these commissions are set forth in those entries.

Winning an award may substantially increase an actor's renown and earnings. The **Emmy Awards** are presented annually to television actors, the **Academy Awards** to motion picture actors. They are among the most prestigious awards given in these respective fields.

Once an actor gains prominence, TV scripts, film scripts, endorsements, commercials, and much more may frequently be offered to him or her. Fees skyrocket and producers and studios eagerly seek the actor for their projects. Indeed, the power of a star is such that just his or her commitment to a project is enough for it to breeze through the normal impediments and be made into a TV pilot, series, or theatrical motion picture.

ACTORS' EQUITY ASSOCIATION. AEA, often referred to as Equity, is a labor union representing actors and stage managers in the live American theater, including Broadway, stock theater, regional theater, road companies, and industrial shows. Because many film and television actors also perform live onstage, they are members of Equity in addition to other unions.

There are three ways in which an actor may become a member of Equity: by receiving an Equity contract as a result of having been cast in a role from an open audition; by having worked approximately fifty weeks in an Equity theater (under the membership candidate program); or by being a member of another entertainment union (AFTRA, SAG, AGMA, AGVA, or SEG) for one year or more and having worked under that union's jurisdiction. There is an initiation fee to join Equity with dues payable every six months.

ACTORS' FUND OF AMERICA. AFA is a national charity organization whose services are available to performers, craftspersons, and technicians working in film, television, and other areas of the entertainment industry. The Actors' Fund distributes money on a confidential basis for needs such as medical care, professional mental-health counseling, and home living expenses. It also sponsors the Actors' Fund Home, a retirement facility in Englewood, New Jersey. The Actors' Fund runs charity benefits to help pay for its services.

ADAPTATIONS. Books, short stories, magazine articles, and plays are fecund sources of ideas or material for feature films, television movies, and miniseries, and yet a creative property in print or onstage will generally travel a long and complicated path before being brought to either a television or movie screen. There are many obstacles to hurdle and a single impediment along the way can cause the entire project to be abandoned.

Before **principal photography** even begins, a preexisting property must be deemed adaptable by a filmmaker, the rights must be procured, a satisfactory screenplay must be written, and financing must be obtained. These are all formidable considerations or undertakings. This entry examines each of these elements individually.

Adaptability. The question of whether a property can be adapted to the screen, and if so, how to do it, is the first one asked by the filmmaker. A novel, for example, is an intricate web of plot and subplots; major and minor characters; multiple settings; numerous themes and motifs; dialogue, inner thoughts, and narrative. A movie can't possibly duplicate a novel—to depict prose visually requires substantial modification—although it can be faithful to the original spirit of the book. This might mean retaining the story in general or a particular element of it, such as a theme or the adventures of an important character. Of course, a director or producer might create a new version of the story, perhaps drawing upon the original but with special focus or a cinematic emphasis.

A written work allows readers to read and stop reading as they choose. To interpret the essence of that work visually in a way that will satisfy viewers and keep them riveted to their seats for one or two hours is often difficult. The "voice" of an author may not reproduce well on the screen. A book or play can be very stylized, in a way unconducive to film adaptation.

What about the characters? Because filmmakers often need bankable stars in order to get financing for a picture, there may have to be substantial roles to draw leading male and female actors. Do the characters and story offer this possibility? Are the roles versatile enough that if some top actors turn them down other actors may be approached?

Indeed, it is usually not the goal of a filmmaker to copy a book or other property onto celluloid, but rather to give it a life of its own, distinct but intertwined with the original work—everything a movie can offer that the printed word cannot. A novel that is straightforward and proceeds in linear fashion is usually more appealing than one with flashbacks or other complex narrative devices.

Best-selling books and hit shows, while having garnered enthusiasm and large audiences, do not always make hit movies. Preexisting book audiences often do not translate into movie or television audiences.

Indeed, careful consideration must be given to the target movie or TV audience of a property. A book might appeal to a particular demographic group, but movies need to attract a much larger audience than books. Consequently, the transformation might require adapting the story, dialogue, action, and other elements for appreciation by a wide audience.

Successful plays are usually considered by Hollywood to be good candidates for adaptations. Many dramatic movies for over-thirty audiences are written by playwrights.

Contracts. Deals for properties are made in various ways. The author of a book usually owns all dramatic rights to the book, and the author's agent might try to sell the rights before or after publication. If the property is considered "hot," an auction might be held. In an auction the agent or publisher sends copies of the book out to a number of producers, who bid separately against one another under an imposed deadline, with a minimum bid set. The rights to musicals and straight plays are usually acquired only after the production has been mounted and proven a critical or box-office success.

The right to adapt a book for film is usually obtained on an option-purchase basis. An option is merely an arrangement in which a producer or some other party purchases the right to make a movie based on the book within an agreed-upon time frame. There is usually a fee paid, often ranging from $5,000 to $100,000, but if a movie based on the book is thought to have great potential, the rights can go for over one million dollars.

The option is no guarantee, however, that a book will get made into a movie. In fact, many optioned properties do not. At the end of the option period, the producer may negotiate anew with the property owner if the producer still intends to make the book into a movie. If the option is not renewed, the property owner is free to sell the movie rights to any other interested party. When an option is negotiated, it is usually a portion of an agreed-upon purchase price, the balance of which will be paid if the movie is actually made.

Whether a movie gets made depends upon many factors: whether financing can be raised, whether there is the support of a studio, whether a satisfactory screenplay is written, whether a top director and stars commit themselves.

A movie-adaptation contract may provide bonuses to be paid to the author if the book achieves certain distinction such as making a best-seller list or being chosen as a featured or alternate selection of the Literary Guild or Book-of-the-Month Club.

In transferring musicals to the screen, the financial terms may be more onerous for the producer. Instead of having to pay a fee to a single individual as the author of a book, the Dramatists Guild contract provides that the creators, composer, lyricist, and play-wright all share in remuneration. Because more parties are involved, the fee may have to be higher.

Screenplay. In general, the rule for adapting a property for the screen is to take the bare plot and characters and create a movie by building scenes, developing characters, conforming dialogue, add-ing elements of suspense, comedy, or drama (not to mention ac-tion), and devising spots for car chases, stunts, and special effects.

While novels may not have a steady pace throughout, a movie must. There generally must be constant movement and the script cannot get mired down with too much dialogue. There must be a definite structure.

There are authors who will protest on creative grounds to the "commercialization" of their works, but unless they have a contrac-tual right of approval (which is rare, unless they themselves are the screenwriters), they will have to go along with whatever changes are made.

Screenwriters often find it necessary to change various elements such as the age, profession, or personal background of characters, the setting, the mood, or one of the subplots. While all these ele-ments may be cut away, it is still possible to maintain the spirit of the property; indeed, that is usually the goal of a filmmaker.

Financing. The best situation for someone selling rights to a property is a deal made directly with a major studio or with a prominent producer who has a right of first refusal with a major studio. This means the producer is obliged to offer a property to a particular studio first. If that studio turns it down, the producer can take the project to another studio. But often an interested party who has taken an option on a property will have to raise the money him or herself, since the costs of making a movie and marketing it are so high (*see* **Financing a Film**). Investors are usually more amenable to getting involved when big-name stars and directors have already committed. In soliciting any of these parties, the filmmaker will use a treatment, or a script, if available. Once producers get all the necessary people to make a movie, they approach investors with the "package."

ADVERTISING IN MOVIES. There are two forms of theatrical motion picture product advertising: commercials that precede the exhibition of a film that audiences have paid to see, and the display of commercial products within the context of the movie. Both forms are controversial with critics maintaining that the moviegoing experience should not be tainted by any kind of commercial advertisement at all.

Individual commercials that precede a film are a source of revenue for theatrical exhibitors, who look for or need income from sources other than box-office receipts to maintain their businesses and to turn a profit. But some major motion picture studios frown upon the practice of showing their films with commercials. In the spring of 1990 two major Hollywood studios, Walt Disney and Warner Bros., forbid theaters in which their films played from exhibiting commercials (but not public service announcements). Research commissioned by Disney indicated that most viewers do not want to see commercials in theaters. The studios' action resulted in an investigation by the Federal Trade Commission for potential restraint of trade, which as of this writing has not been completed. Affected by the FTC decision will not only be theatrical exhibitors but advertisers and their agencies that produce the commercials and specialized companies that place commercials in theaters.

Advertising in movie theaters is desirable for companies that want to reach specific demographic audiences. A motion picture's subject matter and a theater's location enable companies to accurately predict the kinds of audiences who will be seeing films at particular theaters. And without the diversionary elements that can affect TV viewers, movie audiences' full attention stays with the screen.

To meet the high standards of theatrical motion picture exhibition, movie commercials have to be entertaining and of quality. Audiences may object to commercials which are mundane or overtly proselytizing. But those that are artistic, employing effective story lines and special effects or stunts may be well received as they may be perceived as cinematic shorts with a residual message of the promotion of a particular product. Indeed production costs may run into the millions. Some ad agency studies, contrary to movie studio–sponsored research, have found that exciting, theatrical commercials are received favorably by moviegoers.

A second form of movie advertising involves the display of a product within a movie. There is no direct pitch, but merely the strategic placement of a product or product's name in a setting. In some films, actors may even say a particular brand name. Many different kinds of products have been placed by advertisers in feature films, including cereal, soft drinks, jeans, perfumes, candy bars, coffee, cigarettes, beer, and shaving cream. In some movies, more than a dozen different products whose manufacturers have paid for their appearance, may be seen. Some products in movies are advertised by the display of their brand name in a sign.

In considering which movies to place their products in, most companies are concerned that the movie does not offend audiences or is not sexually, racially, ethnically, or nationally objectionable. Indeed, if the product is considered classy, the nature and content of the film is of paramount concern. Consequently, B movies are normally not considered appropriate choices for reputable products. Producers of low-budget films, however, as well as expensive features, seek fees for product placement in their pictures to help offset their production costs.

Fees are the normal form of compensation for product placement in a film, but other forms of remuneration may be used. For example, for prominently showing an outlet of a national fast-food chain in a movie, the chain may plug the movie in an advertising campaign.

Movies based on popular fictional characters for which there already exists a merchandising base are advertising vehicles themselves. The movie serves to promote any products associated with the characters including TV shows and comic books.

The display of commercial products in a theatrical motion picture has been criticized for compromising the creative process for financial consideration. A filmmaker may compromise elements of his film to conciliate advertisers, or the advertisers themselves may have input into the creative process. An advertiser may do a script breakdown and suggest spots where its product could be placed in an attempt, however discreetly, to grab the audience's attention. A scene or line may have to be altered for promotion of the product.

With the release for the home market in March 1987 of *Top Gun*, videocassettes of feature films have carried commercials and been considered an effective medium for carrying advertising messages. Remuneration may be for a fee or a promotional tie-in, as in the case of *Top Gun*, where the advertiser, Diet Pepsi, plugged the videocassette in its TV ads. While consumers may object to being bombarded with advertisements attached to theatrical motion pictures released on videocassette, the flip side of the coin is that the commercials often serve, by offsetting advertising or manufacturing fees or both, to lower the retail price of the videocassette.

Subliminal advertising was introduced to the motion picture arena in the late 1950s and has been the source of much controversy. Subliminal advertising is based on the idea that if a message is repeatedly flashed on a screen for such a brief duration that it is not consciously perceived, viewers will find themselves actually desiring what was flickered before them. Under this theory, for instance, popcorn sales at the movie theater candy counter could be increased by flashing a popcorn message. Its effectiveness was never actually proven and critics considered it less a form of advertising than an attempt at brainwashing.

ADVERTISING ON TELEVISION. Advertising is the primary source of income for television stations and the television networks; for many broadcasters it is the only source. Through the years, television advertising has been the target of much criticism, but one fact remains clear: Without it there could be no free television as we know it.

Indeed, there is a symbiotic relationship between the television and advertising industries. Television networks, affiliates, and commercial independent stations, whose revenues consist predominantly or exclusively of advertising fees, use these revenues to pay for their staff, overhead, and operating expenses, as well as their programming. Television, on the other hand, provides perhaps the most cost-effective medium for advertisers.

If there were no advertisements on television, the public certainly would not want the quality of programming to decrease, nor would it want less coverage of news and sports events. Yet as a commercial industry, how or where would the networks and TV stations acquire the funds to pay their expenses?

Television advertising may be divided into three categories: network, national spot, and local.

Network Television Advertising. Network advertising offers sponsors national exposure for their products since their commercials are broadcast by affiliates around the country. It is by selling advertising time that television networks and local television stations earn most of their income.

In March and April of each year, the networks hold conferences on the West Coast for key advertisers and agencies to describe programs in development for the coming year. The premises of the shows are given, along with information on the producers and cast. This procedure covers sitcoms, dramas, and adventure shows, as well as miniseries and made-for-television movies, and includes prime-time shows, news, sports, and daytime programs.

In May or June the networks announce to the advertising industry what shows will run the following fall and what their time slots will be. Advertisers and their agencies begin planning in which programs they would like to purchase time. The selling season for ad time, called the "up-front" market, begins as early as April and runs until July or early August. The shows' inventory they purchase at this time usually represent between 65 percent and 90 percent of all prime-time ad slots the networks aim to sell. The remaining inventory of the networks, called "scatter," is sold on a quarter-by-quarter basis.

The up-front market is the first sales opportunity the network has for the new season. It normally starts with a part of the day less important than prime time, such as Saturday morning. The network assesses the strength of its schedule in comparison to that of the other networks and predicts how this is going to translate into audience delivery over a full year's period of time.

The idea of the up-front market is to get clients to commit to advertising for a full year. For that commitment they get a lower rate than if they purchase later in the scatter market.

The network's decision of how much to sell in the up-front market is based on various factors, including, importantly, what it thinks the economy will be like. Then it determines how much to ask for spots and packages. Finally the network tries to lay in a certain amount of business in the up-front market that will take it through the year. This basically becomes the network's base that it works off of for the entire year. It doesn't have to sell these time slots anymore, unless a client wants to withdraw for some reason, in which case there might be a penalty to pay.

If the network's schedule is weak or it looks like the economy is going to be soft, principal advertisers may want to put their dollars elsewhere. The network therefore might want to establish a heavier up-front base and try to sell as much as 85 percent to 90 percent of its inventory.

If the network has what appears to be a strong schedule and the year ahead looks to be a bullish market, then it may gamble on the scatter market and sell less up-front. In the scatter market the network can get higher rates because advertisers aren't committing ahead of time. Practically speaking, the networks try to find the right mix of the up-front and scatter markets.

Because advertisers spend such substantial sums of money on the up-front advertising, the networks have in the modern television era promised to deliver certain minimum audiences. For example, a network might guarantee an advertiser that has committed $10 million an audience of one billion women ranging in age from eighteen to forty-nine. The cost-per-thousand women eighteen to forty-nine, then, would be ten dollars. If the show's audience turns out to be lower than guaranteed and the cost-per-thousand turns out to be eleven dollars, the network then produces additional advertising slots—known as make-goods—for the sponsor at no charge to bring the cost-per-thousand back down to ten dollars. The networks each have systems for holding back inventory to back up guarantees for shows whose ratings fail to match those promised. There are no audience delivery assurances, however, on the scatter market. (In June 1990, both ABC and NBC announced modifications in their advertising guarantee policies, which could effectively reduce or eliminate completely the make-goods they have offered.)

Sometimes a network might sell out its prime-time inventory for a particular quarter. An advertiser wishing to buy network ads in that time slot would then have to purchase time from another network or, if all the networks were sold out, might not be able to buy any airtime during prime time. As an alternative, the advertiser could commit to shows in other time periods, such as morning or late night, or purchase ad time in syndication or cable programs.

Advertising rates for particular shows are determined by ratings, but the price may increase or decrease depending on advertiser demand. Ad time for the 1988 Super Bowl went for approximately $600,000 for a thirty-second spot. The cost for the same spot during a prime-time show on a popular network may run anywhere from under $100,000 to $300,000 or more.

When advertisers purchase airtime, they usually are buying it to reach a target demographic audience, such as women eighteen to forty-nine, men eighteen to thirty-four, adults twenty-five to fifty-five, or teenagers. Thus, when an agency decides which network or networks from which to buy, it uses the cost-per-thousand against the target demographic audience as a measuring stick. This is compared to the quality of the package, or the mix of shows that each network has in its package. Advertising agencies and their clients work closely together in developing marketing objectives and strategies. This includes determining the demographics of audiences they want to reach through advertising.

National Spot Advertising. National companies not only advertise on the networks but on individual local TV stations as well. This is called national spot advertising. Its purpose is to advertise products to specific local markets (for example, the Northeast or Southeast) or to supplement network buys.

Local Advertising. Local TV stations deal with two types of clients—national and local. Local advertisers are those with products or services available to local TV markets. They include banks, retail stores, and car dealerships.

Affiliates and independent stations make available spots within and between programs for local advertising. While national advertisers buy network time several months in advance, local stations work within a more flexible time frame, accepting ads a few days or more than three months in advance. Some stations employ the services of a **rep firm** for selling commercial airtime to advertising agencies and media-buying services. Advertisers may buy directly but they usually engage an advertising agency or a media-buying service. Whereas an ad agency performs creative work for its client as well as purchases ad time, a media-buying service only purchases ad time. There are various types of arrangements by which agencies and buying services are compensated, including a commission (percentage), a commission and set fee, or a set fee only. The old standard agency commission of 15 percent is still fairly common, but today agencies will sometimes receive less. Media-buying services work on a lower margin, earning a smaller percentage.

To obtain the best results for its client, the ad agency or buying service will first do media planning. It will determine what media can best be used to reach the client's target audience, when to schedule commercials, where to place the spots, and how frequently they should run. Then it will submit an avail request to local TV stations.

The avail request will ask for advertising rates for specific dates and day parts, that is, the parts of the broadcast day. For example, it might request the rates for daytime, prime access, or for the same time six weeks from then. It might specify that the target audience is women twenty-five to fifty-four and that it wants to use Nielsen's rating schedule (see **Audience Measurement Service**). It will also state the approximate budget.

The station, in turn, will come back and tell what it can offer the advertiser—how many spots, which shows, etc. A negotiation process will ensue, with each party trying to make the best deal it can, until a compromise is finally agreed upon. Station salespersons visit ad agencies and media-buying services not only to negotiate but to pitch specific programs.

ADVERTISING CODE ADMINISTRATION. The ACA is a department of the **Motion Picture Association of America Inc. (MPAA)** that approves all advertising for feature films that have been rated under the industry's voluntary movie rating system. Such advertising includes trailers, television and radio commercials, press books, and print ads. The ACA reviews movie advertising to make certain that it is suitable for all audiences and that it carries the proper rating. Trailers are rated in two categories: G, which designates a trailer is suitable for any audience; and R, which denotes the trailer can be shown only to audiences viewing R- or NC-17–rated films.

AERIAL CINEMATOGRAPHY. Aerial cinematography is filming done from the air. Aerial cinematography is commonly used for scenic shots, car chases, stunts, sports events, and news coverage in motion pictures, commercials, industrials, documentaries, and live television. Most shooting is done from helicopters, with a cinematographer (or camera operator) and pilot aboard, and usually the director (for first unit shooting in motion pictures) or the assistant director (for second unit shooting). With the side door of the helicopter open, the cinematographer sits strapped in behind a mounted camera. A camera may also be mounted underneath the nose of the helicopter and operated by remote control. Widely used camera mounts include the Tyler Mount, Continental Mount, Wescam Mount, and Gyrosphere Mount. Commonly used helicopters for aerial cinematography include the Bell Jet Ranger (which has one engine) and the Aerospace TwinStar (double engine). A two-engine helicopter is generally safer and affords greater flexibility in shooting. FAA regulations in some areas require a twin engine for certain types of flights.

While there are no legal specifications as to how high an aircraft must fly during shooting, the practical standard is high enough to ensure safety, which means high enough to enable a safe auto-rotative (power-off) landing in the event of an emergency. A single-engine helicopter must fly considerably higher than a twin-engine helicopter in order to make a safe power-off landing in case of an emergency. A twin-engine helicopter can fly at almost any altitude, depending on the location, since it is able to propel itself on one engine if the other goes out.

Helicopters normally don't exceed 80 miles per hour during shooting. For scenic shots they are likely to run at 50 mph or 60 mph. Planes or jets are occasionally used for high-speed aerial cinematography.

The cinematographer and pilot work closely together in shooting. It is important that they map out what they are trying to accomplish before going up.

Safety is of paramount importance in aerial cinematography. Sometimes directors will want a certain type of shot without realizing the full dangers of getting it. Whether a pilot accepts a dangerous job is a matter of personal judgment.

To perform aerial cinematography over cities may require authorizations, including a permit to land at a field location. Information on clearances may be obtained from a city's office on motion pictures and television; in other areas, only the permission of the owner of the property over which shooting is done may be needed. This is obtained by having the owner sign a release form. For shooting below five hundred feet it is customary that people in the vicinity be notified. As a courtesy the local police department may be alerted also.

AFFILIATE. An affiliate is a television station that carries the programming of a **network**. There are two types of affiliated TV stations: primary and secondary. A primary affiliate's schedule consists predominantly of one of the networks' programs; a secondary affiliate (often another network's primary affiliate) carries only some of the programs—normally those that are not carried by a primary affiliate.

Some affiliated stations are owned by the networks, but most are held by broadcasting chains and other corporate entities. WNBC-TV in New York, for example, is owned by the network, but the NBC affiliate in Albuquerque (KOB-TV) is owned by Hubbard Broadcasting Inc. WBBM-TV in Chicago is owned by CBS, but the CBS affiliate in Cincinnati (WCPO-TV) is owned by Scripps Howard Broadcasting Company. KGO-TV in San Francisco is owned by Capital Cities/ABC, but the ABC affiliate in Boston (WCVB-TV) is owned the The Hearst Corporation. Each network has more than two hundred affiliates, making free television the only medium capable of reaching virtually 100 percent of the American audience.

Programming. Network programs occupy at least half and up to more than two-thirds of a primary affiliate's weekday broadcasting day (based on a 6 A.M. to 12 A.M. schedule). The remainder is filled with shows of the station's own choosing—self-produced programs, syndicated series, and anything else it wants.

FCC rules stipulate that there may be no contract or arrangement requiring an affiliate to carry all of a network's programing and that an affiliate can preempt programming it deems unsatisfactory or unsuitable. The networks pay affiliates based on the amount of shows they air (see below) and it is, of course, to the networks' advantage that their affiliates broadcast as much of their programming as possible. The networks wish to maintain their schedules as intact as possible to maximize viewing patterns, sales efforts, and national promotion. The networks try to avoid having the affiliates broadcast only their highest-rated shows and not run those that do not perform as well. Affiliates are tempted by programs offered by syndicators and other program suppliers that could pull greater revenues than low-rated network shows. Excessive **preemption** by the affiliate, however, could cause the network to disaffiliate the station and make a new arrangement with another local station. On the other hand, it could be detrimental to an affiliate to move to the number-one network every time its current network is behind the others in the ratings.

As an example of how programming works with primary affiliates, the 1987 schedule offered by the ABC television network follows.

After 12 A.M. ABC affiliates schedule their own programming. They can run shows until the next network feed (at 6 A.M.) or they can go off the air at any time for the day. NBC and CBS at this writing offer programs that extend further into the morning.

The networks offer programming for a substantial portion but not all of the broadcast day, and when the feeds stop the affiliates broadcast programming of their own choosing. The time periods may vary slightly by network and time zone. For instance, NBC offers daytime programming to its affiliates from 10 A.M. to 4 P.M. in the Eastern time zone, and from 9 A.M. to 3 P.M. in the Central and Western time zones. The time periods when network feeds temporarily stop are of special importance to affiliates, since they want to hold or build the audiences they had earlier and keep them for when the network shows resume.

Programming decisions at affiliated stations are made by the program director, who usually needs approval from the general manager. *See* **Independent Television Station** for a breakdown of positions and departments in TV stations.

Sample Programming Schedule

6 A.M.–7 A.M.	"World News This Morning"
7 A.M.–9 A.M.	"Good Morning America"
9 A.M.–11 A.M.	ABC offers no programming. Affiliate has two hours of local or syndicated programming.
11 A.M.–4 P.M.	ABC daytime programming
4 P.M.–6:30 P.M.	local programming (including news shows)
6:30 P.M.–7 P.M.	"World News Tonight" (ABC also has a 7–7:30 P.M. feed of this show.)
7 P.M.–8 P.M.	local programming
8 P.M.–11 P.M.	prime-time programming—sitcoms, dramas, action-adventure, made-for-TV movies, miniseries, films (on Sundays ABC prime time is from 7 P.M. to 11 P.M.)
11 P.M.–11:30 P.M.	local news
11:30 P.M.–12 A.M.	"Nightline"

Network Liaison. Each of the networks has a department that handles relations with its affiliates. This department supplies to the affiliates information on programming, advertising, and anything else of importance or interest. It also has sales representatives who call individual stations to get them to carry ("clear") the network's programs. Since affiliates do not automatically take all of the network's programs, the network will sometimes try to convince the affiliates that it is in their mutual interest to carry specific shows.

A network's department of affiliate relations is in close contact with every other department in the company involved in

31

programming—children's daytime, prime time, sports, news, operations, advertising and promotion, and others. These departments inform the affiliate relations department of program activities and it in turn conveys the information (often by telex) to the stations. The affiliate relations department also lets stations know where network commercials fall in the company's programming, where local spots or station breaks may occur, where there are format changes in network programs, and when specials will be aired.

Network-Affiliate Relationship. Every affiliate has a contract with a network that defines their relationship. Contracts usually cover a two-year term and are renewable. If either the affiliate or the network wants to terminate the contract, it must notify the other at least six months prior to the expiration date, otherwise the agreement is automatically renewed. The FCC has some regulations on affiliation agreements, including the two-year term.

The networks pay fees to their affiliates because in essence they are buying their airtime. The networks in turn earn income by selling commercial time (*availabilities*) during their programs to advertisers. For half-hour prime-time sitcoms, for example, a network would sell the availabilities to advertisers. The affiliate, on the other hand, would sell the commercial airtime at the conclusion of shows (*end breaks*) at the best rate it can get and keep that revenue. For a one-hour show, the affiliate would sell airtime during the middle (*mid-break*). Affiliates can earn additional revenue for broadcasting programs during local periods. Stations buy programs from syndicators and sell local time. They may barter for programs and trade availabilities to syndicators. Affiliates may also produce their own programs and sell the availabilities themselves.

ABC, CBS, and NBC pay affiliates a "network rate," a percentage of an hourly rate for carrying their programs. That percentage is arrived at by negotiations between the network and the affiliate. Various factors determine the amount of compensation an affiliate receives, including the size of the market (city) it is in, the size of the audience it delivers, and the time of day the network programming is broadcast.

Just as advertisers pay commercial rates to local stations based on the size of the audiences their shows will reach, the networks pay their affiliates according to the audiences they can deliver. To determine what the network will pay, the industry uses a unit called "average cost-per-thousand," which is an hourly rate based on the number of homes delivered to the network. Consider, for example, an affiliate that delivers 150,000 homes to a network during a prime-time show that the network is buying at a cost of $20 per thousand. The cost-per-thousand, therefore, is 150 × $20, or $3,000 per hour. If the network rate for prime time was 40 percent, the network would pay the station 40 percent of $3,000, or $1,200 for an hour's worth of programming in prime time. If the network rate for day-time programming was 10 percent, and all other elements were the same, the network would pay the affiliate 10 percent of $3,000, or $300 for each hour of daytime programming. The networks usually send compensation checks to their affiliates each month. Some affiliates in major cities receive more than one or two million dollars annually.

While the affiliates receive fees to broadcast network programs, they share in the costs of delivering the programs. Many programs are delivered live by satellite, although delivery may be by cable or augmented in some geographical areas by telephone lines. (Video-tape may be used for network programs that are not broadcast from a network feed but are aired later.) A percentage of the network rate is deducted from the compensation checks to pay for program delivery. The fee, which is sometimes called a "waiver," is about one-twelfth of what the network determines to be the annual cost of delivery to the station.

Affiliate Ownership. Affiliates are owned by the networks, media and communications companies, corporations, and private individuals. FCC regulations (47 CFR 73.35555) address limitations on multiple ownership of broadcasting stations by any single group, including networks. Under FCC regulation, "No license for a commercial AM, FM, or TV broadcast station shall be granted, transferred or assigned to any party . . . [that] . . . would result in such party or any of its stockholders, partners, members, officers, or directors, directly or indirectly owning, operating or controlling, or having a cognizable interest" in twelve stations of the same service, or fourteen stations if minority controlled. Furthermore, no license may be granted for TV stations that have an aggregate national audience reach exceeding 25 percent, or 30 percent if minority controlled.

Corporations that own multiple affiliates include Gannett Broadcasting (Division of Gannett Co. Inc.), Cox Enterprises Inc., Cosmos Broadcasting Corp., Park Communications Inc., Gillett Holdings Inc., The Times Mirror Broadcasting, and Westinghouse Broadcasting Co. (Group W). Most of these corporations also own a number of AM and FM radio stations.

AGENT, ACTOR'S. An agent seeks employment for actors and represents actors' interests in negotiations with those employing them. The agent finds job prospects for clients, presents actors to casting directors and others who are in a position to hire them, secures auditions, and negotiates contracts.

To establish guidelines for representation of actors, including commission ceilings, SAG and AFTRA franchise agents. (Theater agents are franchised by **Actors' Equity Association**.) The unions set a limit on the agents' commissions of 10 percent of the actor's fee. State laws may deem talent (or booking) agencies to be employment agencies and require that they be licensed. This is the case in California, New York, and many other states.

The agent seeks out new talent and considers actors who come looking for representation. In seeking fresh talent, the agent will attend shows and showcases and pursue recommendations. In some rare cases, an agent will hold auditions. Actors find agents through referrals, listings in registries and directories, and articles in trade publications. In signing talent, the agent considers whether the actor is bookable or not for while the agent may admire an actor's work, he or she may also feel that he or she would only be able to secure the actor limited work.

In seeking employment for clients, agents must make sure the actors are properly "packaged." This includes having good eight-by-ten photos, resumés, and promotional or publicity literature (if available), all updated periodically. With these materials agents recommend their clients to as many casting directors as they can. They might call up and rave about their clients in the hope of securing auditions that give actors the chance to be considered for particular roles and perhaps remembered for future projects as well. Many agents subscribe to Breakdown Services Ltd., a company with offices in Los Angeles, New York, and London, which prints sheets describing new projects in film and television and their casting needs. Agents read these papers and send photos and resumés of clients to the appropriate people.

There are agencies that work exclusively or primarily with actors and those that represent many different types of creative talents in addition to actors, such as recording artists, composers, and authors. Large talent agencies include the William Morris Agency and International Creative Management (ICM).

See **Franchised Agent.**

AGENT, SCREENWRITER'S. An agent seeks out markets for a writer's work or seeks out work for the client on the development of other people's projects. There are agents whose only clients are screenwriters, agents who represent screenwriters and authors as literary agents, and agents who represent writers and talent from all areas of the entertainment industry.

Screenwriters' agents deal with those in a position to get their clients work: studios, producers, packagers, directors, story editors at studios and networks, readers, and actors' agents. In dealing with studios and producers, agents will inquire as to what kinds of star vehicles they may be looking for, what arrangements they may have with directors, and what budgets they are working with. With this information the agents discuss the properties they are representing, and if interest is expressed they will submit one or more scripts.

In order to get a screenwriter work on existing projects in development, the agent tries to "marry" the writer with a suitable property. If a producer is not familiar with a screenwriter, the agent will send the producer copies of the writer's work. A **step deal** is a possibility, both in this situation and when a writer pitches an idea to a producer.

Screenwriters' agents also submit their clients' work to agents of well-known actors in the hope that a package might be assembled and shopped (presented to different studios and producers). The package will not only include a script and a star actor, but perhaps other leading actors, as well as a director and producer. Large agencies, which represent a broad base of established talent from various areas of motion pictures and television, commonly package projects.

Screenwriters' agents work on a commission basis. They receive either 10 percent or 15 percent of a client's gross earnings for a job. Writers' fees vary from job to job and depend on a project's budget. There is an old Hollywood formula, still generally adhered to, that prescribes that the story and screenplay costs should not exceed 5 percent of the budget.

AIR. Air is a colloquialism for airwaves: "on the air." In the United States, its territories, and possessions, the use of airwaves is regulated by the **Federal Communications Commission (FCC)**.

AIRTIME. Airtime is commercial time. Broadcasters (except public and other nonprofit stations) sell airtime to advertisers and it is this resource that is the financial basis of their business.

ALLIANCE OF MOTION PICTURE AND TELEVISION PRODUCERS (AMPTP). AMPTP is a nonprofit corporation that represents the major Hollywood studios, motion picture and television production companies, and film laboratories in the negotiation of collective bargaining agreements with the entertainment industry guilds and unions. The Alliance also represents the industry in dealing with city, county, and state governments. AMPTP collaborates with the Motion Picture Association of America in matters involving federal agencies and legislation. In addition, the staff assists member companies in complying with the myriad laws that affect the employment process, such as state and federal Equal

Employment Opportunity laws, fair labor standards acts, the California labor code, California Industrial Welfare Commission orders, the Occupational Safety and Health Act, and the National Labor Relations Act.

AMERICAN FEDERATION OF MUSICIANS (AFM). AFM is a labor union affiliated with the AFL-CIO that represents musicians, arrangers, orchestrators, and copyists working in motion pictures, television, recording, legitimate theater, and concert engagements. AFM provides minimum compensation (scale) and other terms of employment for its members. Contracts with employers are both national and local in scope. There are national agreements for motion pictures, TV films, and sound recordings, whereas if musicians were to perform on a local television station, they would be covered by the local union's contract. If musicians played on a Los Angeles station, for example, jurisdiction over that employment would be covered by Musicians' Union Local 47 in Hollywood. If the performance took place at a New York station, the employment would be under the contract negotiated by Local 52. Club dates and concert engagements are also under the jurisdiction of the local unions. There are approximately six hundred locals of AFM.

AMERICAN FEDERATION OF TELEVISION AND RADIO ARTISTS (AFTRA). AFTRA is a labor union affiliated with the AFL-CIO that represents actors, singers, dancers, newscasters, weatherpersons, sportscasters, disc jockeys, and others who work in television (videotape), radio, and audio (music) recording. AFTRA television contracts cover such areas as news programs, variety specials, game shows, and daytime soap operas.

AFTRA is an open union and anyone can join. There is an initiation fee and members pay semiannual dues. Dues-paying members of sister entertainment unions pay half the initiation fee and dues. Union agreements provide minimum fees for members, medical and dental plans and pension benefits for those who are eligible, residuals for extended repeated uses of commercials and programs, and other benefits. The union franchises agents, imposing a ceiling on commissions of 10 percent and regulating other dealings of the agent with union members (*see* **Franchised Agent**).

AFTRA is composed of local chapters with more than seventy thousand members in various cities of the United States (there were thirty-seven locals in 1988). These locals are governed by their members and boards of directors, and each local negotiates various contracts pertaining to employment of their members in television and radio stations and other areas. Certain contracts are negotiated nationally, such as those for network shows, commercials, industrial videocassettes and videodiscs, and music recordings.

AMERICAN HUMANE ASSOCIATION. American Humane is a national organization of city and state agencies that serves to prevent abuse of children and animals, and whose Hollywood office is dedicated to guaranteeing the safety and welfare of animals on motion picture and television sets. The Motion Picture Association of America recognized American Humane as the industry's official organization devoted to preventing cruelty to animals in 1939, following a stunt in the movie *Jessie James* in which an actor rode a horse off a cliff and escaped, while the animal crashed into the water below and perished. American Humane was instrumental in having a "Cruelty to Animals Statement of Policy" inserted into the 1980 basic codified agreement between the Screen Actors Guild and film and television producers. The policy provides that producers recognize that "trained animals are available which can perform with realism and without danger of injury or death," that no actor may "perform in a scene . . . in which an animal is intentionally tormented or killed," that prior to any production involving animals the producer must notify the American Humane Association and provide relevant script scenes, and that representatives of American Humane must be allowed on sets to monitor the filming of scenes involving animals.

American Humane promises a four-tiered rating system for treatment of animals in motion picture and television productions. The classification system distributed to the media, reads as follows.

American Society of Composers, Authors and Publishers (ASCAP)

Rating System for Treatment of Animals

Rating	Description
Acceptable	Representatives of American Humane were on the set during filming and acknowledge that scenes in which animals appear to be abused were simulated.
Believed Acceptable	Production was not monitored by American Humane but the association reviewed the script, screened the film, or discussed the production with officials of the film company and determined that animals were not abused or exploited.
Questionable	No American Humane representative was on the set during production and the association has been unable to determine whether animals were abused where it appears they might have been.
Unacceptable	Animals were cruelly and blatantly abused.

AMERICAN SOCIETY OF COMPOSERS, AUTHORS AND PUBLISHERS (ASCAP). ASCAP is a **performing-rights organization** for composers, lyricists, and music publishers that collects fees from broadcasters and other users of music and pays members performance royalties when their compositions are included in the society's sample survey of performances on radio, television, and other areas. ASCAP has classified performance as *feature, theme, background,* or *jingle.* Each use generates a certain number of "performance credits," which varies depending on, among other things, the type of use, the particular medium in which the performance takes place, and, in the case of network television, the number of stations interconnected and the time of day of performance. The monetary value of a credit can change from quarter to quarter, depending on ASCAP's distributable revenue for that period and the number of ASCAP performances processed.

See also **Broadcast Music Incorporated; Music Licensing, Film.**

ANCHOR. The anchor is the chief reporter of a local, network, or cable television news program. Considered to be the main attraction of the newscast, an anchor is typically good-looking and well-groomed, and is expected to have sensitivity and style.

Anchors wield much power in the newsroom and often influence the character of their show. They may conduct live interviews, and they often participate in writing news copy. An anchor usually has years of experience in television journalism, perhaps as a correspondent. The salaries of anchorpersons are relatively high; a leading network anchor can earn an annual salary in excess of $1 million.

ANIMALS. Animals, like people, may be cast in starring and minor roles in films and on television programs. But unlike their human counterparts, animals, or rather their owners, do not enjoy some of the benefits of the profession. The entertainment unions, for example, do not accept animals as members, and consequently animals do not qualify for any union benefits (such as minimum fees). Contractual arrangements are made between the producer and the animal owner.

For owners of animals that have become immensely popular, however, merchandising rights may be valuable. The names and likenesses of well-known performing animals may not be used without their owners' consent. Often a studio is the owner of a starring animal's "name," using several similar-looking animals to play the role. Animals are also used on television commercials, for which their owners earn a flat fee. Residuals are not paid for rebroadcasts.

The **American Humane Association** is a recognized industry watchdog for abuse of animals on movie and television sets.

ANIMATION. To animate is to create seemingly spontaneous lifelike movement through specific mechanical means. Animation is used in many forms—for cartoon shorts, full-length feature films, TV-show introductions, combinations of live action and animation, clay-model animation, commercials, titles and logos—but there are three basic animation processes: cel, stop motion, and computer.

Cel Animation. Cel animation is the process of sequentially photographing individual drawings, using a motion picture camera that exposes one frame at a time. Each *cel* (from celluloid, the original material used) shows a slight change in position of whatever is depicted. When the developed film is viewed at the correct speed (twenty-four frames per second), the sequence of drawings creates the illusion of movement. The life, energy, and spirit of the character depend on the skills of the animator.

The traditional animation process follows the steps outlined below.

- *Script.* First, the idea for an animated property has to be developed into script form. There are screenwriters who specialize in animation. Writing a screenplay for animation is somewhat different than writing for live action because animation allows the freedom to exaggerate reality.
- *Storyboard.* After a script is finalized, an artist illustrates it with a series of drawings called a storyboard to give the director and animators a scene-by-scene account of the script.

  Storyboard pages consist of anywhere from six to twelve panels; together they read like a comic book. During this stage, the director works with the layout artist to determine where on the screen the characters should be. This process, known as staging, is analogous to the **camera blocking** of scenes in a live-action movie. The director also communicates the mood of the piece and the initial timings to the animators. For a commercial, the creative team of the ad

41

agency usually prepares the storyboard, although the production house may be asked to contribute.

- *Layout.* Using the storyboard as a guide, a layout artist now must design each scene. The storyboard is the initial visualization of a concept; the layout is an elaboration of the storyboard. The layout has more camera directions, more details on character positioning, and it is scaled to working size. The characters must be posed in relation to the backgrounds. Scenes are broken down into sequences, each of which may have several backgrounds. All the background drawings in the film are done to the scale of the final art. The animators animate the characters over outline tracings of the layouts. For an in-house animation project, the layout artist, the storyboard artist, and the director may be the same person.
- *Character Design.* Artists design characters for a story based on previous rough sketches. Then color models of the characters are painted on cels. These color models are executed by colorists, who choose the appropriate shades of the characters. These acrylic cel vinyl colors may be bought premixed from the manufacturer.

  Serial cartoons and commercials use recurring characters, so character design may simply consist of an update to give the characters a fresh look.
- *Background Painting.* In a stage presentation, the set, or backdrop, behind the actors provides the space in which they will perform the given scene. In an animated film, the backdrop, or background, is an illustration that creates an environment for the animated characters. The background painter is a skilled draftsperson, colorist, designer, and media technician all in one. The cel painter, on the other hand, is not required to do anything more than fill in the colors on the acetate cels. As the backgrounds are completed, the color models of the characters are placed over them, and any adjustments in their colors are made at this time.

In some cases, the backgrounds may be live-action film, such as was used in the motion picture *Roger Rabbit*, where the animated characters, or toons, were optically matted over "live" backgrounds and interacted with the live actors in the scene.

- *Recording.* Three audio elements—voice, music, and sound effects—are recorded onto separate quarter-inch magnetic tapes. In a sound studio, actors read and act out the dialogue. This is followed by the recording of the music (which may be an original score or prerecorded music) and sound effects. In some cases, music is designed to fit the visual. Two tracks are usually used for each element, but eight or more may be used. The audio elements are kept separate until the final mix. A rough mix of the sound track is made on a quarter-inch tape, and this is transferred to 35-mm film. The first mix is for the animators.

- *Track Analysis.* In a process called track analysis, or track reading, the sound track is broken down by an editor into words (or syllables for lip syncing), beats for the music (if there is music), and sound effects. (Lip syncing refers to the vocal synchronization of the sound track to the mouth movements of the character on the screen, be it live or animated.) The 35-mm film with these elements on the audio track is run through a synchronizer, or frame counter, which enables the editor to determine exactly on which frame of film the sounds being analyzed come in and go off, and in which frames the vocal syllables change.

This information is put on exposure sheets. An exposure sheet, a visual guide to the sound vibrations on the track, looks like an enlarged legal-size piece of paper with eighty lines. Each line, indicated by the numbers 1 through 80 on the left margin, represents a frame of 35-mm film. Eighty frames are equivalent to five feet, or 3⅓ seconds, of animation (the film runs at twenty-four frames per second).

The dialogue, music, and effects from the track are written vertically on the left edge of the sheet, next to the frame numbers. The animation must coincide with the numerical breakdown of the sounds or the action will be out of sync with the track. Music is broken down into sounds, and the length of each sound is broken down into frames. This allows the animator to determine the speed of the action.

• *Animation.* Using the exposure sheets and the layouts, the animators draw the action. The director, who has decided the key poses (or basic moves) of the characters, discusses them with the animators and tells them what the characters should be doing in each scene. With the poses laid out by the director, the animators are responsible for designing the moves of the characters and adding expressions and emotions that complement the action and dialogue.

The pace of a scene or sequence is established at the layout stage. By determining how many drawings there should be and where they should go, the animator sets the timing. The animator's drawings develop the characters within the established mood. Mood is also developed by the background artist, who establishes the lighting for the scene.

The drawings done by the animator are actually rough poses (called *extremes*), which need to be cleaned up and developed further. The roughs are cleaned up by an assistant animator who will make sure that the finished drawings have characters that look like those on the model sheets. The process of filling the drawings between the extremes is referred to as *in-betweening*. Sometimes an animator will in-between his or her own work, but often an assistant will do it. If the animation is limited, with movement confined largely to the characters' mouths and eyes, there will probably be no need for in-betweening.

The characters being animated are not always completely drawn on the same sheet of paper. In films using limited animation techniques, the moving parts are separated into several levels. Any part that is not moving is simply held in that setup, and only the levels on which there is movement are changed. This technique saves time and money in drawing, inking, and painting. In full animation, the entire character is drawn on one level since it has to be redrawn for each frame whether it is moving or not.

Timing is crucial in animation. Observation, experience, and acting ability provide the animator with a sense of what will look real and dynamic. An experienced animator can "feel" how long an action should take.

The number of animators on a project depends on its complexity. Although many different animators will work on the same project, their professional ability enables them to draw characters consistently. The more animators involved in a film, the more difficult it becomes to control character design. For feature films, animators who have similar drawing styles will "share" a character in order to keep the design consistent.

- *Pencil Testing*. Preliminary animation is done on specially prepared and cut sheets of paper. The paper is different than regular bond drawing paper in the sense that it does not have a manufacturer's water mark on it, and it is cut to a 35-mm aspect ratio (10¼ × 12½). (Some paper is cut for Cinemascope and Vistavision.) Most animators use a blue pencil to block out the action (electronic copiers cannot see blue), and then, on the same sheet of paper, redraw the character with a black pencil. In order to confirm the accuracy of the poses, these pencil drawings are shot in sync with the audio track on black-and-white film or videotape. This process is referred to as a *pose test*. If the key poses work, they will be in-betweened and shot again in sync with the track. This is called a *pencil test*. Pencil tests are done so that the animators and the director may check the movement and timing of the animated characters. If the action does not work, it will be reanimated and pencil tested once again. When the work is acceptable, the cleaned-up drawings will go to the inking department for transfer to acetate cels.
- *Xerography*. When animation was first introduced to the film industry, the drawings were done on paper cels. Con-

sequently, each frame of the entire scene had to be redrawn for each frame of film, whether it was moving or not. With the advent of commercial animation, it became apparent that a way had to be devised that would save time and cut cost. Transparent sheets of cellophane paper were used (they were placed over the pencil drawings on registration pegs, and traced by inkers who used India ink and brushes), and this way any drawings that were not moving could be drawn once and held on the bottom level, while the moving parts could be animated on second and third levels.

Coloring was done with water-based tempera paint, and the cels were washed and reused in order to save the cost of new ones. This technique was used until the invention of the Xerox machine. The Xerox camera (a dry copier), which was commonplace in animation studios since the late 1920s, became an invaluable tool to the industry when Ub Iwerks, of the Disney studio, modified one of the machines so that it would make the copy directly onto the cel. This process preserved the spontaneity of the animator's original drawings and eliminated the need for hand inking. The Xerox line was thinner and more desirable than the heavier brush lines. However, the machine would print only in black, so the colored hand-drawn lines were forsaken for the more accurate and time-saving Xerox copies. At that time, the copiers could make one reproduction in approximately two minutes. The Xerox 3100 LDC copier was the industry standard by the early 1970s, and could make about six copies per minute. Hand tracing is still used in high-quality theatrical films while the Xerox is used almost exclusively for video.

- *Pegging.* The animation is done on paper cels that have registration holes punched on the bottom edge. These holes fit over the pegs on the animator's drawing table, and match the pegs on the camera stand table. The drawings must be registered one over the other or it would be impossible to control the animation. The drawings, done on paper, are put through the copying machine but do not come out registered to one another. Therefore, the plastic cels must have registration holes punched along the bottom edge. The punched edge is cut off (peg strip) and placed on the registration pegs over the original drawing. The transparent copy is then placed over the drawing, and fastened to the peg strip that was previously removed with clear tape. This process is tedious but faster than using the older machines, which made a one-to-one registered copy.

- *Ink and Painting.* Even though the Xerox machine has taken over the job of copying the animation, it has not eliminated the need for inkers in the paint department. Colored match lines still have to be hand-painted where two different colors come together, or where the edge of a character has to match the shape of some object on the background. If an animated character has to walk through a doorway that is painted on the background, the edge that matches the doorframe is not photocopied. Instead, it is inked in the same color as the character's costume. Such lines are called *self-trace lines.*

The actual drawings are on the front side of the cels. The cels are painted on the reverse side to eliminate the texture and tonal changes of the brush strokes. Since the colors are somewhat transparent, darker tones would show through if painted over the lighter tones. Therefore, the dark tones are painted first. The paint is spread up to the line that separates the adjoining color. When the lighter color is applied, it can "slop over" the line since it will not show through the darker color.

At the same time, an artist makes final renderings of the backgrounds, usually on watercolor paper, which is paper specially made to accept watercolor paints or watercolor dyes. When all the color roughs, or layouts, are approved, the background artist will make this *final rendering*, which is the ultimate painting, the piece of art that will be used in the film and seen by the viewing audience.

- *Checking.* After all the scenes are painted, a checker makes sure they are all camera-ready. All the match lines must be accurate (for example, when a character is twisted around a door, the edges of the character must match the edges of the door). Accidental paint splatterings are then scraped off the cels (a painter may have slopped over a line), and the colors are checked for leveling so they are consistent when all the levels in the setup are registered one over the other.

• *Polishing.* Polishing is a cleaning process in which the cels are cleaned to make sure that there are no fingerprints, dust, or stray paints on them. This is important because contamination can cause flares or flashes.

• *Shooting.* The cels, or each setup (background plus all character levels), are shot one frame at a time. Each setup is shot twice, which is referred to as *shooting on twos*. This is standard for animation unless a movement is very fast. In cases where a character is talking fast, the lip sync will be shot on ones (every successive frame), while the other levels are on twos. If the entire character is moving too fast to be interpreted in ones, the animator may elect to draw two poses on one frame. Ideally, the setups are laid out so that the level that is moving the most is on top. This way the camera person does not have to remove all the levels to change cels that are animating on the bottom. If the maximum of four levels are used in a given scene, four levels must be maintained even if there is artwork on only one of them. This ensures that there will be no density changes in the overall color of the scene. For example, if the character is broken up into four levels, and only the eyes (Level D) are moving, only this level is changed. If the eyes alone are not moving, but the whole head is (Level C), the eyes from Level D are drawn on Level C with the head, and a blank cel will replace Level D in order to maintain color density throughout the scene. If the following scene is using the same background, but only two levels are moving, two blank cels will have to be used to maintain continuity in color density. Different systems are used for labeling the levels; letters and numbers are commonly used. If the mouth and head are intended to move, there may be three levels; and if the arms are also supposed to move, there may be four levels (this depends on the kind of animation being done; there may be a level for every moving part). The parts that are moving are drawn separately so that the rest of the body does not have to be redrawn.

When the camera person receives the artwork, the scenes are put in different stacks (arranged by level) on a table next to the camera. The camera person sets up the cels as they are laid out on the exposure sheets made up by the animator (the artwork is numbered), and usually shoots two frames of film at a time. Then the drawings are replaced with the next setup (there may be three or four cels in a setup), and the process continues in this manner.

Since animation technique relies on visual retention, two frames of the same drawing must be shot consecutively. The eye sees the two frames as a single image. If three frames at a time were shot, a viewer might sense a *popping* from drawing to drawing because visual retention would start to fade out when the next drawing came up, depending on the type of motion and the spacing of the drawings.

The drawing's popping from pose to pose is an animation problem in the sense that the animator gives the instructions to the camera person. The popping occurs if the drawings are too far apart or shot on three frames or more. Drawings that are very close together (perhaps the thickness of a pencil line apart) will not pop if they are shot on threes or even fours. This is done in the case of a moving hold, where the animation is coming to a very soft stop, or if the movement is very slight but long in duration.

The camera is mounted on a stand and is placed directly above the cels. The height of the camera depends on what field is being shot. The standard animation format is a twelve-field; that is, a frame that is twelve inches wide. The camera can be adjusted to shoot anywhere from a two-field to a twelve-field (or beyond, depending on how big the art-work is).

The most popular stand used by animation cinematographers is the Oxberry. The Oxberry has four motorized peg bars that travel from right to left and an optional floating peg bar that moves up and down on a horizontal plane. Every function on the Oxberry stand is computer-programmed. Some brands of camera stands are not computerized.

The length of a shooting depends on its complexity and on how many levels are required. The average thirty-second commercial has about 250 to 300 setups, which takes several hours to shoot. If a cameraperson is working with five or six levels, it might take five hours or more to shoot a thirty-second commercial. For a half-hour show, there would be about six hours of camera time per minute; thus, for twenty-eight minutes, there would be 168 hours of camera time.

- *Workprint.* After the cels are shot, a workprint is made in a lab. A workprint is the first contact print off the original negative, and is used for cutting and screening purposes. It does not need to be edited because the animator has done the editing in making exposure sheets. However, if a scene is not acceptable and has to be reshot or reanimated, it will be cut out and replaced at a later time.
- *Audio Mix to Picture.* After the workprint has been cut and synchronized with the audio tracks (there may be more than eight tracks), they are mixed and then transferred to one track. If a composite film is to be made, the track will be transferred to an optical negative. There is no need to do this for television, though, since the videotape is made directly from the interlock.

An interlock is the combined screening of two elements that are on separate reels. Reel one is the workprint (picture) and reel two the audio track, which is on a magnetic strip of film corresponding to the same size as the picture. If a transfer is being made to videotape, the interlock will be composed of the picture negative and the audio mag track. If one is going to a composite release print, then the interlock will be composed of a picture negative, and the audio must be transferred to optical negative film.

- *Composite Answer Print for Theatrical Motion Pictures.* If the animation is being prepared for film, the sound track has to be transferred to an optical negative. The optical negative is then combined with the picture negative to make a color-corrected release print.
- *Transfer of Negative to Video for Television.* If the animation is being prepared for television, the interlock (which includes the mixed audio track and the picture negative) is transferred to a one-inch videotape (the master dubbing tape), and a protection master is made also. From the master dubbing tape, ¾-inch or ½-inch videocassette copies may be made, depending on how the copies will be distributed.

Stop-Motion Animation. Stop-motion, or *model*, animation refers to the motion picture photography process of shooting an object, exposing one or two frames (most film cameras will shoot one frame), moving the object a fraction of an inch, shooting the object again, then repeating the process. When the film is played in real time, the object appears to be animated, or moving. With the stop-motion process, almost any three-dimensional object can be animated. Shooting a small model in stop motion to simulate the movement of a large object is commonly done.

Computer Animation. Computer animation, or computer graphics, refers to three-dimensional geometric shapes generated and manipulated in space by a computer. The computer can change color, reassemble scenes, and recycle animation, thereby expediting production and saving on man-hour costs. Special machines translate computer images from diskettes to film or video. At this writing, there is no practical way to animate characters using a computer.

ANSWER PRINT. An answer print is the first composite print of a film made from a duplicate of the edited original color negative film and the sound track. As the first print of image and sound, it is essentially a prototype of the release prints. It is screened by the producer, director, and director of photography to see where corrections, usually for color and sound, are needed. If changes need to be made—for example, a scene may be too green or too yellow—then laboratory technicians will re-time the negative and make the necessary changes, then obtain a second answer print. This process will be repeated until a print is finally approved, at which point release (color-positive) prints will be made for theatrical distribution. These are the films that are actually shown in movie theaters.

ANTHOLOGY. *See* **Television Programming Genres.**

ART DEPARTMENT AND PROP DEPARTMENT. The tasks of designing the visual elements of a motion picture or television show, obtaining props, and dressing sets are handled by members of the art department and the *prop* (short for property) department.

The roles of these two departments are closely related, and some crew members' roles may overlap depending upon such factors as budget, how much work is involved, whether locations are being used, how much time is available, and the rules of the local union. Job titles and functions may also vary from production to production. The table that follows on pages 54–55 summarizes the traditional or general responsibilities of the various members of art and prop departments of film and television production.

ART DIRECTOR, TELEVISION. A television art director creates sets for a television series or program and is ultimately responsible for designing the look of the show. The sets should not only be appropriate to each scene but to the overall nature of the show. It is also vital that the arrangement of a set enable flexibility in operating the cameras.

The art director will begin by reading the script and sketching some initial impressions. Then in a meeting with the director, the sketches will be discussed, ideas exchanged, and the script reviewed scene by scene with respect to the set design. Details will be worked out, with the art director adding specific instructions such as, "In this scene I need a door downstage left." Using floor plans of the set, the art director or the assistant art director will then draft designs for the scenes. The sets are built in construction shops (*see* **Shop Craftsman**). When a set is completed, it is shipped in pieces to the studio, where it is put together by the studio carpenters.

Television series are taped (or filmed) on sets located in production studios. While a series is on the air, its main set changes very little, if at all. In the studio there may be a small number of additional sets (*swing sets*) that can be designed as needed.

The art director may also be involved in location shooting. If an exterior (outdoor) scene is needed, the art director will design it. For interior scenes done on location, where furniture, drapes, or lamps have to be brought in, the art director will supervise the setup of these props.

The art department of a TV show has a weekly budget. It may range from $5,000 to $10,000 for sets, and less for props. A sitcom, for example, might have a weekly budget of $8,500 for sets and $7,500 for props, or $16,000 total. Since the budget is usually planned for an entire season, the money appropriated for one show can run over the average and another show can run under, so long as the final expenditure meets the overall budget.

Another important figure in the art department is the set decorator, who confers with the art director and studies sketches to find furnishings and props that realize the art director's set concept. An outside prop person takes care of all the arrangements with regard to purchase orders and shipping. Inside prop persons unload the trucks and dress the sets. An assistant art director might be involved not only in drafting but supervising the dressing of the sets. The positions in the art department, and even their functions, might vary from show to show.

An art director's qualifications may include college courses and programs in art, production design, or architecture. Many art directors begin by designing sets for theatrical productions. Art directors generally are hired because of their reputations, track records,

Art Department

Title	Medium Works In	Depart-ment	Function
Art Director	Film	Art	Serves as either a local production designer or an assistant to the unit production designer
Art Director	Television	Art	Creates sets based on the script that complement the functions of the scenes
Construction Coordinator	Film		Supervises the construction of sets; liaison between art director and construction crew
Construction Illustrator	Film	Art	Makes conceptual sketches of the script to assist in designing sets and laying out shots
Inside Prop Person	Television	Art	Dresses sets with props
Matte Artist	Film	Matte	Paints backgrounds for matte shots
Outside Prop Person	Television	Art	Acquires props
Production Designer	Films and Television	Art	Is responsible for the artistic look of the production; is the chief designer

Continued on next page

Continued from previous page

Property Master	Film	Property	Acquires and maintains the action props (guns, swords, brooms, etc.)
Scenic Artist	Film	Art	Creates backdrops and other background paintings to represent a third dimension
Set Decorator	Film	Property	Supervises the dressing of the set
	Television	Art	Obtains props that convey the intended look of the set, such as furniture
Set Designer	Film and Television	Art	Devises scale diagrams of the set (showing such details as floors and windows) so the carpenters can build it
Set Dresser	Film	Property	Physically carries props onto and dresses the set; set props include furniture, pictures, and curtains
Shop Craftsman	Television	Art	Supervises the building of objects to be used on sets, such as doors, walls, and furniture
Set Painter	Film and Television	Art	Paints sets and objects, often to create the illusion that they are other than what they are
Title Artist	Film and Television	Art	Draws lettering, sketches, and portraits that may appear in the credits

and referrals. Some have agents who more often serve to negotiate contracts than to obtain work.

ASSISTANT DIRECTOR. *See* **Director, Motion Pictures, First Assistant; Director, Motion Pictures, Second Assistant.**

ASSOCIATED ACTORS AND ARTISTES OF AMERICA (Four As). Four As is an international union of nine prominent entertainment unions that determine the jurisdictions of its member unions, resolves jurisdictional disputes, monitors reciprocal agreements between its members, and supports its members in labor and contractual disputes with management. The association was founded in 1919 to represent entertainment unions to the American Federation of Labor, which merged in 1955 with the Congress of Industrial Organizations to form the AFL-CIO, a voluntary federation of U.S. labor organizations. The nine affiliated national unions that comprise Four As are: Actors' Equity Association, American Federation of Television and Radio Artists, American Guild of Musical Artists, American Guild of Variety Artists, Hebrew Actors Union, Italian Actors Union, Associación Puertorriqueña de Artistas e Tecnicos del Espectaculo (for Puerto Rican actors), Screen Actors Guild, and Screen Extras Guild. The member unions of Four As exercise jurisdiction in their respective fields of the entertainment business.

ASSOCIATIONS, TRADE, PROFESSIONAL, AND HONORARY. There are numerous organizations in the motion picture and television industries that comprise people and companies of a particular trade or profession and which serve to further the common goals of their members.

These associations conduct research related to their trade or profession, present awards, represent their trade or profession to the public and the government, and disseminate reports of their activities. Unlike **unions**, however, trade, professional, and honorary associations do not serve to negotiate industry-wide contracts with employers for their members. Membership in professional and trade associations is normally available to individuals and companies active in their fields; for honorary organizations, individuals must have achieved recognition or met minimum requirements as prescribed, such as a certain number of years of professional work experience.

The table beginning on page 58 lists associations and the trades, professions, and fields they represent.

AUDIENCE MEASUREMENT SERVICE. An audience measurement service is a company that, using statistical samples of television households and specially designed techniques or devices for monitoring viewing choices, estimates the size and composition of audiences watching television programs both nationally and locally. The results of these surveys are published as **ratings and shares**, numbers which indicate the relative popularity of shows and the demographics of their audiences. Ratings and shares are used to establish advertising rates, to help advertisers and their agenciesdecide which shows to buy (in terms of how much they can afford and the audience they will reach), and to help networks and stations determine whether to continue, drop, modify, or reschedule programs.

Historically, the A. C. Nielsen company has been the most prominent audience measurement service in television, but the other major companies, AGB Television and Arbitron, are competitive. All three publish their audience estimates as reports which are subscribed to by the networks, television stations, television producers, syndicators, and advertising agencies.

Nielsen's measurement of network prime-time viewers is called the Nielsen Television Index (NTI) and its estimates of local TV station audiences is the Nielsen Station Index (NSI).

Until a few years ago, diaries were the main technique used to measure national TV audiences. Respondents filled out forms to record their TV viewing habits. Then during the fall of 1987 AGB and Nielsen implemented a *people meter.* The Nielsen people meter is a system consisting of a hand-size remote-control unit and an electronic monitoring device that is placed on top of or beside the

Trade Associations

Trade, Field, or Profession	Association
actors, film	Academy of Motion Picture Arts and Sciences
actors, television	Academy of Television Arts and Sciences
agents	Association of Talent Agents
art directors, film	Academy of Motion Picture Arts and Sciences
art directors, television	Academy of Television Arts and Sciences
audio mixers	Cinema Audio Society
base film manufacturers	International Tape Association
broadcast engineers	Society of Motion Picture and Television Engineers
cable programmers	National Federation of Local Cable Programmers
cable programming suppliers	National Cable Television Association
cable system operators	National Association of Television, Program Executives National Cable Television Association
camerapersons	Society of Motion Picture and Television Engineers

Continued on next page

Continued from previous page

casting directors, film	Academy of Motion Picture Arts and Sciences Casting Society of America
casting directors, television	Academy of Television Arts and Sciences Casting Society of America
commercial producers	Association of Independent Commercial Producers
composers, film	Academy of Motion Picture Arts and Sciences
composers, television	Academy of Television Arts and Sciences
costume designers, film	Academy of Motion Picture Arts and Sciences
costume designers, television	Academy of Television Arts and Sciences
critics, television	Television Critics Association
directors, film	Academy of Motion Picture Arts and Sciences
directors, television	Academy of Television Arts and Sciences
directors of photography	American Society of Cinematographers Inc.
documentaries	International Documentary Association

Continued on next page

59

Continued from previous page

Trade, Field, or Profession	Association
editors, film	Academy of Motion Picture Arts and Sciences American Cinema Editors
editors, television	Academy of Television Arts and Sciences
engineers, film	Society of Motion Picture and Television Engineers
engineers, television	Society of Broadcast Engineers Society of Motion Picture and Television Engineers
entertainment management personnel	Financial and Administrative Management Executives
executives, film	Academy of Motion Picture Arts and Sciences
executives, television broadcast	Academy of Television Arts and Sciences Academy of Motion Picture Arts and Sciences
film distributors	Motion Picture Export Association of America
hairstylists, film	Academy of Motion Picture Arts and Sciences
hairstylists, television	Academy of Television Arts and Sciences
home video production companies	International Tape Association

Continued on next page

Continued from previous page

independent video producers, directors, technicians, and writers	Association of Independent Video and Filmmakers
journalists, broadcast	Academy of Television Arts and Sciences
makeup artists, film	Academy of Motion Picture Arts and Sciences
makeup artists, television	Academy of Television Arts and Sciences
merchandise licensing companies	Licensing Industry Merchandisers' Association
motion picture theater operators	National Association of Theatre Owners
networks, television	National Association of Broadcasters
news directors	Radio-Television News Directors Association
personal managers	National Conference of Personal Managers
producers, film	Academy of Motion Picture Arts and Sciences
producers, television	Academy of Television Arts and Sciences
professionals in broadcasting, advertising, and cable	International Radio and Television Society Inc.

Continued on next page

61

Continued from previous page

Trade, Field, or Profession	Association
program executives, television	National Association of Television Program Executives
projectionists	Society of Motion Picture and Television Engineers
public television stations	National Association of Public Television Stations
publicists, film	Academy of Motion Picture Arts and Sciences
publicists, television	Academy of Television Arts and Sciences
radio stations and networks	National Association of Broadcasting
rerecording mixers	Cinema Audio Society
rep firms	Stations Representatives Association
scenic designers, television	Academy of Television Arts and Sciences
screenwriters, film	Academy of Motion Picture Arts and Sciences
sound editors	Motion Picture Sound Editors

Continued on next page

Continued from previous page

sound effects editors, film | Academy of Motion Picture Arts and Sciences

sound mixers, film | Academy of Motion Picture Arts and Sciences

sound recording technicians | Society of Motion Picture and Television Engineers

special effects artists, film | Academy of Motion Picture Arts and Sciences

studio and transmitter operators and technicians | Society of Broadcast Engineers

stuntpersons | Black Stuntmen's Association
Stuntmen's Association of Motion Pictures Inc.
Stuntwomen's Association of Motion Pictures Inc.
Society of Professional Stuntwomen

subscription TV | Subscription Television Association

technicians, motion pictures | Society of Motion Picture and Television Engineers

technicians, television | Society of Motion Picture and Television Engineers

television programmers | National Association of Television Program Executives Inc.

Continued on next page

63

Continued from previous page

Trade, Field, or Profession	Association
television stations	National Association of Broadcasters, Television Bureau of Advertising
theater operators	National Association of Theater Owners
video retailers and wholesalers	Video Software Dealers Association
video equipment companies	International Tape Association
writers, television	Academy of Motion Picture Arts and Sciences

TV set and is attached by a wire to the back of the set. Every member of a household is assigned a number which he or she presses when starting to watch television. Information about viewing activity is then automatically stored in the meter for analysis by Nielsen the next day. It can be safely predicted that techniques and tools for estimating audience sizes and demographics will continue to evolve as programmers and advertisers continue to search for more accurate information about who is watching what.

See also **Network; Rating and Shares, Television.**

AWARDS. Awards are presented in the television and motion picture industries to honor the achievements of creative people, technicians, and workers, and to bring attention to the mediums. The awards, usually given on an annual basis, are presented by many of the professional trade associations, unions, guilds, honorary societies, and other organizations that constitute the industries. Information on major awards in television and film appears in the following table.

Awards

Name of Award	Field	Sponsor or Administrator
Academy Awards	film	Academy of Motion Picture Arts and Sciences
American Video Awards	music videos	National Academy of Video Arts and Sciences
American Women in Radio and Television Awards	radio and television	American Women in Radio and Television
Artios Awards	casting	Casting Society of America
Awards for Cable Excellence (ACE)	cable television	National Academy of Cable Programming
Christopher Awards	film and television	The Christophers
Circle Awards	film	New York Film Critics
Directors Guild Awards	film and television	Directors Guild of America
Alfred I. duPont–Columbia University Awards	broadcast journalism	Columbia University

Continued on next page

Continued from previous page

Name of Award	Field	Sponsor or Administrator
Emmy Awards	television	Academy of Television Arts and Sciences
Gemini Awards	Canadian film and television	Academy of Canadian Cinema and Television
Gold Medal Award	communications	International Radio and Television Society Inc.
Golden Globe Awards	film and television	Hollywood Foreign Press Association
Golden Palm Award (Palm d'or)	film	Cannes Film Festival
Golden Reel Awards	film and television sound editing	Motion Picture Sound Editors
D. W. Giffith Awards	film	National Board of Review of Motion Pictures
Humanitas Award	television writers	Human Family Educational and Cultural Institute
Image Awards	blacks in entertainment industry	National Association for the Advancement of Colored People

Continued on next page

Continued from previous page

Iris Awards	local programming production	National Association of Television Program Executives
Key Art Awards	posters in film and television	*Hollywood Reporter*
Life Achievement Award	film	American Film Institute
MTV Music Video Awards	music videos	MTV
National Board of Review Awards	film	National Board of Review
NATO Awards	film (box-office sales)	National Association of Theater Owners
Patsy Awards	animal performance in film and television	American Humane Society
Peabody (George Foster) Awards	broadcasting	University of Georgia School of Journalism
Publicists Guild Awards	film publicity	Publicists Guild
SAG Annual Achievement Award	entertainment and humanitarianism	Screen Actors Guild

Continued on next page

67

Continued from previous page

Name of Award	Field	Sponsor or Administrator
Saturn Awards	science fiction and horror film	Academy of Science Fiction, Fantasy and Horror Films
Television Critics Association Awards	television programming criticism	Television Critics Association
Video Software Dealers Association Awards	videos	Video Software Dealers Association
Writers Guild Awards	scriptwriting	Writers Guild

B MOVIE. Under the old Hollywood studio system, B movies were budget movies. They cost less and lacked the names or stars who appeared in features, or A movies, of that era, though they were often coupled with those features as the second billing of a double feature. Films made by independent producers often had small budgets also and were considered B movies.

Beginning in the 1950s, low-budget movies generally referred to low-budget exploitation films. These include many of the science-fiction films of the 1950s, the motorcycle movies of the 1960s, and the black exploitation and drug films of the 1970s. Companies were formed for the sole purpose of making these low-budget exploitation films.

Today, a B movie is sometimes designated as a **low-budget movie**, although the money needed to finance a contemporary low-budget movie, which could be about four or five million dollars, exceeds the cost of many a major feature of Hollywood's golden era.

B-movie classics include the Charlie Chan movies of the 1930s, *The Big House* (1930), *Hollywood Boulevard* (1936), *Stranger on the Third Floor* (1940), *Face Behind a Mask* (1941), *Cat People* (1942), *I Walked with a Zombie* (1943), *Detour* (1946), the Ma and Pa Kettle movies of the 1950s, *The Thing* (1950), *Creature from the Black Lagoon* (1954), *The Little Shop of Horrors* (1960), *Wild Angels* (1966), *Student Nurses* (1970), *Shaft* (1971), *Superfly* (1972), *Caged Heat* (1974), and *Savage Streets* (1975).

BARN DOOR. *See* **Grip Equipment.**

BARTER SYNDICATION. *See* **Syndication.**

BELOW-THE LINE. Below-the-line is a budgetary term that refers to the production costs of making a movie, including technical and craft labor, construction, materials, and fees. The expenses that are below-the-line include money paid for grips, gaffers, electricians, makeup artists, set directors, property masters, sound mixers, camera equipment rentals, film, developing, costumes, transportation, location fees, music, titles and opticals, and insurance. Talent salaries, advertising costs, and other negotiables are **above-the-line** expenses.

See also **Above-the-Line; Budget, Motion Pictures.**

BEST BOY. A best boy is an assistant lighting electrician or, in some cases, an assistant grip. In the electrical department, the best boy is the second electrician and would take over the gaffer's responsibilities if needed. While the film crew is filming one scene, the best boy is helping the crew set up the next scene.

The National Association of Broadcast Employees and Technicians (NABET) Local 15 in New York has defined the specific duties of the best boy, or second electrician. According to the NABET electric department safety manual, the second electrician must know: "the third electrician's duties (*see* **Electrician, Third**); how to tie-in (pull the power out from a main electrical box with tie-in clamp and bring it to the set or area where shooting is taking place); how to measure load balance; how to mark power distribution; how to trim arc lights, and maintain and set gaps; how to start, run and refuel generators; A.C. and D.C. tie-ins; how to determine generator output terminals; safety rigging pertaining to working with electric equipment; first aid; how to make emergency repairs on lighting equipment; fusing; cable capacity; functions of basic tools of the trade (and to have them); simple rigging; how to read a volt, ohm and amphere meter; how to use gels and diffusion material; how to operate a camera regulator (a machine used to maintain constant voltage flow); how to operate light fixtures; how to bulb, operate and ground HMI's."

Males have traditionally performed the duties of the best boy, but in recent years women have been occupying the position with increasing frequency. There have been efforts to change the term to "best person."

See also **Gaffer (Electrician).**

BIDDING. *See* **Syndication.**

BIT PART. *See* Actor.

BLOCKBUSTER. *See* Hit Movie.

BLOCKING. *See* Camera Blocking.

BOOK ADAPTATIONS. *See* Adaptations.

BOOK AUCTION. *See* Adaptations.

BOOM. *See* Sound Recording, Production.

BOOM OPERATOR. *See* Sound Recording, Production.

BOUNCE CARD. *See* Grip Equipment.

BOX-OFFICE CHARTS. Box-office charts are tables published in trade publications that state the weekly and total rentals of the top-earning motion pictures as well as other information. Both *Variety* and *The Hollywood Reporter* publish U.S. and international box-office charts.

BROADCAST MUSIC INCORPORATED (BMI). BMI is a **performing-rights organization.** Founded in 1940 by several hundred radio broadcasters, the organization pays royalties to composers, songwriters, and lyricists for public performances of their works.

For performances of musical works on television, BMI pays different royalty rates according to distinctions it makes with regard to the type of performance (feature, theme, or background music), whether the broadcast is network or local, and, if it is network, what time the performance is broadcast. Payment is also made for performance on public broadcasting stations and cable TV stations with which BMI has licensing agreements.

A feature performance is defined as one that "constitutes the main focus of audience attention at the time of performance" and

71

requires the singers or instrumentalists to be on camera except when the music is part of a dance number that is the main focus of audience attention.

A television theme is defined as one that "comprises both the opening and closing musical works performed on a program." If the work is performed at any other time during the show, it is credited at background rates.

Background music is defined as "music used other than as feature or theme." There are separate rates for background music on game shows, made-for-TV movies and theatrical films, news and public affairs programs, and for entrances and exits.

As an example of how a feature song on television can earn royalties for the composer, suppose Margaret Songwriter had her work "Love Is My Favorite Subject" performed on a 1987 prime-time network variety show. BMI's prime-time rate in 1987 was $9.00 per network station, therefore, if the network averaged 200 stations, Margaret and her publisher would share a minimum of $1,800 for the single performance.

See also **American Society of Composers, Authors and Publishers (ASCAP); Music Licensing, Film.**

BUDDY MOVIE. *See* **Film Genres.**

BUDGET, MOTION PICTURES. A motion picture budget is an estimate of the total cost involved in the making of a motion picture broken down into categories. Major studio budgets are prepared by specialized departments (often called Production Finance and Budgeting or Theatrical Finance and Estimating); the budgets for independent production companies are determined by freelance feature estimators or production accountants. Budget sheets, forms divided into various categories such as story, cast, set design, location, music, sound, editing, and insurance, are used as aids in estimating specific costs.

There is no standard method for calculating a budget, as each type of expense is subject to the individual requirements of a film. The wardrobe costs for a contemporary feature film would be relatively small, while those for a period piece (one set during the American Revolution, for example) would be high. Costumes for a period piece would have to be rented or manufactured, which would be substantially more expensive than buying the wardrobe at retail stores.

Although budgets vary greatly in size, there are a number of conventional processes by which they may be broken down. For example, expenses may be calculated in terms of preproduction, production, and postproduction. Preproduction expenses are those necessary to bring the project to the commencement of principal photography (the first day of shooting). This may involve such costs as book rights and screenwriter fees (for several drafts of the script). Production expenses are those for shooting the film. A production board, or stripboard (basically a shooting schedule), is used to show where production will take place—indoor sound stages, locations, or both. From this it can be determined how many days are expected to be spent shooting on each set. Expenses for crew, construction, location, stunts, and other production essentials can be estimated, and with the addition of information on actors' salaries, the budget for production may be determined. Postproduction costs are those for editing, music, rerecording, and other areas necessary to achieve an **answer print**. The total of all costs will yield a final figure, and several budgets may be drafted until one is finally approved.

Expenses are designed as **above-the-line** or **below-the-line**. The former applies to up-front, fixed costs such as fees for the director or screenwriter, and the latter designates variable costs including those for postproduction. Expenses are categorized as follows:

ABOVE-THE-LINE:

story	director
screenplay	cast
continuity and treatment	bit parts
producer	

production staff
production operating staff
set design and construction
set operations
film and laboratory
wardrobe
makeup and hair styling
set dressing
lighting
transportation
locations

studio rentals
tests and retakes
special effects
editing
music
opticals and titles
miscellaneous
publicity
insurance and taxes
licenses and fees
contingency

Theatrical motion pictures are generally categorized as being low budget or high budget. Although these are relative terms, a **low-budget movie** generally ranges in cost from $100,000 to $6 million, while a **high-budget movie** can cost over $10 million. Any movie whose cost is between these ranges could be considered one or the other. There is also what is sometimes referred to as a **no-budget movie**, one whose cost is relatively marginal ($100,000 or less). No-budget movies are made by young or inexperienced filmmakers and budgets may not even be calculated for them.

BUSINESS MANAGER. A business manager administers an entertainer's finances. There are many services a business manager may perform on behalf of a client, including collecting income as it is due and making sure it arrives on time and in accordance with contractual agreements, investing money, paying bills, negotiating contracts, performing tax work, and advising the client on financial matters. A business manager may handle a client's finances only as they relate to the entertainment industry or may handle all aspects, professional and personal, of the client's financial life. Business managers are usually certified public accountants, but anyone may serve as one, as there are no licensing requirements. Business managers represent a variety of people from the entertainment field, including actors and actresses, directors, producers, singers, composers, and dancers. For their services business managers charge a straight fee (by the hour, month, or year) or work on a commission basis (usually about 5 percent).

BUTTERFLY. *See* **Grip Equipment.**

C

CBS TELEVISION NETWORK. One of the three major commercial **networks,** CBS was organized in 1928 when its founder, William Paley, acquired ownership of a group of radio stations. As the Columbia Broadcasting System expanded its operations, soon becoming the largest radio network in the United States, it precociously recognized the potential for the rapidly evolving television broadcasting technology. On July 13, 1931, it began experimental television broadcasting in New York, and ten years later began regular black-and-white weekly broadcasts over its WCBW-TV station in the same city, which became WCBS-TV in November 1946. With Television City in Hollywood, CBS launched the industry's first full-scale production studio.

CBS was also successful in its early ventures into the record business, and because of FCC monopoly restrictions it sold its interests in other fields, such as musical instruments, toys, and magazine and book publishing. In 1985 Loews Corporation, whose main holdings are in hotels, insurance, tobacco, and watchmaking, increased its share of CBS stock to 24.9 percent, thereby becoming the largest stockholder and preventing an unfriendly takeover. In an effort by CBS to strengthen the core business, network broadcasting, management prompted company-wide layoffs.

In 1988 CBS sold its record division to Sony for a reported $2 billion. Today CBS owns television stations, radio stations, and home-video production and distribution interests. The CBS Broadcasting Group is composed of six divisions: television network, entertainment, sports, news, local television stations, and radio.

For most of commercial television history, CBS has been the network leader in prime-time ratings, having the highest-rated shows in almost every year from the mid-1950s through the mid-1980s. During the late 1980s, however, CBS lost its top position to NBC.

CBS has traditionally been strong in the TV news area. The network began the first regular TV news program in 1948 with Douglas Edwards as anchor. Journalism legends such as Edward R. Murrow and Walter Cronkite gave CBS its reputation as a quality news broadcaster.

CALL SHEET. A call sheet is a report prepared daily during the production of a movie that outlines the work of the following day's shooting, including:

- Which scenes will be shot.
- Which cast members are in those scenes.
- What time actors have to be in makeup and when they are to be on the set.
- Which special effects will be used.
- Where shooting will take place and directions for getting there.
- Which equipment and props crew members or departments will be using.

There are usually different calls (work requests) for the different crew members. Assistants and regular staff members typically report to the set earlier than key members to prepare for the shoot. There also may be different calls for the assistants and regular crew members.

A call sheet is prepared by the first or second assistant director, with approval from the **unit production manager**. It is typed and photocopied by the **production office coordinator (POC)** and distributed on the set before the end of that day's shooting.

CAMEO. *See* **Actor.**

CAMERA BLOCKING. Camera blocking is a run-through of a scene to determine approximate camera positions. The actors rehearse the scene and the camera operators track them with the cameras in the same manner they would use in an actual take. Blocking is done before actual rehearsal, and extras or stand-ins may substitute for the leading performers. Just before the take, a full dress rehearsal is done in which all participate.

CANNES FILM FESTIVAL. *See* **Film Festival.**

CARPENTER. *See* **Shop Craftsman.**

CASTING DIRECTOR. The casting director is the individual responsible for searching for, auditioning, and recommending actors who, due to physical appearance and acting ability, are best suited to the roles called for in a script.

The casting director is the link between the director and the acting community. Casting directors, many of whom are former actors or directors themselves, are specialists who keep abreast of the vast pool of acting talent, a task that directors have little time for. They scout new actors, maintain working relationships with agents, hold auditions, recommend people for parts, and negotiate contracts with actors.

A successful casting director has an extensive knowledge of actors in the film, television, theater, and advertising industries, though the extremely large number of emerging, unemployed, and active thespians makes it difficult for casting directors to bear in mind every available actor. The casting director uses various resources to aid the search for appropriate talent. Resumés and photos, union books with pictures and profiles of the members, trade publications, trade services, and videotapes are all helpful. Developing a network of associations with agents is also important. A good casting director keeps an eye on actors already performing in theater, the movies, and television as well. The casting director is on the lookout for talent anywhere and at any time.

Casting directors are categorized as either independent or in-house. Independent casting people are free lancers, hired by producers and directors for specific projects. In-house casting directors are affiliated with a motion picture studio, production company, advertising agency, or television network, and work exclusively on their company's productions.

A casting director begins work on a new project by reading the script. The casting director then visualizes the leading roles and supposes actors who might be right for the parts. The next step is to discuss the possibilities with the director. The casting director offers preliminary ideas and tries to get a sense of the kinds of actors the director envisions in the various roles. The two discuss which performers might be right for specific parts. The casting director will consider the director's ideas when carrying out the talent search. It is the director who will usually make the final casting decisions.

Besides acting talent, there are many factors that may be considered in casting a part: age, personality, mannerisms, physical qualities, ethnic characteristics, accents, and any special talents required. Often specific combinations of these are needed. Another consideration is the chemistry between actors.

In searching for talent, the casting director relies on contacts and in some cases solicits agents' recommendations through companies such as Breakdown Services Ltd. (*see* **Agent, Actor's**). Based on detailed character descriptions in service bulletins, agents submit photos and resumés of clients whom they feel would be suitable for the roles.

The casting director reviews the candidates, and those deemed potentially suitable are given appointments to audition. Since the largest pools of acting talent are located in Los Angeles and New York, it is often necessary to hold auditions in both these cities. This is done in one of two ways. The casting director may hold auditions in both cities, or the producer might simply hire New York and Los Angeles casting directors and make final decisions from their selections.

This screening and audition process is used when the main characters will not be played by "name" actors. Stars usually meet with the director and may take a **screen test**.

Anywhere from a few to a hundred or more actors may audition for a single part. When a director does not have a clear-cut picture of a character in his head, or an unknown is being selected for a major role, the casting director may need to see a substantial number of actors.

At auditions, actors read sides selected by the casting director. A *side* is a compilation of a character's most difficult scenes. A person up for a large role will probably act out a few different scenes. Actors usually pick up their sides the day before their audition but are sometimes asked to do a **cold reading.**

An audition may run anywhere from ten minutes to a half-hour.

Since there are many actors who try out for a single part, perhaps only one out of every five to ten of them will be asked back. Those who are given callbacks then audition before the director, producer, executive producer, or some combination thereof. The director usually has the ultimate decision-making power.

Readings and screen tests may continue for several months. In film, the director may have to clear certain decisions with the producer; in television, network personnel often must be consulted. After final decisions are made, the casting director notifies the actors' agents and proceeds to negotiate contracts. The casting director now serves as the liaison between the producer and the actors' agents.

The producer or unit production manager gives the casting director a budget, which is broken down into estimates of how much each actor should be paid. The casting director is allowed flexibility with regard to these figures but must not exceed the overall budget. Thus, if ten thousand dollars is saved on one part, he or she can spend more for another if necessary. A casting director finds the best talent available and negotiates the best possible price. ·

A casting director also hires extras, who register directly with the casting offices. During shooting, a casting director and the extras will be in touch on a daily basis so the casting director can provide them with information about such things as what to wear, how much makeup to put on, and the location of filming for the following day. There are no auditions for extras.

Casting directors who work for studios, production companies, and networks are salaried employees. An independent casting director's fees vary from film to film depending on the scope of responsibilities. The independent casting director might be asked to cast one role over a three-day period or hundreds of roles, for an epic film, over the course of a year or more. Reputation is also a factor in establishing a fee.

There are no licensing or educational requirements for becoming a casting director. Although good instinct is a requisite for success, the casting director must also understand relevant union contracts and rules and be a competent negotiator. There is no union for casting directors, but there is a professional association, the Casting Society of America.

Just how important is the casting director's job? Suffice to say that the right actor or ensemble can be the fuel that propels a project to mega-success. On the other hand, even with the right script, director, and other elements, less than perfect choices for the roles could mean a film or TV series' demise.

CELEBRITY BROKER. A celebrity broker specializes in booking talent, particularly major stars, to endorse products in television commercials. Since the association of a famous actor with a product tends to increase sales, advertisers often want celebrities to promote their products. The celebrity broker is there to fill that demand.

The celebrity broker serves as a liaison between the advertising (or corporate) community and the entertainment industry. If an advertising agency has a creative concept that requires a celebrity, the broker secures a suitable spokesperson whose fee fits within the client's budget. Representatives of advertising agencies or corporations could contact the large talent agencies that represent stars directly, but they usually do not know the specifics of celebrity availability and endorsement fees.

First, an advertiser calls a broker and conveys its concept for a particular campaign. The broker in turn gives a general idea of who is available within the budget range of the advertiser. The agency decides on a celebrity and the broker attempts to hire that person. He or she will contact the entertainer's personal manager or booking agent, or perhaps call or write directly to the celebrity. The broker serves the interest of the advertiser and tries to negotiate the best deal possible.

Celebrity brokers usually work on a percentage basis. Their commission for finding talent and negotiating contracts is commonly 10 percent of the celebrity's fee, but each deal is different and the commissions can vary according to individual circumstances.

Celebrity brokers do not serve as actors' representatives, but rather find and contract talent on behalf of advertisers. They are free to work with anyone and, in addition to working with motion picture and television stars, they might secure sports figures, politicians, and other distinguished persons.

To be a celebrity broker requires years of making contacts in the entertainment industry and dealing with actors or their representatives. In securing talent for advertisers, brokers have to know who to contact to determine interest and negotiate deals. They may have to convince personal managers and agents why a particular endorsement is in their client's best interest. People who enter this field may have a background in advertising or management, or be former actors themselves.

CEL ANIMATION. *See* **Animation.**

CENTURY STAND. *See* **Grip Equipment.**

CHARACTER ACTOR. A character actor is an actor who plays stereotypical roles such as gangsters, maids, army sergeants, secretaries, or maniacs. Character actors' roles are usually integral to plot and action but subservient to the roles of the leading men and women. Character actors often begin their careers by playing a certain type of role and thereafter are typecast due to physical appearance and association with that role.

CHILDREN'S MOVIE. *See* **Film Genres.**

CHILDREN'S TELEVISION SHOW. *See* **Television Programming Genres.**

CHRISTMAS MOVIE. Christmas movies are released anytime between Thanksgiving and New Year's Day. The weeks prior to and after Christmas, when schools and colleges are closed, traditionally compose one of the strongest box-office periods of the year. Winter temperatures and increased family spending during the holiday season also contribute to the box-office surge.

Movies deemed to have blockbuster or highly commercial potential are often targeted for release during this period. A movie that is completed after the summer, for example, might be held up for release until at least Thanksgiving. Major Christmas movies greet the public with extravagant advertising and publicity campaigns. *See also* **Summer Season, Motion Pictures.**

CINEMATOGRAPHER. *See* **Director of Photography.**

CLIFFHANGER. The cliffhanger is used by television programs in which a show concludes with one or more major characters being involved in a situation, the outcome of which is uncertain and seemingly unresolvable. The dilemma promises to be resolved in the next episode. The purpose of this device is to leave the audience "hanging," wondering about the outcome and eager to tune into the next episode. Many prime-time soaps and dramas use cliffhangers on their last show of the season. Promotional mileage is gained by exploiting the up-in-the-air ending in the interval between seasons. The movie serials of the 1940s and 1950s were the predecessors of today's television cliffhangers.

CLIP BOARD. *See* **Grip Equipment.**

CLOSED-CAPTIONING. Closed-captioning is a system in which a device called a decoder is attached to a home television set and interprets an electronic code so that television shows designated as closed-captioned appear with subtitles on the screen (white letters on a black background). This enables those who are hearing-impaired to enjoy television. Closed-captioning is also used as an educational tool, helping children to strengthen their reading skills while watching television.

Closed-captioning works in the following way: The dialogue of a show is set in captions and recorded onto a magnetic disc, whose data in turn is inserted into line 21, field 1 of the television signal. This data is transmitted in the form of an electronic code and converted into the subtitles that appear at the bottom of the screen.

A television set without a decoder cannot receive captions. Only programs that have been electronically encoded can be watched with a decoder installed.

For a program to become closed-captioned, consent must be obtained from the producer and there must be a sponsor to pay for the costs of captioning. Various groups sponsor closed-captioning, including private companies, the federal government, and the networks. The use of closed-captioning grew from sixteen hours per week in 1980 to 145 hours in 1987 on free television and pay cable TV. Hundreds of home videocassettes are also available in closed-captioned format.

Only a handful of companies do closed-captioning. These include the National Captioning Institute and WGBM in the United States, and the Canadian Captioning Development Agency (CCDA). The National Captioning Institute (NCI), a private nonprofit corporation, has spearheaded the closed-captioning movement in the United States. The NCI not only is responsible for the majority of closed-captioned programming on American television, but also has been active in consumer research, congressional advocacy, and the promotion of closed-captioned television.

COLD READING. A cold reading is a reading of lines from a script without the benefit of preparation. In holding auditions, directors, producers, and casting directors sometimes do not give out scripts in advance. The actors are not given an opportunity to *warm up* (prepare in advance). Reasons for holding cold readings may include a directorial strategy or logistics. A director may want to test an actor's spontaneity or it simply may be impractical to make copies of the script for everyone auditioning for a part.

COLOR CORRECTION. Color correction is a process that makes the color of film consistent throughout. Because film is shot outdoors and indoors and in different locations for each, the different color temperatures of the light in each location results in color bias. Skylights, for example, may be of one particular color and room light another. In this process different colors are added to the film, such as yellow to a blue-cast film, to make it look more neutral. Color correction then changes the color balance of film.

COLORIST. *See* **Animation.**

COMEDY. *See* **Film Genres.**

COMMERCIAL. A commercial is a paid announcement promoting a product, business, or service that is broadcast on a television network or station, or a public-service message for which airtime is provided free of charge by a network or station. Contrary to popular belief (due to former rules), the **Federal Communications Commission (FCC)** does not limit the number of commercials or the amount of commercial time that may be run during any set time period on television. The National Association of Broadcasters, similarly, has no restrictions regarding the length or quantity of commercials. Rather, the amount of commercial time aired is decided by the stations. However, the stations are restricted by the understanding that excessive commercial time counts against a station trying to renew its FCC license.

Television is one of the most effective ways to advertise commercial products and services to mass audiences. Like other media, advertisements may be targeted for specific demographic groups. Audiences of television programming are studied by their makeup—sex, race, education, and income. But television offers benefits that print publications cannot. A catchy jingle, for instance, serves as an indelible reminder of a product. Skilled actors can persuasively impart a message that in print might not have the same impact upon the consumer. While print advertisements are generally messages, television commercials are mini-stories, with the moral being to buy the produce or use the service. Adept camera work, attractive actors, and action all bring a script to life and serve to make TV commercials effective. Another advantage of television over print advertising is that TV viewing is free and its ads are likely to reach more people. The rates of advertising on television are competitive with print fees.

Commercials vary in content, but commonly they are vignettes that attempt to motivate people to buy a specific product. The message can be subtle or blatant, but commercials tend to be quick and impact-oriented. Commercials usually run ten, fifteen, thirty, or sixty seconds.

Commercials are a source of income for those who perform in them. Stars who endorse products, in particular, may earn large sums of money. However, exposure in commercials may undermine a performer's credibility, and consideration must be given by the celebrity to the product being touted. The Federal Trade Commission (FTC) prescribes certain guidelines pertaining to claims made by endorsers. For example, a spokesperson must actually use a product at the time the endorsement is made, and the endorsement must be a true reflection of the person's opinion of the product and not contain deceptive claims.

Composers and copyright owners earn royalties when their music is played in commercials. The performing-rights organizations each have their own methods of calculating payments to composers, lyricists, and publishers for the use of music in a commercial.

See also **Advertising on Television.**

COMMUNICATIONS ACT OF 1934. A legislative act created the **Federal Communications Commission (FCC).** Radio broadcasting was a young but burgeoning industry in the United States in the 1920s and early 30s. As people began to make it their preferred medium for news and entertainment, broadcast stations cropped up to meet the demand. At first the airwaves were cluttered, but in 1927 the Radio Act created a commission to license stations and assign frequencies to them.

By 1933, electronic communications—radio, telephone, and telegraph—had expanded to the point that President Franklin D. Roosevelt ordered a study on how the government should deal with this growth. As a result of this research, Congress passed the Communications Act of 1934, which created a single agency, the FCC, to be responsible for establishing and overseeing all broadcasting policy in the United States. As television evolved, its regulation also became subject to the FCC, and the Communications Act has been amended through the years.

COMPLETION GUARANTOR. A completion guarantor is a company that guarantees for a fee (the completion bond fee) that a film will be completed on time and on budget. A completion guarantor guarantees to a financier (usually a bank) that a motion picture will be made in compliance with the contract negotiated between the producer and the studio or the distributor; to wit, the film will be made according to the script, a specified director and stars will be employed, and the running of the picture will be as agreed upon.

During production the producer will submit on a regular basis (usually weekly) cost reports detailing what has been spent to date and projected expenses for completion of the film. If the bond company sees or anticipates a problem in production, it may send a person to the set to supervise. The bond company has the right to sign every check, and to make sure the bills are being paid and other areas are being carried out properly. And though it is rarely done, the bond company has the right to shut the production down if the cost of completing and delivering the picture would likely exceed the cost of abandoning the production and repaying the financier its cash-outlay-to-date. The guarantor also has the right to replace the producer, director, or any of the cast, if such cast or crew member is the cause of an unacceptable or unreasonable delay.

In the event that the film is not submitted by the delivery date, or if it goes over budget, then there may be a claim against the guarantee (the bond). The guarantor could then be required to repay the loan, in which case it would take over the lender's position, or if additional financing is needed to complete the project, it can advance the funds to do so. The bond company serves as a kind of insurance policy to a financier that a film will be completed on time, on budget, and in such a manner as to conform to the requirements of the distribution agreements and other related contracts and documents.

See also **Financing a Film.**

COMPUTER ANIMATION. *See* **Animation.**

CONSTRUCTION GRIP. *See* **Grip.**

CONTINGENCY. A contingency is a sum of money or percentage of the overall budget of a motion picture agreed upon between the production company and the financier that is not itemized but is ready to be used to finance filming should production be halted by inclement weather or *force majeure* occurrences or if materials or other costs that were not provided for in the budget are deemed necessary. The contingency varies from film to film and is proportionate to the specific risks and material needs of the picture.

CONTINUITY. Continuity refers to the seamless professionalism which is characteristic of a commercial-quality film. Continuity serves to achieve the audience's willing suspension of disbelief. It is necessary to have continuity of action, movement, dialogue, direction, art, lighting, sound, wardrobe, props, hairstyles, makeup, and virtually anything else that gives a film a continuous air of believability. Because one scene may be filmed over an extended period of time, care must be taken that the characters are dressed in the same costumes, have the same hairdos, and are wearing the same makeup during each take. If different microphones are used, adjustments must be made for consistency. The **script supervisor** makes sure that everything is exactly in position from one scene to the next. As scenes are shot out of order, a continuity breakdown is made, indicating the composition of each scene, which can be referred to at any time during production.

When the actors "get into" their roles in front of the camera, they make believe that what they are doing and what is going on is real. But if any element of the film's continuity is interrupted—the screen direction changes, an actor's tie is suddenly open, the wine on the table is missing, the windows are open instead of closed—the audience will be distracted. In such cases, the audience is reminded that the people on the screen are only acting, and that the world they are watching is illusory.

CONTINUITY BREAKDOWN. *See* **Script Supervisor.**

COP/CRIME SHOW. *See* **Television Programming Genres.**

COPYRIGHT. The law in the United States that governs copyrights is title 17 of the United States Code, which in its latest general revision is commonly known as the Copyright Act of 1976. It is divided into eight chapters and has been amended. Section 102 of the law provides that copyright protection exists for original works of authorship fixed in any tangible medium of expression in the following categories: 1) literary works; 2) musical works; 3) dramatic works; 4) pantomimes and choreographic works; 5) pictorial, graphic, and sculptural works; 6) motion pictures and other audio-visual works; and 7) sound recordings.

The concept of copyright in the United States has its roots in the U.S. Constitution, based on preexisting English law, which provides for authors to have the exclusive right to their works "to promote the progress of science and arts."

The term *copyright* is used in many senses. It may refer to an original work of authorship, any of the exclusive rights to reproduce an original artistic work, or the law of a country covering and protecting original works of authorship. Copyright laws enable creators and rights owners to license or sell their properties and thereby be financially rewarded for their labors. Anyone who uses a copyrighted work without permission of the owner is violating the statute and is subject to subsequent penalties.

Since motion pictures and television programs are creative works, the copyright law, in essence, allows industries to thrive on these creative formats.

Movies and television programs contain copyrightable elements, and copyright registrations are therefore made for them. In a movie, the script, which contains dialogue and plot, is copyrighted. Music and choreography are copyrightable also. On television, the questions on a game show, the patter of a talk show, or the script of a sitcom or drama is copyrightable. Elements may be registered separately or a work may be registered as a whole. Movies and television programs are subject to copyright protection regardless of their nature: Theatrical films, documentaries, biographies, sitcoms, news programs, cartoons, talk shows, even home movies and amateur films are covered by law.

Application forms for registration of a claim to copyright may be obtained from: Copyright Office, Library of Congress, Washington, D.C. 20559. The Copyright Office also has a hotline, which can be called twenty-four hours a day to request the forms. (Callers leave their name and address on the tape and requests are filled promptly.) The hotline telephone number is (202) 707-9100.

Registration of claims to copyright for works in any of the categories afforded copyright protection is made in five basic classes: PA, SR, TX, VA, and SE.

Class PA is used for "works of the performing arts." Published or unpublished works prepared for the purpose of being performed directly before an audience or indirectly by means of any machine, device, or process are registered in this class. These include motion pictures and other audiovisual works, screenplays, choreographic works, musical scores and songs (with or without lyrics). Registrations are made with Form PA.

Class SR, or "sound recordings," is used to register published and unpublished works consisting of a fixed series of sounds—musical, spoken, or otherwise. The music embodied on records and tapes (including movie sound track scores) are registered in this class. Form SR is used to register works in this class.

Class TX is used to register published and unpublished "nondramatic literary works." Works that are registered in this class, with Form TX, include short stories, books, poetry, advertising copy, and catalogs.

Class VA is used to register published and unpublished works of the visual arts. Works that are registered in this class, with Form VA, include photographs, prints, fine and graphic art, diagrams, advertisements, and pictorial labels.

Class SE is used to register published and unpublished serials. These are works issued in successive parts having chronological designations and intended to be continued indefinitely. Works that are registered in this class include newspapers, magazines, and journals. Registrations are made with Form SE.

The Copyright Office also uses other forms for particular types of registrations. Form RE is the renewal application used to extend the term of copyright protection for works (of any class) that were in their first term of copyright protection on January 1, 1978. Works copyrighted after January 1, 1978, do not have a renewal period.

Form CA is used for supplementary registration, that is, to amplify or correct information given in the original application form.

COPYRIGHT NOTICE. On March 1, 1989, the United States joined the Berne Convention for the Protection of Literary and Artistic Works. This international convention, formed in 1886, provides protection for the literary and artistic works of the copyright owners whose countries adhere to the convention. Adherence to this treaty has changed the statutory requirement that copyright notice be placed on all publicly distributed copies of works (this would include motion picture and audiovisual copies*). Copyright notice is no longer required for works published for the first time on or after March 1, 1989, but is strongly encouraged by the Copyright Office. This is so an infringer will not be able to make a claim of innocent infringement, which could result in a reduction of damages in an infringement suit.

Section 401 of the Copyright Act of 1976 prescribes the form of notice, which comprises three elements:

1. The symbol © or the word *copyright*, or the abbreviation *copr*.
2. The year of the first publication of the work.
3. The name of the owner of the copyright, or an abbreviation by which the name could be recognized, or a generally known alternative designation of the owner. Example: © 1987 Genius Productions Inc.

---

*By *copies*, it is meant film, videotape, and other materials from which the work can be visually perceived, either directly or with the aid of a machine. The term *motion pictures* covers theatrical films, television programs, cartoons, and all other audiovisual works.

Copyright Registration Summary

Work	Class	Form
Advertisement (for a movie or TV show)	TX or VA—TX if text is predominant, VA if visual matter is predominant.	TX or VA
Cartoon	PA	PA
Continuity	PA	PA
Idea for a movie or TV series	TX or VA. An idea itself is not copyrightable, but the expression of the idea is; copyright protection would only extend to this.	TX or VA
Motion picture (theatrical documentary, etc.)	PA	PA
Motion picture videotape	PA	PA
Orchestration	PA	PA
Scenario	PA	PA
Score	PA	PA
Screenplay	PA	PA
Shooting script	PA	PA
Song	PA	PA

Continued on next page

Continued from previous page

Work	Class	Form
Sound track	SR	SR
Television program or pilot or episode of a series	PA	PA
Title of a movie or TV series	a title cannot be copyrighted	
Treatment	PA	PA

If the audiovisual work contains previously copyrighted material, such as old film footage, the year date of first publication of the compilation or derivative work is sufficient.

COPYRIGHT PROTECTION IN FOREIGN COUNTRIES. The United States enjoys copyright relations with many foreign countries by virtue of being a signatory of common copyright agreements and other arrangements. Hence, works registered in the United States receive copyright protection in these countries. The United States is a member of the Buenos Aires Convention, Berne Convention for the Protection of Literary and Artistic Works, Universal Copyright Convention, Geneva, Universal Copyright Convention, Paris, Convention for the Protection of Producers of Phonograms Against Unauthorized Duplication of Their Phonograms, and the Convention Relating to the Distribution of Programme-Carrying Signals Transmitted by Satellite.

COPYRIGHT PROTECTION, U.S. The U.S. copyright law provides for copyright protection upon fixation. For example, once a writer sets to paper a screenplay, that work is protected under the federal copyright law (*see* **Fixed Work**). Registering a work with the Copyright Office is not necessary to acquire copyright protection for a work, although registration is necessary to initiate an infringement suit. Upon fixation, copyrights for a work belong to the creator, or author. If the work is made under an employee- or work-for-hire agreement, ownership is vested in the employer. Certain components of motion pictures or television programs are often created under work-for-hire agreements, such as the script and the music.

COPYRIGHT REGISTRATION, DURATION, AND RENEWAL OF MOTION PICTURES. Both published and unpublished motion pictures and other audiovisual works may be registered for copyright with the U.S. Copyright Office. The application used for copyright registration of these works is Form PA, and among the motion pictures that may be copyrighted are the following:

- animated films
- commercials
- documentaries
- educational films
- feature films
- industrials
- music videos
- television programs
- television series

   To copyright a published or unpublished motion picture, the applicant must send to the Register of Copyright, Library of Congress, Washington, D.C. 20559 the following elements:

- Form PA, completed and signed.
- For a published motion picture, one complete copy of the best edition of the film; for an unpublished motion picture, a complete copy, or either an audiocassette of the complete sound track or prints (enlarged frames) representing every ten-minute portion of the picture.
- Written material such as a script or synopsis in which the contents of the picture are described, including the theme

95

and a plot summary, along with the title, credits, length, date of first broadcast on television (if this has occurred), and the date when the work was completed on film or video (called *fixed* under the law).

• The application fee.

The Copyright Office offers agreements that relax the deposit requirements for published motion pictures, to allow filmmakers to have more prints in circulation and to relieve the burden of small filmmakers from depositing film prints by initially depositing a videotape instead.

Under the Motion Picture Agreement, which is a contractual agreement between the depositor and the U.S. Government, the copy deposited for registration will be returned by the Copyright Office after it is examined. The depositor must hold on to an archival copy for two years and the Copyright Office may recall the copy within two years.

The Supplemental Property Agreement provides for signatories to the MPA to deposit a copy other than the actual print (called the *best edition*) that was published, such as a videotape. The Copyright Office may recall a best edition copy within two years. The Motion Picture Supplement allows independent filmmakers who only have ten or fewer 35-mm or 16-mm film prints of a motion picture to deposit a ¾-inch videotape for up to five years. At the end of the five years the Library of Congress will request a best edition copy of the film. To qualify, the depositor must meet the criteria for independent filmmakers as set forth by the Library of Congress.

Under the law it is not mandatory to register for copyright a motion picture that is published (ready for distribution to theaters, distributors, networks, stores, or others, or when at least one print or videotape is publicly distributed) or unpublished, but there are certain benefits in doing so, including the following: It is a prerequisite for instituting an infringement suit; it enables statutory damages or attorneys' fees to be recovered for infringements that occurred before registration was made (the law allows a three-month grace period following the date of publication to make registration); in a judicial proceeding the certificate of registration constitutes *prima facie* evidence of the validity of the copyright and of the facts stated in the certificate; and it places on public record the name and address of the copyright owner, which may facilitate licensing arrangements. Additionally, the law requires that a work published in the United States be deposited within three months of publication. If a deposit has to be made anyway for a published motion picture, it might be advantageous to just go ahead and make the registration.

In the application for copyright registration, space two requests the name of the "author(s)." Since most motion pictures are made as a **work-for-hire**, the author would normally be the studio or production company, even though many people may have creatively contributed to the project. If individuals who creatively contributed were not "employees for hire," however, their contributions should be noted in space two, and if individuals not "for hire" and an employer claim authorship, both parties should also be noted in space two.

If a television series is being copyrighted, each individual show (episode) must be registered separately (when available) to receive the benefits of copyright registration. Each new program embodies creative expression, including dialogue and perhaps music, and these elements may not be covered by a previous registration.

The copyright law provides terms of copyright (for works created after January 1, 1987) as follows:

1. For works made for hire a term of seventy-five years from first publication or one hundred years from creation, whichever expires first.
2. For works in which a person is the author, the life of the author plus fifty years after the author's death.
3. For a work jointly prepared by two or more authors who were employees for hire, fifty years after the death of the last surviving author.

Again, most motion pictures are made as works for hire, so the "seventy-five years from publication" or "one hundred years from creation" would most often apply. As a practical example, if a feature film was fixed and theatrically released in 1988, copyright in that motion picture would endure for seventy-five years, or until 2063. At that time the work would fall into the public domain, and anyone would be free to use or copy it as desired without permission. However, if derivative works were prepared from the original copyrighted work, copyright protection in the new, additional elements would still be under statutory protection.

For motion pictures that were copyrighted between January 1, 1950, and December 31, 1977 (that is, in their first term of copyright), a renewal must be filed for copyright protection to continue. Renewal registration is done by sending Form RE properly completed and the statutory fee to the Copyright Office in the twenty-eighth year of copyright, before December 31 of that year. Copyright protection will be lost if renewal registration is not made within the time limits set forth by the statute. Proper renewal will provide for a second term of statutory protection for a total of forty-seven years.

If a motion picture was copyrighted before 1950 and renewed so that it was in its second term before 1978, its second term was automatically extended by the Copyright Act of 1976 for an additional nineteen years, or a total of forty-seven years. For example, if a documentary was copyrighted on October 15, 1948, and renewed between October 15, 1975, and October 15, 1976 (its twenty-eighth year under the old copyright law), statutory protection will endure until 2023.

COPYRIGHT REGISTRATION OF A SCREENPLAY OR OTHER NONDRAMATIC LITERARY WORK. A published or unpublished screenplay, or other written nondramatic literary work, is registered with Form PA. A claim to register the copyright is made by sending the following to the Copyright Office:

1. Form PA, properly completed and signed.
2. A deposit of the work as follows: If unpublished, one com-

plete copy or phonorecord; if published, two complete copies or phonorecords of the best edition of the work (if the work was published before 1978, send two complete copies or phonorecords of the work as first published; if the work was first published in a country other than the United States, one complete copy or phonorecord of the work as first published, regardless of the date of publication).
3. An application fee.

These elements should be mailed in one package to: Register of Copyrights, Copyright Office, Library of Congress, Washington, D.C. 20559.

COST REPORT. *See* **Production Accountant.**

COSTUME DESIGNER. A costume designer creates, selects, or coordinates the costumes worn in motion pictures and on television programs. He or she is expected to provide suitable outfits for any historical period. Costumes are designed or chosen to evoke the authenticity of a period and to complement the plot, the settings, and the personalities of the characters.

A costume designer's creation of a wardrobe for a cast is often a lengthy process. The designer begins by reading the script, to get a sense of the intention and mood. The story, the historical era, the geographical location, and the characters all suggest specific styles, colors, and accessories. Research is often necessary, particularly for period stories or those set in foreign places. Paintings, books, and old photographs are useful sources. Authenticity is important because an anachronism disturbs a film's continuity (*see* **Continuity**).

Other factors that help determine the final selection of costumes include makeup, hairstyles, set design, and lighting. Also, the costume designer must accommodate the vision of the director.

Because a costume is to a large extent the physical externalization of a character, actors often want to have creative input in this area. The costume designer talks with the actors about their characters and the story. It is important that both parties have a similar sense of the character, at least sartorially.

To determine the number of costumes to be worn by each actor, the costume designer breaks down the script into screen days. Some movies, for example, might cover only one day in the life of a character, others might cover a number of years. A **script break-down** tells the costume designer when screen days begin and end and consequently how many costumes the characters will need. Variations of costumes are noted as well. For example, a character about to leave his house during the winter will need a topcoat and a hat.

For feature films, it is important that the costume designer know what clothes are to be worn on each day of shooting, since scenes are often shot out of sequence. If Scene 43 is being filmed on a particular day, for example, the costume designer need only refer to the script breakdown to see what costumes and additions (coats, hats, etc.) are required for that scene. The **shooting schedule** tells when each scene will be shot.

Whether costumes are specially designed for a production, rented from a **costume house**, or purchased from a retail store depends upon a few major factors, mainly budgetary. For films with large budgets the costume designer may provide only drawings and then have the costumes made from the drawings pending his or her approval. Bids are obtained from various costume houses to find the most inexpensive supplier, or to find the house the designer feels will construct the costumes best. Costumes for stars are often custom-made since high-budget projects can afford this luxury.

Another option for costume designers is to rent outfits from a costume house. It is usually cheaper to rent existing garments than to make new ones. If basic costumes can be rented and modified (by adding to, subtracting from, or both), then a lot of money can be saved. (Most houses require rented costumes to be returned in their original condition, however.)

Costumes can be assembled from items found in retail stores also. Many film, television, and theatrical productions buy costumes new from department stores, boutiques, and designer showrooms; or used, from secondhand stores, resale shops, and antique clothing stores. Script requirements as well as budget limitations frequently necessitate shopping for, rather than designing, a wardrobe.

All the members of a cast, from the principal actors to the extras, wear costumes that have been either specially designed or selected. Although assistants may handle extras' costumes, primary responsibility for all costumes falls to the costume designer.

There are no educational or licensing requirements to work as a costume designer, but certain skills are necessary. All costume designers should have sewing and drawing skills. Many have a master's degree in costume design or a related field. To get work it is usually necessary to be a member of the local costume designer's union, since most television shows and movies are produced under union contracts. Also, local union regulations stipulate who may construct costumes and whether the work must be done in a studio wardrobe room or in a union shop. In order to become a member, a certain level of skill must be demonstrated and an exam must be taken.

One way for a novice to gain the experience necessary to build a portfolio is to serve an apprenticeship with a mentor of a local costume designer's union. Involvement in regional theater or low-budget movies is another option for the novice. In the beginning, work may have to be done for free or for only a small stipend, but the contacts and experience gained from an apprenticeship make it extremely worthwhile.

See also **Wardrobe Supervisor.**

COSTUME HOUSE. A costume house is a company that supplies costumes for motion picture, television, and theatrical productions by renting out its stock or by making new costumes for outright purchase. A costume house typically will have thousands of costumes in inventory. Except for minor alterations (like taking up a hem or tightening the waist of pants), costumes usually have to be returned in their original condition. If a costume is cut, dyed, or changed in any way so that it cannot readily be restored to its original condition, there will be a charge. Costume houses are not used when costumes may be bought from retailers. Contemporary clothing, for example, may be purchased from boutiques or attire of the 1930s might be found at a thrift shop. Sometimes a store will get a credit line such as "Wardrobe supplied by _____." Uniforms, such as those of policemen, firemen, and the armed forces are rented or made by costume houses. Fees are based on such factors as the cost of the costume, the quantity rented, and the duration of rental, which is typically by the day or week. The terms and conditions of rental or purchase are delineated in a contract.

COUNTER-PROGRAMMING. *See* **Independent Television Station.**

COVERAGE, CINEMATOGRAPHY. Cinematography coverage refers to all shots made for a scene other than the master shot. Coverage allows the film editor to cut from one shot of a scene to a shot of the same scene from a different angle.

COVERAGE, SCRIPTS. This term is used by story editors and readers in reference to written reports on new scripts and treatments that are read and considered for development. A coverage usually ranges from one to five pages. The first page of a coverage is an evaluation sheet where the reader rates the various elements of the script such as plot, structure, characters, dialogue, and commercial appeal. The reader then rates the script itself as one of the following: pass, consider, recommend, highly recommend.

CRANE. *See* **Grip Equipment.**

CREDITS, HOW TO READ MOVIE AD. Advertisements that appear in newspapers and magazines for feature films sometimes befuddle the public (not to mention some industry workers) with the line of credits that appear immediately below the illustrative part of the ad and the title, and right above the acting and key crew credits. There may be several names of entities and while the contributions or roles of such entities vary from picture to picture, a sample line of credits with a brief explanation of the participation of the entities follows to illustrate their nature.

1	2

Hilltop Pictures Presents in Association with CopperVision Partners II

3	4

A Film from Floral Park Pictures A Royalston Company Production

5

Fading Fast

6

Distributed by Valley Stream Distribution

Name or Title	Role or Contribution
1 Hilltop Pictures	the studio could be partially financing the film, could have agreed to buy the film for a set price after completion (a negative pickup), or could have agreed to distribute the picture thereby completing the structure to allow bank financing. Its participation gives credibility to bankers so financing can be arranged. The studio provides its distribution, promotion, and advertising apparatus.
2 CopperVision Partners II	limited partnership investing in the film.
3 Floral Park Pictures	the limited partnership most pic-closely identified with the specific picture, often formed just for the ture; also a financial investor.

Continued on next page

Cucoloris

Continued from previous page

Name or Title	Role or Contribution
4 Royalston Company	individual production company that may have developed the idea or script of the movie. It could be the company of the producer, star, or agency that packaged the film.
5 *Fading Fast*	title of the film.
6 Valley Stream Distribution	distribution arm of the studio or a separate distribution company.

CUCOLORIS. *See* **Grip Equipment.**

CUT. *See* **Final Cut; First cut.**

CUTTER. *See* **Grip Equipment.**

DAILIES. Dailies are preliminary film clips, processed daily by a laboratory, that enable the director and cinematographer to analyze recently shot footage. Since motion pictures, TV films, and documentaries are shot over a period of time that can range from weeks to months, it is necessary to monitor on a daily basis the results of filming.

DEAL MEMO. A deal memo is a shortened version of the contract made between a studio and an independent producer for the production of a motion picture that highlights the terms of the arrangement. The deal memo includes the name of the project, the approximate starting date, the producer's fee, and any special conditions or contingencies, but does not go into the detailed boilerplate provisions of the final contract, which is generated at a later date by the studio's legal department. A deal memo is written with the understanding that both parties have agreed to the terms and confirms a studio's intention to pick up an independent producer's film when completed. It also can be used by a producer to interest a bank in lending money to a production, but the producer must supply the complete, full-fledged contract before financing may be issued.

DEVELOPMENT, MOTION PICTURES. Development is the stage prior to **preproduction** during which an idea, outline, treatment, or screenplay is further elaborated or developed. A screenwriter, for example, presents to Interstellar Pictures an idea for a movie about a military group that buys a country in a politically strategic location in order to take over the region. Interstellar loves the idea and thinks the movie will be a blockbuster, but they need to know more about the project. The screenwriter says, "Terrific, I'll develop it with you and won't take it to any other studios, provided we agree upon a fee for me to research the idea and write a screenplay." Once the project has a narrative structure, Interstellar will have final approval on the project. The decision as to whether a studio will take on a project is made by the head of production.

The development stage may contain any of the following procedures:

- The shaping of a story idea into an outline or treatment.
- The writing of a script from an outline or treatment.
- The rewriting of the script as many times as necessary.
- An analysis of the commercial potential for a property.
- The marketing of the project to stars and directors by studios, producers, agents, and packagers.
- The drafting of a stripboard (production board).
- The preparation of a budget projection for the film.
- The producers' attempt to gain financial backing from studios and banks (*see* **Negative Pickup**).

Studios, independent producers, actors, and directors may employ development workers to find material appropriate for them. Development workers regularly meet with agents and writers and go through scripts, novels, unpublished manuscripts, and articles in literary and consumer magazines to find material suitable for putting into development.

It is an axiom in the industry that "most movies never get made," meaning most scripts in development and books under option do not get produced. Because movies are so expensive to make—the cost of a feature film usually ranges from $10 million to over $20 million, and marketing adds several millions more—tremendous prudence is exercised in deciding which projects to undertake and which not to.

Since the odds of a film being made are slim, some producers, directors, actors, and screenwriters have several projects in development at once. This practice serves as insurance that films will continually be launched. Scripts are submitted to studios either alone or as part of a package, which may include a star, a producer, or a director, or any combination of these. Frequently, projects that have been in development for years are canceled. But cancelation is not necessarily the end of the line for the scripts. Once a writer is out of turnaround, a contractual agreement in which a script's rights revert to the author, the script may be offered elsewhere.

See also **Turnaround Deal.**

DEVELOPMENT, NETWORK TELEVISION. The development department for prime-time programming at a network is responsible for screening ideas and creating concepts for new series, commissioning scripts to be written from promising ideas and concepts, ordering pilots of scripts, and ultimately submitting pilots to programming executives.

Writers and producers have *pitch meetings* with network development people during which they propose ideas for new series. The development department generally meets only with established writers and producers because of time constraints and the legal risks involved in meeting with novice writers, who might later claim idea misappropriation. The development department then commissions pilot scripts for the ideas with the most encouraging possibilities. In considering types of shows to commission scripts and pilots for, development often responds to ideas emanating from a vice president or even the head of the network.

Pilot scripts are written around story ideas. Then development reevaluates the script in terms of plot, characterization, setting, demographic appeal, and other factors such as freshness, competition, and long-term potential. Approximately 20 to 25 percent of all scripts submitted are chosen to be produced into pilots.

When the development department decides to consider a show, usually only a pilot is commissioned, but occasionally a series of episodes is ordered. If a star agrees to do the pilot, for example, development might commit to extra episodes. Producers of dramas often want to make a two-hour pilot. This way, if the pilot is rejected, they can try to sell it to other markets as a movie. Development screens the pilots and submits those they consider meritorious to the network's head of programming.

The development season begins in late May or early June, sometime after the announcement of the fall schedule. First, pilots of scripts are ordered, a process which may continue through November. Decisions as to which pilots will be scheduled for the fall season are made by April or May. The number of pilots each network orders varies, but choosing only six out of thirty-five pilots ordered for one season is not an unusual occurrence.

Sometimes pilots that do not get selected for the fall later become mid-season replacements for shows that are canceled due to low ratings. Though some mid-season replacements are developed as such, most development work is geared to the fall season.

Development department budgets vary from network to network, but a standard budget might allow a particular network to allocate funds for fifteen one-hour scripts and twenty-five half-hour scripts. The overall development budget, which counts producing pilots as its largest expense, is usually several million dollars.

Network prime-time development primarily takes place at a network's California offices, even though the networks also have development departments in New York. Comedy and drama may have separate development divisions.

DIALECT COACH. A dialect coach is employed to help actors speak a foreign language with native authenticity or speak with an authentic foreign accent.

A dialect coach uses a variety of methods to inculcate an accent in a client. Primarily, instruction consists of the coach speaking lines in a particular dialect and the actor repeating them. An actor's lines also can be transcribed phonetically to bring out the desired accent. American actors commonly engage dialect coaches to help them learn everything from Southern drawls to Japanese accents. Actors who come to the United States to work and whose native language is not English often employ dialogue coaches to hide their foreign accents.

DIALOGUE EDITOR. A dialogue editor "cleans up" the dialogue track of a film in postproduction. The dialogue editor makes sure the actors' lines are audible and comprehensible, and background noise is consistent in scenes where it is present. Any actor whose dialogue needs fixing dubs in the part for synchronization to the picture at a sound studio. The dialogue editor also checks for pops, clicks, hums, and other extraneous noises on the sound track. Dialogue may be unacceptable for a variety of reasons: The director's cues might be audible in the background of a scene; a scene may not have been acted out properly; the director might want to change or add lines to improve the story; different microphones may have been used at different points in the film. Even when an actor accidentally hits a microphone during a scene, the dialogue editor is responsible.

DIRECTOR, MOTION PICTURE. The director is the creative "captain" of a movie production crew who guides the entire filmmaking process from preproduction through editing. The director's vision affects every aspect of the production, including casting, location, set design, actors' performances, cinematography, lighting, costume, makeup, hairstyles, stunts, special effects, editing, music, and sound mixing. Making a theatrical movie requires the efforts of a large ensemble of performers, craftspersons, and technicians. The director maps out the production strategy and supervises all stages of a picture's artistic journey. The director's job begins long before principal photography commences. A renowned director may be part of a package put together by a producer or agent, though more often the director is hired after financial backing has been secured.

In **preproduction** the director is involved in the following areas:

- *Screenplay.* The script is the blueprint from which the director creates the film, and therefore it must be in a polished form before production begins. A script may go through several drafts (and writers) before finally approved. The director usually works closely with the screenwriter and often suggests changes.
- *Crew.* The director interviews and chooses the key members of the production team, such as the cinematographer, the casting director, and the script supervisor. Then the unit production manager usually hires the rest of the production team, although the director will oversee this, perhaps recommending specific people.
- *Casting.* The director gives general casting suggestions to the casting director. After the casting director has narrowed

down the pool of candidates, the director auditions them himself, sometimes ordering screen tests. For starring roles, the director may forego the casting procedure and hire actors based on their reputation and star potential.

- *Set Design.* The director may have a look in mind for the film. Although the set specifications are often described in the script, the director and production designer must translate the script's suggestions into a set that complements the director's vision.
- *Shooting.* The director meets with the cinematographer to discuss lighting effects and scene angles.
- *Costumes.* The director discusses his ideas for wardrobe with the costume designer.
- *Shooting Schedule.* The director approves the shooting order, which is prepared by the assistant director, and the time allotted for each scene.
- *Locations.* The director approves locations chosen by scouts.

The director supervises the entire shooting of the principal photography for a film. Production may take place at several locations simultaneously. At the beginning of each day of filming, members of the crew arrive early on the set to make technical preparations. Before shooting begins, the actors must go through hair, makeup, and wardrobe. Meanwhile, the camera and sound people block scenes and determine how they will cover them. The director oversees all these preparations.

At the scheduled time, the cast and crew converge on the set, and rehearsals and shooting begin with the director in charge. The director decides when a shoot begins and when it ends and how a scene is to be covered. The director may cut the action at any time or order the entire scene to be re-shot. The director also works with the actors, suggesting how they might improve their delivery, actions, gestures, movements, expressions, and interplay.

Working from prepared notes, the director oversees the work of the cameraman, discussing each shot and the lenses to be used. (A 35-mm lens, for example, gives a wide-angle effect; a 50-mm lens, on the other hand, gives less of an angle, making the background appear closer.)

Dailies are made of each day's shooting and the director views these to determine if the film is progressing satisfactorily. If not happy with the results, the director may order a re-shooting. The reason could be anything from an artistic flaw to wanting to shoot from a different angle. A director's perfectionism is limited only by a film's budget.

Indeed, during production it is essential that the director keeps an eye on the budget. Going over budget may burden the producer, who is responsible to the studio, creditors, and investors, and may even jeopardize the completion of the film. A portion of the budget is allotted for each department, but often funds are funneled to where they are most needed. For example, if an expensive crane shot is needed during the principal photography, the director might use fewer extras in another scene.

During principal photography, production reports are prepared at the end of each day summarizing the work executed. These are sent to the studio or **completion guarantor.**

The director is integrally involved in postproduction. Editing, music scoring, special optical effects, the sound tracks, re-recording, and answer prints are all attended to by the director.

The 1987 Basic Agreement negotiated by the Directors Guild of America establishes that the director must be involved in all aspects of postproduction if he or she so chooses, and extends the director's authority over a film or television production until the *director's cut*—the production exactly as the director wishes it to exist—is turned over to the producer. Upon delivery of the director's cut, the producer sometimes alters the production for commercial reasons. It is at this point, rarely reached, that challenges to the director's vision may occur.

The image of the director is one of the most ingrained stereotypes to emerge from Hollywood—dictatorial, importunate, egotistical, petulant—yet the role of the director in a film is also perhaps the least understood. The director is a blend of artist, authoritarian, visionary, craftsperson, and oracle. The legends stem from the reputations of some of the more fiery personalities who have occupied the director's chair through the years. The director is often a silent hero behind the success of a film or the salient culprit for a picture's failure.

DIRECTOR, MOTION PICTURES, FIRST ASSISTANT. The responsibilities of the first assistant director are outlined by the Directors Guild of America:

PREPRODUCTION RESPONSIBILITIES

- Organizes preproduction with unit production manager.
- Prepares a stripboard.
- Prepares the shooting schedule.
- Supervises location searches (at the request of unit production manager).

PRODUCTION RESPONSIBILITIES

- Assists director on the set.
- Supervises crew.
- Prepares day-out-of-day schedules, which are organized by character appearances rather than chronologically.
- Overseas the preparation of call sheets.
- Supervises extras.
- Obtains minor contracts.

The Guild's agreement states that a producer "may not assign the duties of a first assistant director to extra player coordinators, production assistants, or persons in positions in which the assigned duty has not been customarily performed in the motion picture industry" and that there can be "no alteration of job titles to evade or subvert" the responsibilities of the first assistant director.

See also **Directors Guild of America Inc.**

DIRECTOR, MOTION PICTURES, SECOND ASSISTANT. The Directors Guild of America defines a second assistant director as "an assistant to the first assistant director in conducting the business of the set or the location site" and designates "key second assistant directors, second second assistant directors, and additional second assistant directors" as being included in the term *second assistant directors*.

During production the second assistant director:

- Prepares call sheets and processes requisitions for extras.
- Prepares production reports on a daily basis.
- Distributes script revisions and call sheets to cast and crew.
- Arranges for accomodations and food for cast and crew.
- Coordinates with cast and crew so that production may commence at the designated time each day.
- Supervises extras with the first assistant director.
- Serves as a liaison between the production office and the first assistant director.

The Guild's agreement provides that the producer "may not assign the duties of a second assistant director to extra player coordinates, production assistants, or persons in positions in which the assigned duty has not been customarily performed in the motion picture industry" and that there can be "no alteration of job titles to evade or subvert" the second director's responsibilities.

See also **Directors Guild of America Inc.**

DIRECTOR OF PHOTOGRAPHY. The director of photography is the person who imparts a photographic style to a film or videotape based on the script and the director's vision (and within the confines of the budget). He or she executes the artistic look of the film or tape by designing and overseeing the lighting, choosing the camera lenses, supervising the camera movement, determining the framing and angles—always in consultation with the director. This art of photographing action or scenes-in-motion is called cinematography. While *cinematographer* is the historic term used to describe the person who supervises this aspect of filmmaking (or sometimes the person who operates a camera), the job classification most commonly used today is director of photography.

Director of Photography

The director of photography chooses the lighting and camera equipment, which is physically moved and set up by the **grips.** On high-budget films the director of photography does not do the actual shooting but sets up the shot and directs the *camera operator* who makes the moves. There is often only one camera operator although there may be more depending on the needs of the scene. In filming a dangerous stunt, for instance, there may be a half dozen cameras to cover the stunt from many angles. This is done so the stunt will not have to be repeated. But there will be only one director of photography supervising. For dramatic film scenes, however, there is almost always only one camera.

The director of photography is hired or recommended by the director or the production company. For films this position is usually filled well in advance of the principal photography so the director of photography may read the script and discuss ideas with the director, as well as examine locations, order equipment, and carry out other relevant preproduction work.

Discussions with the director will involve such elements as lighting, composition, mood, camera moves, and cutting pace, with consideration given to the budget. For TV movies, for example, which customarily have tight budgets, there may not be time to give a signature look to the work as it is done at a rather fast pace. Ultimately, the film is the director's, to make the decisions that will affect the movie's final look.

The budget will also determine what equipment and how much personnel is used. The director of photography, for example, might ask the **gaffers** for five HMI's. But it must first be determined if there is enough power and personnel to accommodate this. If there is not, an alternate way of effecting the setup will have to be devised.

Lighting for films is a complex and technical subject, indeed, an art that the director of photography has mastered through years of study and experience. In shooting, many different kinds of lights and pieces of equipment are used, determined by such factors as whether filming is being done indoors or outdoors or during the day or the evening. The director of photography must consider the movement of the sun during shooting; how to compensate if the weather changes, such as from sunny to cloudy since continuity must be kept; and if there are cover shots (e.g., can the camera go to tighter shots and make them look sunny even though it's raining heavily?). In short, the director of photography will use anything from his or her bag of tricks to help make the shot.

The director of photography may go to an exterior location before shooting and plot where the light is best. One consideration is how big the shot is supposed to be. All factors will be evaluated with respect to the look to be achieved for a particular scene. A strategy is worked out with a plan of what equipment to use within budget. The director of photography may feel, for example, that the ideal lights for a particular scene would be arc lights. But as these are expensive to use and require certain kinds of generators, an ample crew, and much trimming, a producer may request less expensive illumination.

For shooting done in a studio, the director of photography will first evaluate the shot by asking, has it changed?; what's the master shot?; what's the sequence of shots after that? Then he or she directs the crew, telling the gaffers where to put the lights, and the grips where to put the cameras.

The physical setup of lighting and equipment can be very time-consuming. For a commercial, for example, hours may be spent getting the desired illumination for a can of peas or a roll of toilet paper. On a big film set, that luxury may not be available, considering high-paid stars and union casts.

Ideally, a prelighting will be done for films. The crew comes in before shooting and works out a rough scheme of the actual lighting. After or while **camera blocking** is being done, it is determined where and how the lights should be placed (the camera blocking determines the lighting). When the actors come in for the shooting, adjustments in lighting are made for their faces, changes in action, and changes in camera moves. But with prelighting, much of the technical work is accomplished beforehand.

Before actual shooting begins there may or may not be several rehearsals. It depends on how complicated the scene is and other such factors. If, for example, a scene involves three car crashes and the camera is to follow the action on a moving dolly, there may be several rehearsals in slow motion before the cars actually crash to make sure all the technical aspects are worked out.

During the actual shooting the director of photography is trying to get the right look. This requires an awareness of the continuity of lighting, the direction of the lighting, and the quality of the lighting; and an ability to think ahead to where the script is going. When the shooting of a scene or sequence may be continued at a later date the director of photography has to remember how the lighting was, where the actors were, where the camera was located, and other related elements.

In some productions the director of photography may operate the camera, but for major feature films there is always a separate camera operator. This enables the director of photography to concentrate on the overall picture—the lighting, composition, movement, feeling—while someone else handles the technical end of working the camera—turning the wheels and framing, looking for gremlins in the frame and focus, and so on.

The director of photography will usually light a wide shot differently than a medium or close-up shot. For example, consider a big street scene with a crowd: a group in the foreground and another in the background. For the wide shot, the group in the background does not have to be lit as carefully. Lighting may be used to just edge and fill them a bit; the audience will know it is a group of people. For close-ups of faces, more time on the lighting will be spent, with more modeling.

The director of photography is concerned with composition: how all the elements within the frame aesthetically fit together. If there is too much head room on an actor, for example, the camera will be lowered. Composition is analogous to a still photograph. There is a frame and within that frame are certain elements, such as an actor, objects, an environment. Composition uses these elements in a way that can please or distract the audience and add to the psychological impact of the story.

Different types of lenses can affect the composition. The scale of a frame can be changed by using a wide angle, medium length, or telephoto lens. A longer lens can be used to cause the background to become softer, which results in an actor popping out more from the background.

Composition is distinct from lighting, although there are nuances in composition that can be affected by lighting. Light can be used, for example, to make certain areas pop out or recede more than others. This is referred to as giving an image more depth.

The director of photography will sometimes collaborate with the production designer or art director to enhance the director's vision. While the production designer is responsible for the environment of the film—designing the interior sets, accentuating what is needed in exteriors—the director of photography might make a suggestion such as, "Let's have a beige wall instead of a white wall." For an interior shooting he or she will obtain a floor plan from the production designer or art director to plan where to place the lights and where the sources of electricity are.

Sometimes the distinction is made between a director of photography and a cinematographer, indicating that the latter also operates the camera. While directors of photography can and sometimes do operate the camera, they usually do not, and concentrate instead on lighting, composition, and other areas.

On a union feature film production under the director of photography, there customarily would be a camera operator, a first assistant camera operator, a loader, gaffers, and grips. The director of photography would tell the camera operator how to frame up the shot and make the camera moves.

The camera operator looks through the camera to guide and frame it as the action unfolds. When the director of photography has selected an angle, the camera operator executes it, doing the physical panning and tilting and moving the camera. But the camera operator must not only carry out orders but have an artistic sense himself; he or she may have creative leeway on the shoot, depending on his or her relationship with the director of photography, a relationship based on trust and taste. The director must rely on the camera operator for the successful execution of the scene photographed.

Director of Photography

As 35-mm camera equipment is cumbersome, the camera operator will have assistants. The first assistant is responsible for setting up and adjusting the camera, including focus pulling during camera moves. When the distance of a subject in front of the lens changes, the focus changes, and therefore the lens has to be adjusted. The focusing ring on the lens must be changed to accommodate the distance that is changing between the subject and the camera. The first assistant will have a hand on the lens and adjust it according to where the action is moving, towards or away from the camera.

The first assistant has to be very accurate in focusing the lens, particularly when high-speed lenses are being used. Often a tape measure is used to measure various distances between the camera lens and where the action is, and then a mark is put on the lens. In this way the first assistant can "eyeball" when to pull focus, according to the action.

A loader, or second assistant, loads and off-loads the magazines. Magazines are light-proof containers that hold the film and fit onto the camera.

There are several brands of 35-mm motion picture cameras, but three popular ones for feature film production are the Panaflex, made by Panavision Inc.; the Arriflex, made by Arriflex Corporation; and the Moviecam Super America made by Moviecam F. G. Bauer Film Technik. Directors of photography believe that a different camera lens gives different looks, such as a crispy or a more cosmetic look.

In postproduction, the director of photography may have the opportunity to go through a film, after it has been edited, to do the timing. He or she may, for example, peruse a scene at the lab and say, "Here's the shot I like of the actor. The saturation of color is good. I like the density of the print, the darkness and lightness of it. This is what I want to maintain throughout the rest of the scene." The technical quality of the coverage may be different owing to the inherent nature of film stock, the lighting, and the camera angles as some lenses read differently. The director of photography tends to be most involved working in features and less involved in commercials.

A person may work up to the position of director of photography from various routes. Often one will have previously served as an assistant camera operator, camera operator, or gaffer. The routes are generally through camera or lighting, although others break in through film editing and other areas. Many colleges offer relevant courses.

DIRECTORS GUILD OF AMERICA INC. (DGA). The Directors Guild of America is a labor union representing directors, assistant directors, unit production managers, associate directors, stage managers, and production assistants to major and independent motion picture companies, television networks and stations, educational and industrial filmmakers, commercial advertising sponsors, and other industry employers. Through the process of collective bargaining, the Directors Guild periodically negotiates agreements with the Alliance of Motion Picture and Television Producers (AMPTP). The Directors Guild also negotiates contracts with more than fifteen hundred other employers. The agreements cover DGA members working in the United States and foreign countries.

A national board of directors consisting of twenty-one voting members is elected at periodic conventions. This board determines DGA policy, which is carried out by its ten officers and administered by a national executive director and regional executive secretaries. Sub-councils determine specific policy for their respective categories of membership.

Eligibility for membership in DGA depends upon the category of work. To sign a contract of employment for a DGA position offered by a producer, one must become a member of the Guild. In 1990 the Directors Guild had more than nine thousand members.

DISTRIBUTION OF NETWORK AND SYNDICATED SHOWS. Network television programs are distributed by satellite to their affiliates. The programs, on videotape, are fed to a satellite and picked up by the affiliates, which air the show live or tape it for later broadcast.

Distribution of syndicated shows is different. It can work in either

119

of two ways. A master videotape can be used to feed a satellite and the show can be taped by local stations, which feed it to customers, or dozens or hundreds of copies of a show can be made and shipped to each of the stations that have bought that program. The number of stations that have bought the show and such financial considerations as how much it will cost to make dubs (copies) and ship them, will help determine which course is chosen.

DOCUDRAMA. This term refers to a television movie or miniseries based on a fictionalized true story. As its name suggests, a docudrama lies somewhere in between a documentary and a drama. A docudrama is based on fact but usually contains fabricated conversations and exaggerated characters. In essence, it applies literary license to the commercial needs of television. Real-life events, such as sensational murders and kidnappings, are frequently distorted for heightened commercial potential. The lives of important historical figures are also common fodder for the docudrama.

DOCUMENTARY. *See* **Film Genres, Television Programming Genres.**

DOLLY. *See* **Grip Equipment.**

DOLLY GRIP. *See* **Grip.**

DOLLY TRACK. *See* **Grip Equipment.**

DOTS. *See* **Grip Equipment.**

DOUBLE. A double is an actor, usually a **stuntperson**, who substitutes for an actor when the action may be too dangerous for the original actor or the original actor is not available for shooting. The double must physically resemble the original actor.
See also **Stand-In.**

DRAMA. *See* **Film Genres; Television Programming Genres.**

DRIVE-IN THEATER. A drive-in is an outdoor movie theater where patrons watch the film from inside their parked cars. Drive-in theaters are an endangered species. At one time they flourished in the towns and suburbs of America, but because high real-estate taxes, substantial insurance rates, increasing land values, and dwindling attendance made it more profitable to sell the theater grounds, many drive-in theaters have been sold or gone under. At one time the potential of drive-in theaters appeared promising. In 1948 there were 820 drive-ins in the United States and this increased to 3,730 in 1969. But by August 1987 there were only 2,086 screens.

DRY RUN. A dry run is the rehearsal of a scene without the camera following the action.
   See also **Camera Blocking.**

DUBBING. Dubbing is the recording of sound onto a film sound track for the purpose of editing, continuity, modifying a story line, changing the lines of an actor, or translating dialogue. Dubbed sound must be synchronized to the picture.

ELECTRIC DEPARTMENT. The electric department of a film or television production may consist of a gaffer, third electrician, and an electric crew. The gaffer is the chief electrician, the best boy the second electrician. They are the supervisors for the rest of the electrical department.

See also **Best Boy; Gaffer (Electrician); Electrician, Third.**

ELECTRICIAN THIRD. The third electrician serves under the gaffer and the best boy in a film or television production. The New York Local 15 of the National Association of Broadcast Employees and Technicians (NABET) requires a third electrician to know: "names of lighting fixtures; sizes of cables; names of hangers and brackets; simple knots; how to bulb and hang fixtures; how to coil cable and to know the routing and distribution of cables; names of connectors; basic electricity (A.C. and D.C.); how to lamp all A.C. lighting fixtures; set etiquette (that it, proper etiquette on the set and the chain of command); light trimming; functions of basic tools of the trade and to have them; names of gels and diffusion materials; associated grip equipment."

EMMY AWARDS. The Emmys are awards of merit presented annually to recognize outstanding achievements in national television programming. Prime-time Emmys are given by the Academy of Television Arts and Sciences (ATAS) in Los Angeles in categories which include performing, directing, writing, programs, cinematography, costume design, makeup, music, lighting direction, film editing, videotape editing, and sound mixing.

Daytime Emmys are presented by the National Academy of Television Arts and Sciences in New York City and by ATAS in Los Angeles. Daytime Emmys usually are presented for categories such as outstanding drama series, outstanding children's series, outstanding talk service show, outstanding lead actor in a drama series, and outstanding game show host, among others. The International Council of NATAS maintains liaisons with broadcasters throughout the world and gives out international Emmys. The individual chapters of NATAS present local awards.

The name *Emmy* was suggested in an ATAS board meeting in October 1948, by Harry Lubcke, a television engineer. He derived the name from *Immy*, the nickname for the image orthicon tube. Previous to this Syd Cassyd, the founder of ATAS, suggested the name *Ike*, a derivative of iconoscope. But as the iconoscope was shortly replaced by the image orthicon tube, the name became outdated. (Another conflict was that Dwight D. Eisenhower, who was considering a run for president, had the same nickname.) A contest was held for the symbol for the award trophy, and a sketch by designer Louis McManus was selected.

The first Emmy Awards ceremony was held in Hollywood on January 25, 1949, for programs aired during 1948. Winning an Emmy attracts more work and higher fees for an actor.

ENGINEERING DEPARTMENT, TELEVISION STATION. *See* **Independent Television Station.**

EPISODE. An episode is a single show that is part of a television series. Sometimes a series may have special episodes which run in length twice as long as the normal show. A **pilot** is an introductory show, not necessarily an episode since there is no promise of future shows. If a series runs along enough, the episodes may be accumulated in order to sell the series for **syndication.**

See also **Pilot.**

EVANGELICAL TELEVISION SHOW. *See* **Television Programming Genres.**

EXHIBITOR. Exhibitors, or movie theaters, may be divided into two types: chains and independents. A chain is a company with screens at more than one location, usually at least three. An independent theater is one whose proprietor owns only that one facility, and perhaps an additional one.

A single facility may comprise several screens and is often called a multiplex. A relatively recent innovation in theatrical exhibition, multiplexes have substantially increased the number of screens across the country. Multiple screens under one roof increase the chances for the theater owner to make more money, since overhead costs such as rent, heating, insurance, and staff may not be considerably more for a multiplex than they are for a single-screen theater. While multiplexes increase the cinematic fare available to the public at a single location, some have criticized them for reducing the size of screens to accommodate more rooms, which makes viewing movies less pleasurable.

A movie theater that is part of a national chain typically employs certain personnel. The theater manager supervises operations of the house and is responsible for the smooth running of the facility. He oversees everyday operations including the hiring of personnel, the handling of money, the management of ticket inventory, and the flow of customers, and is ultimately responsible for the handling of film (although the projectionist directly works with it; in some theaters the manager also functions as the projectionist). Often the manager's job becomes more important when the home office is closed, that is, during evenings and weekends. (The home office's division manager is usually on call, however, if not making rounds.) Because theaters operate so many hours during a week, most have at least two managers, who work on a rotating basis.

The projectionist runs the machine that plays the film and is responsible, theoretically, for showing the film in synchronization with the sound and in the correct reel order. With machines having some degree of automation, it is not unusual for a single projectionist to be responsible for more than one screen at a time. Most theaters that operate on a seven-day-a-week, noon-to-midnight basis, however, employ at least three projectionists, who work on a rotating basis.

Theaters also employ cashiers (a few who rotate), ticket takers (the doorman is a ticket taker), the ushers (who may rotate with the ticket takers). The ticket taker takes the consumer's ticket, tears it in half, and returns a stub. The usher escorts latecomers to seats and handles any problem with respect to the audience or technical exhibition of the film (he or she will report any problem to the manager or projectionist). In some large theaters there are resident stagehands or electricians. Porters clean the theaters.

There are also people who run concession stands, where popcorn, ice cream, candy, and soft drinks are sold. A concessions stand may be part of the theater company or owned by an outside vendor, in which case that firm pays a percentage of the revenue to the theater and hires the people who run the stand.

A theater chain will have a headquarters, and, depending on its size, regional offices. Some chains operate theaters in only a single city; others own theaters across the nation.

The division manager, or manager's manager, oversees theater operations for a specific territory or city. He makes sure that the individual theater managers are doing their jobs properly, that the theaters are supplied with displays and advertising materials, and that prints are supplied timely and orderly.

The film buyer is responsible for negotiating and making contractual arrangements with distributors for exhibition of movies at the chain's theaters. There is often more than one film buyer, and in some chains a vice-president may serve as a film buyer. An advertising and publicity person oversees these respective areas, and handles co-op advertising where appropriate.

In the home office there are also one or more accountants. They function to check over box-office statements from the theaters as well as oversee the reporting of information to the film distributors and the computing of moneys that are due them. There might also be a head of theater operations (or executive vice-president), who deals with the unions to which theater personnel belong and to whom the division managers report.

Many independent theaters obtain films through theater booking services (*see below*), but, as mentioned, the major chains employ film buyers. The film buyer acquires films through negotiation or sometimes bidding. Bidding is a practice in which the distributor offers to license a film for a specific date and period of time and the chains make their best offer of financial terms for the right to play the film (either exclusively or with other theaters, depending on the distributor's arrangement). The bid is then written and guaranteed, meaning that if the theater bids $100,000, it must pay that sum, regardless of its box-office receipts. A large amount of buying is done by negotiation, however. Oral agreements are followed up by written contracts, and negotiation is often based on trust and existing relationships. A theater chain will customarily deal with a variety of distributors.

Because distributors usually release motion pictures in a particular sequence and under a particular marketing plan, chains often deal with the same group of suppliers for ease of administration. Since there are often not enough new films released evenly throughout the year to take care of all the screens all of the time, however, there is room for independent distributors to get their product played. Still, the major distributors are the main suppliers of films, and without them there wouldn't be enough product to fill all the screens throughout the year. Major distributors are almost always responsible for the blockbusters.

In addition to box-office receipts and concession revenues, a theater may also derive income from other sources. Theaters may receive fees for screen advertising, advertising signs in the lobby, and for making space available in the lobby for the distribution of movie magazines.

The sizes of theaters vary widely. They range from less than one hundred seats in small rural theaters to more than one thousand in large city theaters. An average-size theater in a major city would contain approximately five hundred seats; a small-size theater would have less than three hundred.

Many theaters are equipped only to play 35-mm films, though some are equipped for 16-mm and others may also play 70-mm. The quality of sound is very important in theaters and most have noise-reduction systems such as Dolby.

A multiplex usually has one manger working at a time, one staff that rotates among the auditoriums, and may or may not have a common cashier. There may be one or two projectionists, depending on the number of screens. Multiplexes usually have common concession stands and common restrooms. The projection booths may be completely separate or semi-common. If two auditoriums are adjoining, there may be one large projection booth with different projectors. These may or may not be synchronized, so that one print could be run through both projectors and the same film would play in the two auditoriums simultaneously, although almost always a multiplex will have different films playing in each auditorium.

Box-Office Receipts. Admission fees to movie theaters are divided between the theaters and the distributors of the films that play there (which may be motion picture studio branches or independent firms). Distributors receive a percentage of the box-office gross after the theaters recoup their overhead, or *house expenses.* Through the weeks that a film plays, the distributor's share decreases and the exhibitor's increases. Such factors as the policies of the distributor, location and size of the theater, how badly the exhibitor wants the film or how desperately the distributor wants to book it, the time of the year, the competition, and length of time the film is booked for may determine the split.

For first-run films, box-office receipts for the first or second week are commonly split in a ratio ranging from 70–30 to 90–10; that is, after house expenses are deducted, 70 percent to 90 percent goes to the distributor, 30 percent to 10 percent to the theater. As a practical example of a 90–10 split, assume that an exciting new picture takes in $115,000 at a Chicago theater in its first week and the house expenses are $15,000. The first $15,000, then, is retained by the theater. Of the remaining $100,000, the distributor gets $90,000 (the *rental fee*) and the theater keeps $10,000.

When splits change and in what proportions are negotiable, but they can change anytime after the first week, often in increments of 10 percent. Beginning with the second week of a film booked at 90–10, for example, and continuing every seven days for the next four weeks, the distributor-exhibitor split could be 80–20, 70–30, 60–40, and 50–50. Distributors usually require a guarantee that their percentage of box-office revenues will not be, after house expenses are recouped, less than a certain minimum percentage of the gross receipts. Guarantees range from 30 percent in small markets to 75 percent in large ones. Certain films (such as foreign ones) may be rented on a flat-fee basis.

Distributors sometimes require theaters to pay guarantees for the right to play certain new films (those deemed potential blockbusters). In these cases the stipulated amount is taken off the gross before house expenses are deducted and the balance is split. In New York guarantees could run as high as $50,000 or more. Quite often in deals such as these, advertising costs are split in the same percentage as the profits. For example, if the theater is paying 90 percent of the net receipts, the distributor pays 90 percent of the advertising costs. Such arrangements are known as co-op deals. The terms of rental, including guarantees and splits, are contained in an agreement between the theater and the distributor.

Theater Booking Service. The day-to-day job of operating an independent movie theater is replete with such normal business functions as bookkeeping, administration, supervising a staff, keeping up the facilities, and maintaining and upgrading equipment. However, many independent exhibitors aren't set to handle the complex and time-consuming tasks of screening new movies, dealing with many different distributors, negotiating contracts for renting movies, and attending film festivals. For these purposes they retain specialized firms known as theater booking services.

A booking service handles the booking and buying functions on behalf of the theaters it represents. It is essentially an agent who works for the theater owner. On a regular basis, the booking service informs theater management of what films are available, makes recommendations, gives the distributors' terms of rental, and books films (arranges for them to be shown).

It is vital that a booking service know all the new movies that are released and properly guide its clients with respect to which ones to rent. To stay on top of the new releases, it maintains associations with studios and distributors, attends previews held by distributors, travels to film festivals around the world, and peruses advance synopses, critiques, and reviews in trade publications.

The theater makes the final decision as to what to rent, but it heeds very carefully the suggestions of its booking service. If it wants another movie, however, the service will try to obtain it. The booking service contacts the appropriate distributor and if the film is available negotiates a deal on behalf of the theater.

Booking services charge fees for booking films into theaters. There are various factors that determine the fee, including the volume of business the theater does, whether the theater plays first- or second-run movies, and the particular services that are provided.

Booking services are relatively small operations. The number of employees a firm retains is proportionate to the number of clients it has. Typically, there would be a president, vice-president, booker (who arranges for films to be played in the theaters), buyer (who handles the terms of rental and payments), cashier (who administers box-office statements and billings), controller, and secretaries.

EXTERIOR SET. *See* **Set.**

EXTRA. An extra is a background actor for film or television who has no lines. While the individual contribution of an extra is marginal, the group effect is vital to the realism of a scene. They are human decorations necessary for proper ambience. The camera may sweep over their faces, but they primarily serve to help create a particular atmosphere.

Extras usually supply their own costumes. Formal dresswear, uniforms, hats, and expensive outerwear are valuable accoutrements for obtaining employment. Some casting directors keep notes or maintain computerized information on the wardrobes and physical qualities of extras. During production, the casting office usually tells extras what to wear on the set.

Extras are used in settings such as parties, speeches, card games, social dances, and crowds. Under union regulations, they may be granted allowances for providing specified items such as motorcycles, skis, cameras, golf clubs, luggage, and wigs. The Screen Extras Guild (SEG) is a national union that represents extras, except in New York, where extras belong to SAG.

See **Screen Actors Guild.**

FAIRNESS DOCTRINE. The Fairness Doctrine is a defunct policy of the Federal Communications Commission that required broadcasting stations to "afford reasonable opportunity" to cover contrasting viewpoints on significant controversial public issues. When the Fairness Doctrine was announced in 1949, it generated controversy for numerous reasons. Because it was unclear who was to determine the importance of a controversial issue, the Fairness Doctrine actually inhibited stations from presenting controversial issues. The threat of sanctions, in a worst-case scenario, included the revocation of the station's broadcasting license. In August 1987 the FCC voted the Fairness Doctrine unconstitutional, although some members of Congress have since attempted to codify it.

FEDERAL COMMUNICATIONS COMMISSION (FCC). An independent agency of the government, the Federal Communications Commission, established by Congress with the **Communications Act of 1934**, is responsible for regulating interstate and international communication by television, radio, wire, cable, and satellite in the United States (and Puerto Rico, the Virgin Islands, and Guam).

The FCC has a number of regulatory powers. It has the authority to:

- Either on its own or in response to individual petitions for rule-making license frequencies for new types of services.
- License television stations for five-year terms.
- Ensure that stations serve the public interest through their programming.
- Review the records of a TV station at renewal time and, depending on the station's record in serving the public interest, renew or cancel the station's license.
- Consider applications to build or sell stations.
- Grant permits for the construction of stations.
- Ensure that stations grant political candidates equal opportunities.

Federal Communications Commission (FCC)

- Ensure that stations do not broadcast advertising that is false or misleading.
- Require licensees to identify their stations (either visual or spoken for TV broadcasters) by call letters, the name of the area they serve, and their station's name or channel, if desired (the FCC prescribes a format and times for such announcements).
- Conduct investigations to determine if stations are complying with FCC rules.
- Limit ownership of television stations by the same owner to twelve.
- Fine a station or revoke its license for broadcast of language considered obscene by FCC standards.

The FCC is commonly believed to have a number of powers that it, in fact, does not have. The FCC *cannot:*

- Either limit or establish a minimum number of commercials a station or network may broadcast per hour.
- License networks.
- Prohibit any entity from creating a network.
- Censor programs.
- Prohibit a station from broadcasting an opinion.
- Investigate a station pursuant to receiving complaints that it is suppressing or distorting news reports (unless extrinsic evidence is supplied).
- Prohibit stations or networks from broadcasting identical programs.
- Regulate advertising.
- Review advertising rates as a normal procedure.
- Interfere with a station's right of free speech in broadcasting.
- Select material for programming.
- Rate television programs or films.
- Regulate promoters of sports events or team owners.
- Promulgate guidelines on volume.
- Ban programs on which persons or groups are parodied or criticized.
- Require stations to broadcast in color or in stereo.

- Regulate closed-circuit television (such as systems in offices or in stores).
- Become involved in disputes resulting from the submission of scripts by the public to TV stations, networks, and producers.

The public may send comments or complaints to the FCC about a particular station. Licensees must comply with applicable regulations and laws (*see* **Television stations, federal regulation of**); those found to be in violation risk losing their licenses or being denied their renewal. There are many seemingly questionable practices by stations, however, that do not violate laws or FCC rules. The FCC encourages viewers to send written comments and suggestions to stations, which may provide constructive criticism on programming and policies. The FCC requires stations to keep these in a public file, available for examination by the community, for three years.

Criticism that violence and sexual material on television was not in the public welfare prompted a study by the FCC in February 1975 ("Report on Broadcast of Violent, Indecent and Obscene Material"). The agency concluded that government interference could stifle creative programming and that the First Amendment guarantees freedom of expression. However, broadcasters were urged to announce when programming might be offensive to some viewers.

The FCC is administered by five commissioners appointed by the President with the approval of the Senate; one commissioner is appointed chairman by the President. The terms are for staggered five years. Commissioners may not have a financial interest in a broadcasting entity.

FILM EDITING. The production of a motion picture may take many weeks, even months, to complete. During that time thousands of feet of film are exposed. It is not unusual to shoot as much as 250,000 to 500,000 feet (46 to 100 hours) of film on a major motion picture. The finished film, when it is released, will run about 9,000 to 12,000 feet (about two hours or less). To add to the complication, the film is not shot in chronological order and it is usually shot with a single camera, one angle or scene at a time. This means that the same line of dialogue, the same actions, are repeated over and over. In order to create a cohesive motion picture that tells the story or conveys the ideas that the script intended, the film must be edited into its final form. The film editor and the editing staff must apply all their creative skills and experience to assemble a film that enhances the director's style. A good editor has a strong sense of where to make a cut, how to create flow, how to accent the director's rhythms, or even how to edit against those rhythms.

During the editing process, the editor works with a silent picture (a work print) and a separate magnetic sound track. After a day's shoot, the film in the camera (which is negative stock) is sent to a motion picture laboratory to be developed. A positive print is made from the developed negative. However, only selected takes of the negative stock are printed. While the film is being processed, a sound studio transfers the sound corresponding to the selected takes to 35-mm sound film (film with a magnetic stripe on it). While film is shot, the sound is recorded on quarter-inch tape with a syncpulse, which keeps the sound synchronized with the picture (*see* **Sound recording, production**). After the film is printed and the sound is transferred to the prints, the two elements are delivered to the editing room.

At this point, the editing crew synchronizes the dailies by aligning the clapstick that is seen on the film with the sound of the clapstick on the sound track. The clapstick is an identification slate that is snapped at the beginning of each take. The frame showing the clapstick hitting is the point where the sound track is synchronized. For example, if "Scene 1, Take 1" is being synchronized, the editor's assistant marks an X on that frame of the picture where the blur of the clapstick stops. When the assistant hears "Scene 1, Take 1" and hears the stick clap, it is matched up with the marked picture frame so they are in perfect synchronization. After the dailies are synchronized, they are usually rechecked for accuracy by the editor or an assistant.

Each day, the dailies are screened with the director. After the director finishes the filming for the day, a meeting is held with the editor during which the dailies from the day before (which are now synchronized with the sound) are screened. The director and the editor decide which takes they prefer.

The next step is edge-coding, a mechanical process in which a series of matching numbers are stamped on the edge of the picture and sound track, so when the film is cut up into pieces the synchronization will not be destroyed. The coding consists of two letters and four numbers, starting with AA0001, then a foot later, AA0002, and so forth until AA9999. Then the coding would pick up with BB0000 and continue similarly with other letter prefixes. There are other coding machines that use different variations of this system.

After the film has been coded, it is sent back to the editing room, where it is logged onto printed sheets. Logging, or cataloging, is the system by which an editor keeps track of takes. When an editor cuts up the film into pieces, the pieces can be identified by referring to the log sheets and the code number on the film. The log sheets are a record of what was printed, listing the scene number, the take number, a one-line description of the scene, the code number, the latent image key number (which is a number printed on the film by the company that manufactured the film stock), the camera roll number, and the sound roll number.

After logging, the film is broken down into the small rolls—the individual takes—that were selected by the director while screening the dailies. The editor is now able to begin the editing process.

The editor assembles the footage that has been broken down the day before until all the footage has been exhausted. This is called a *first-cut*, or the *editor's cut*, of the film. Although the director has control in selecting the takes from the dailies, the experienced editor has total control over the first-cut. Once the first-cut is completed, it is subject to changes by the director.

There are different ways an editor can operate to achieve similar ends. Some editors write the changes or requests that the director has made on the script. Other editors write the changes directly on the film using a grease pencil. Then the editor views the shots of a scene taken from different angles, decides which coverage is best, marks the film where it is to be cut, and assembles the chosen pieces of film. This process continues until the assembled pieces form the first-cut.

After the editor has completed the first-cut, it is shown to the director. Most directors do not look at the edited footage until the editor has completed the first-cut. For a feature film it usually takes one or two months after the director has completed shooting for the editor to get the first-cut. Television features are edited much faster because of budget and time restrictions. Most editors of TV features take about a week to complete their cut after the director has finished shooting.

Once the editor has completed the first-cut, the editor and the director view it together. They work in conjunction until the director is satisfied.

After the film has been edited to the director's satisfaction, the opticals must be added to the work print. Opticals can be titles, credits, special effects, dissolves, wipes, freeze frames, and any other added visual effects. If the director or editor decides a certain effect is needed, the editor sends the appropriate segment of the negative out to a specialized company known as an *optical house*. The optical house will make a new negative which incorporates the effect and then makes a positive print from that. The new negative will be sent back to the laboratory and the editor will put the positive print back into the work print.

Complex visual effects are done by special-effects companies. Detailed work with miniatures and complicated puppets often is begun during the principal filming of the script.

After the positive prints, including opticals, are spliced into the editor's work print, the visual part of the movie is completed.

Once the director is satisfied with the visual aspects of the film, the work print is sent to a negative cutter. A negative cutter makes the negative film conform to the editor's work print. Copies of the film will be made from this final negative.

The negative cutter finds the pieces of negative film stock that match the pieces of film in the work print by using the latent image key numbers printed on the film by the manufacturer of the film stock. A certain amount of care is necessary because every time the negative is spliced one frame is lost due to overlap. The editor has more freedom with the work print because splicing tape is used. Splicing tape lets the editor change cuts with an ease not available to the negative cutter. With most movies the negative is not cut until the audio portion is done, allowing the director to make additional last-minute changes.

The audio track of a film includes dialogue, sound effects, and music.

Once the picture of the film is completed, the director and editor sit down with the composer and sound editor (or sound editing crew) and spot the film. *Spotting* consists of determining at what points or intervals in the film sound effects and music should go.

The film is run forward and backward, and the director or editor dictates to the sound editor unusual effects wanted at certain points in the film.

The sound editor builds the sound effects on separate tracks, and splits up the dialogue into separate tracks. Sometimes one or more actors will be called into the sound studio to redo dialogue because various words did not come out clearly on the sound track. This is called *automated dialogue replacement* or ADR. The dialogue has to be rerecorded, or dubbed, into the sound track at the exact point where it belongs. The sound editing might take from several weeks to several months to prepare.

Meanwhile, the composer is writing music for the film. The composer and the sound effects editor are each given their own copy of the work print to work from. Should there be any changes made in the film after they receive their copies, they must have the alterations made on their duplicates or else the timing will be out of sync when they're ready for the final mixing session. Usually a few days before the mixing session, the composer goes into a sound studio with anywhere from one musician to a 120-piece orchestra and records the music for the film. Whether recording on sixteen-, twenty-four-, or thirty-two-track tape, the music eventually mixes down to three or four tracks for the final sound mix of the movie.

When all the sound effects tracks, dialogue tracks, and music tracks are completed, there are a number of separate sound tracks that must be combined, or mixed down, into one master sound track. (In New York, this combining is referred to as a *mixing session*, in California a *dubbing session*.) Ultimately there could be over one hundred tracks. The master sound track will either be a three-, four-, or six-track master on 35-mm magnetic film.

The master sound track is made in a sound studio usually under the supervision of the director. To prepare for the mix, mixing sheets, also known as *cue sheets*, must be prepared. The mixing sheets list exactly what is on each sound track and at what footage. In the mixing studio there is a footage counter under the screen which tells the mixing engineer exactly what foot and frame is being viewed at all times. The mixing engineer can stop, go forward or backward, and record over anything. Thirty-five-millimeter feature films are recorded on one-thousand-foot reels. A feature will average about twelve reels, each reel being about eight to ten minutes in length. One reel, with all its separate sound tracks, is mixed at a time.

In New York there is usually only one mixing engineer working at a sound console, whereas in California there usually are three. The number of sound tracks there are depends upon the complexity of the film. The mixing engineer blends all these tracks onto one master track. The engineer has control over the volume and equalization (treble, mid-range, and bass components of the sound) for each track.

Before the composite print is made, the master sound track must be transferred to an optical track negative. Prior to the making of the optical track negative, the recorded sound is in magnetic form. Digital sound is sometimes used, but until the new technology is totally phased in, the magnetic sound is, most often, transferred to an optical sound track.

The master sound track is put into a transfer machine, which has six heads that will blend all the tracks into one track. This in turn is fed into an optical sound recorder, which translates the magnetic impulses into optical impulses. These optical impulses are recorded onto the raw film stock in the recorder. This is then developed, resulting in an optical track negative. Some feature films have a magnetic sound track instead of an optical sound track on their prints, but usually only on 70-mm prints for special limited runs.

The optical track negative and the picture track negative are used to make the final composite print. The negatives are not physically combined, they are kept separate. However, they are put together photographically to produce the composite print on positive film stock. This process is called *printing* and produces the film that is delivered to the distributor. The final composite print has a picture which takes up most of the space on the frame, with the sound track printed along-edge of the picture frame.

Recently, film editors, primarily those who work on filmed television shows, adopted computerized video-editing techniques that save time and labor. The editor, working on one of these systems, never has to make a splice or even touch a piece of film in any way. In many cases there is not even any film in the editing room, only videotape and/or disks. In 1987 it was estimated that 60 to 70 percent of all filmed television shows were edited in this way. A few feature motion pictures have even been edited on these systems.

The film is shot using conventional single-camera motion picture techniques, but after it is developed at the laboratory, the developed negative is sent, along with the quarter-inch sound track master tape, to a film-to-tape (telecine) video transfer facility. There the picture negative and the quarter-inch tape are synchronized and transferred onto a one-inch videotape master. This one-inch master, called the *telecine master,* is then used to manufacture multiple copies on half-inch or three-quarter-inch videocassettes and/or videodiscs which are used as source material in the editing process. This is, in effect, the editor's work print.

The editor, director, and producer view their dailies on a video monitor from one of these cassettes. All of the same decisions and selections that are made in the projection room with film dailies are made at this time. The assistant editor uses another of these tapes or a videodisc to enter a log of its scenes into the editing system's computer data base in a manner similar to the log sheets made for film.

There are several editing systems currently in use (Editflex, Editdroid, Montage, Laseredit, CMX) and they all are referred to as *off-line editing systems*. All of these systems are computer-based, and they all use multiple copies of the source material in multiple playback machines to permit random access of the scenes to be edited.

The editing techniques used with these systems are identical to those with film from a creative standpoint, but the mechanics are reduced to pushing buttons. There is no winding, no splicing, nothing to physically handle. A scene is marked for a cut by pushing a button and spliced into the edited sequence by pushing another button. The computer will remember where each edit is made.

While the source material used is essentially a composite format (that is, the picture and sound on the same tape or disk), the computer deals with picture and sound edits separately. This gives the editor the same flexibility allowed by physically cutting the film.

When the editing is complete and everyone is satisfied, the computer is asked to produce an *edit decision list*, or EDL, which can be in the form of a paper printout, punch tape, or computer data disk. The EDL will be used during what is called the *on-line* editing session to manufacture an edited one-inch master videotape from the telecine master videotape.

The telecine master that was made during the original film-to-tape transfer is put on a video playback machine and a blank roll of one-inch videotape is put onto a recorder. This blank tape becomes the electronically edited master. The EDL is loaded into the on-line editing system's computer, creating a data base that is used to make the edits.

The source tape on the playback machine will shuttle back and forth, transferring each clip or cut to the edited master on the recorder, placing them in the proper order, and leaving an unrecorded hole on the tape for any material that is not on that source tape roll. When all the cuts on that source roll have been transferred, the process is stopped and the operator is asked by the computer to put up the source tape roll containing the next cuts. This continues until all the cuts have been transferred and the edited master is complete, a process called *auto assembly*. During the auto assembly, titles may be added, optical effects may be created, and the color balance of each cut may be corrected.

After the on-line edit is complete, the sound track is transferred from the edited master onto two-inch, multi-track audiotape for *audio sweetening* (dubbing or mixing in film terms). Sound effects, music, additional dialogue, etc., are added to this tape and then mixed to create the final sound track.

If the production is to be exhibited as a video, the final mixed sound track is then laid back onto the edited master. If the production is to be exhibited as film, the on-line edit is not done and at some point the original film (print and/or negative) is edited to conform to the final off-line edited video. The remainder of the editing process, including the addition of sound track, is carried out in the conventional film manner.

FILM EDITOR. The film editor arranges selected takes and cuts into a motion picture. Film editors are usually hired late in pre-production by the director. Before principal photography starts, the film editor reads the script, noting special situations such as optical effects and matte shots, and meets with the director to discuss how the director envisions the film to be shot. After shooting commences, the film editor views the dailies in the evening with the director, taking notes on the director's feedback, and then makes cuts with selected takes of the dailies. When sequences are completed they may be edited.

A picture may be best served by having only one editor—for consistency in style and perspective—but sometimes there is so much footage that additional editors are needed. In such cases there would be a supervising editor in charge.

The hiring practices for film editors has changed greatly over the years. In the past, all the major studios had an editorial department with a staff of editors. The editors were assigned to a picture by the department head after consultation with the producer. Now, except for television production companies, there are no editorial staffs; almost all editors work free-lance and the director will have final approval. Many directors have an editor who will always cut their pictures. A few directors are also editors and will cut their own pictures.

Some editors work only on feature motion pictures, while others do television films exclusively. Many, however, work in both mediums. Most of the feature film editors have agents who negotiate for them, while most television editors negotiate their own deals.

The film editor generally hires an assistant and other editing room staff. The sound-effects and dialogue editing staffs are hired after joint consultation between the editor, director, and producer. The composer generally hires a music editor.

FILM FESTIVAL. There are two types of film festivals: industry and public. Industry film festivals are regularly held throughout the year in different locations around the world. Their purpose is to showcase new films and talent; to serve as a central marketplace where movies may be screened and buyers and sellers of film may do business (that is, foreign distribution); to serve as a marketplace where filmmakers may raise financing or cut deals for new projects; to bring attention to the industry; to pay tribute to workers of the industry; to serve as a forum for city, state, and foreign film-liaison offices to attract filmmakers; and to promote the particular locales where they are held as potential locations for shooting films, television movies, and miniseries. Indeed, film festivals are events publicized heavily in trade and consumer press. Paparazzi and journalists are ever-present.

Film festivals run from a few days to one month, and the number of films screened per festival can range from a few hundred to a thousand. Competitions are often held for a selected group, with an international jury selecting the best film.

The Cannes Film Festival is perhaps the best known and most glamorous industry film festival. Other prominent film festivals are held in such locations as Milan (the festival called MIFED), Montreal, Vancouver, Melbourne, Tokyo, Munich, Rio, Barcelona, Seattle, and Athens, Ohio. Announcements of these are made in trade journals.

Film festivals for the general public are usually held to showcase foreign movies, classics, and other films that local audiences are not customarily given the opportunity to see. Motion pictures that relate to a particular theme such as comedy, or a certain ethnic group, a legendary star or director, or promising new talent are common as well. There are film societies, often associated with cultural or educational groups or centers, that serve to sponsor these film festivals.

FILM GENRES. Films are produced in a variety of genres, not only for artistic expression but for commercial purposes—that is, to cater to the tastes of paying audiences. The various genres of films are characterized by subject matter, characters, settings, dialogue, language, cinematography, stunts, special effects, and other elements. Many movies are actually hybrids of two or more genres or are subgenres of a broader category. For example, there are films that combine horror and comedy, and a whodunit movie may be considered a particular type of mystery. Indeed, many names for genres have entered our vocabulary and some genres may only be distinguished by slight nuances. The following table contains the names and brief descriptions of several motion picture genres.

FILM GENRES

Genre	Description
Action-adventure	"Good guys versus bad guys" as they face one another in frenetic pursuit of rewards or other goals with stunts catalyzing the action.
Buddy	Two sidekicks, usually having opposite personalities, meandering through predicaments and adventures.
Children	Real-life or animated characters involved in situations and actions that amuse youngsters.
Comedy	Many different forms (slapstick, black, etc.) in which exaggerated real-life characters react to improbable situations, keeping audiences laughing.

Continued on next page

Continued from previous page

Genre	Description
Documentary	Cinematic account of real-life event, situation, dilemma, or crisis using the actual people involved, as opposed to actors.
Drama	A story of human conflict with real-life characters; also an all-inclusive genre for stories characterized by strong emotion and keen dialogue.
Horror	Vicious monster, creature, alien, or human preys on and kills people; meant to terrorize both the innocent characters and the audience.
Monster	Same as "horror."
Mystery	Protagonist attempts to solve a murder or crime that grows more intriguing or life-threatening to him as the probe deepens.
Pornography	Explicit (soft- or hard-core) material intended to arouse sexually.
Revenge	Vile characters who harm or take advantage of innocent people are fought by the protagonist, who struggles but eventually kills or defeats them.

Continued on next page

Romance	Two attractive lovers attempt to hurdle obstacles and difficulties to unite or reconcile their affections.
Science fiction	Futuristic story of a contemporary theme involving human beings and aliens; special effects usually heavy.
Spy	Superhero who is attractive, agile, powerful, and cunning involved in insuperable situations where the stakes are great and the superhero always triumphs.
Suspense	Protagonist involved in life-threatening situation and tries to overcome enemy or bring to justice.
Teen	Irreverent statements on society involving young protagonists; fantasies of adolescents acted out, for whom it is designed to appeal; often includes energetic music score; script contains profanities and expressions in vogue, an important element to lending credibility to the story.
Western	Timeless issues confronted in the setting of 19th-century western United States; classic conflicts of good and evil.
Whodunit	Protagonist tries to find the mystery killer, and as the plot unfolds the audience is kept guessing as to the identity of the culprit, who often turns out to be a most unlikely suspect.

FILM LABORATORY. After film is shot, it goes to a photographic laboratory where it is processed, enabling it to be shown on a motion picture projector. **Dailies** are sent to film labs for developing, and when they are returned, they are screened, edited, and made ready for theatrical distribution.

Film arrives at the lab in cans (often one thousand feet of film per can). There are several different kinds of processing. As an example of how processing works, consider the Ectochrome method of processing:

1. A silver image of the film (negative) is developed. When the motion picture camera takes the picture, an ionic silver image results. This step changes the ionic silver into metallic silver, which is a black-and-white image.
2. The metallic silver image is reversed. The metallic silver is changed back into ionic silver and any silver that is still in ionic form (that is, was not exposed to light in the first developer and consequently not converted) is chemically exposed to become metallic silver. This step, done in what is called a reversal bath, results in a reverse, or positive image.
3. Color is added to the film. The film goes into what is called a *color developer*, where dye clouds attach to it. Dye clouds circle and grab onto the metallic silver image in different quantities to produce different colors.
4. The film is placed in a bleach bath, where the metallic silver is converted back to ionic silver.
5. A fixer removes the ionic silver, leaving a dye image on an acetate base.
6. The film is stablized, a process that removes some of the dye-couplers. Dye-couplers are undesirable, as they could later yellow.
7. The film is dried, respooled, and returned to an editing facility or to the producer.

Another common process of film developing is the ME2 System (with 52-47 film). It is a less expensive method than Ectochrome, but the film that results does not last as long. Film labs usually charge for processing by the foot.

FILM LIBRARY. *See* **Stock Footage Library**.

FILM RATING SYSTEM. Theatrical motion pictures released in the United States are rated in terms of suitability for viewing by children and teenagers under seventeen by a Film Rating Board sponsored by the Motion Picture Association of America (MPAA), the National Association of Theatre Owners (NATO), and a group of independent movie distributors. The Board consists of seven parents and a chairman, who rate films in various categories including profanity, sex, violence, and theme. After viewing a film, the Board assigns one of five ratings to it: G, PG, PG-13, R, and NC-17; these are certification marks and can only be legally applied by the trademark owner. If a producer believes a rating is inaccurate, an Appeals Board may be requested, comprised of twenty-two members of MPAA and NATO, as well as independent motion picture distributors, to review the film. A rating can only be changed by a two-thirds vote by the Appeals Board. The Classification and Rating Administration was created in November 1968 to help parents decide or recommend what films their children should see.

The film ratings system is shown on page 148.

FILM RELEASES. Approximately four hundred to five hundred theatrical motion pictures are released each year in the United States. This includes films made by major studios, independent producers, and foreign producers, as well as documentaries. The foreign films are a potpourri of English-language, dubbed, and subtitled movies.

Certain weeks of the year or seasons attract larger audiences than others, so there might be more releases during those times. Holiday seasons (*see* **Christmas Movie**) and the summer (*see* **Summer Season**), for example, are traditionally high-volume periods at the box office.

Film Ratings

G	General audiences	"All ages admitted"; the Rating Board deems that no elements of the film are considered offensive.
PG	Parental guidance suggested	"Some material may not be suitable for children"; some violence or profanity is contained in the picture and the Rating Board advises parents to either see the film or investigate it further and use their own discretion in deciding whether to permit their children to see it.
PG-13	Parents strongly cautioned	"Some material may be inappropriate for children under 13." This rating is intended to alert parents that the language, violence, or nudity in the film is not such that an R rating is warranted, but that the content may not be considered appropriate for youngsters. It was instated in July 1984.
R	Restricted	"Under 17 requires accompanying parent or adult guardian"; the movie contains mature material and parents should consider whether they want their children exposed to this before they take them to see the film.
NC-17		"No children under 17"; the film contains material that is adult-oriented and the theater may deny admission to anyone under 17. This designation replaced in September 1990 the X rating, which was not trademarked by the MPAA when it established the voluntary rating code and which became associated with hard-core pornography. Pornographic filmmakers consequently were able to advertise their movies with one or more X's, and may still continue to do so.

Not all films are released nationally at first. Some films are test-marketed or released on a regional basis to sample their potential. A film that is released nationally may play on a thousand or more screens. In an average month there may be about one dozen releases by major U.S. studios and two dozen from independent distributors.

FILM, SOURCES OF INCOME. Since studios do not usually recoup their production, advertising, and marketing costs for a film from domestic box-office revenues, they rely on ancillary sources to not only break even but to earn substantial profits. The potential sources of income for a film are as follows:

- Rentals (first-run and all subsequent releases).
- Television licensing fees from networks, independent TV stations, and cable and pay-TV systems.
- Videocassette and videodisc licensing advances and royalties or sales.
- Merchandise licensing advances and royalties.
- Foreign revenues from all the sources above.

Music publishing rights and sound recording (**sound track album**) rights generate additional income for the studio if it owns these rights.

Music publishing rights accompany ownership of the songs that are in the picture, which might earn income from radio airplay and other areas of public performance, record sales (both from a sound track album and cover records), sheet music, songbooks, band arrangements, and other print materials and advertising jingles.

Sound recording rights accompany the ownership of musical, vocal, and spoken sounds, which are a separate class of copyright. The sound track of a motion picture may be commercially released and generate revenues for the film studio if it owns the sound recording rights. Studios would license the master recordings (sound tracks) to a record company, which would release and pay royalties on singles, LPs, compact discs, and cassettes. Some movie studios are affiliated with record companies.

FILM STOCK. From original cinematography and sound recording to release printing, the original visual image and sound record undergo several transfer and duplication stages. The original image requires several intermediate printing steps and intermediate film stocks.

The different types of film stock used for 16-mm and 35-mm color and black-and-white motion picture photography is summarized in the table that begins on page 151.

FILM AND TELEVISION AGENCIES, STATE AND CITY. Film production is no longer confined to studio sets associated with old Hollywood. Today, films and television shows are regularly produced in cities throughout America. State and city film and TV agencies promote an area's resources to filmmakers. The benefits that may be incurred economically and prestigiously are the raison d'être for the agencies. Local movie productions translate into tax, trade, and labor benefits for an area, and serve as a boost for tourism as well.

Film agencies work with producers and location managers to help them find desirable locations to shoot. These agencies also help obtain licenses, permits, and accommodations. They aggressively seek the business of producers by taking out ads in trade publications, attending industry film festivals, offering literature on the area, and maintaining photograph files of local sites. Many local studios have been built to accommodate filmmakers' needs and serve as a further draw. Producers prefer to shoot outside of California both for the realism that an authentic location offers and for the reduced labor costs.

FINAL CUT. The final cut is the edited and finished film. The Directors Guild of America's 1987 Basic Agreement provides for the director to make a *director's cut*. However, the producer may make further changes to the director's cut for commercial reasons. The final cut is the cut approved and released by the studio or producer.

See also **First Cut.**

Film Stock	Explanation
Color negative film	Used for color motion picture photography. It is the film that originally captures the action and is shot through the camera. It is used for 16-mm, 35-mm, and 65-mm shooting and comes in medium speed and high speed. High-speed film is more sensitive to light and can often be shot under existing conditions as opposed to medium-speed film, which is shot under normal daylight or studio lighting conditions.
Color positive film	Printed from the color negative used for the dailies. It becomes the work print. The same film type is used for the answer print, and for theatrical release prints.
Color reversal film	Camera original film which yields a positive image. Prevents going from a negative image to a positive image. A reversal (chemical) process yields a positive image. There are a few different types of reversal stocks, which may be divided into original camera stocks and print stocks. Both can be projected because they both have a positive image. The reversal print stock is simply designed to make a duplicate of the camera original stock or to make a series of copies or prints of the original negative. Color reversal film is normally available in 16-mm and super 8-mm.

Continued on next page

Continued from previous page

Film Stock	Explanation
Color reversal intermediate stock	By means of a color reversal chemical process, a master positive and a duplicate negative of a camera negative are made in a single step.
Sound recording film	Designed to transfer the magnetic recording of dialogue, music, **Foleys**, and sound effects (the composite mix of a studio master) into a corresponding analog optical signal on a black-and-white emulsion (that is, an optical image on sound recording stock).
Black-and-white camera film	Black-and-white equivalent of color negative film. It comes in 16-mm and 35-mm stock and at low, medium, and high speeds.
Black-and-white duplicating stock	Equivalent to color internegatives except that it is black and white. If several prints are to be made from the black-and-white camera negative without ruining the negative, a duplicate negative is made, which requires an interpositive. The duplicate negative is then printed onto black-and-white positive stock (the equivalent of color positive) and is used for dailies, work prints, answer prints, and release prints.
Titling stock	A high-contrast stock that is normally a record of the art or titling work. It is usually incorporated at the duplicate negative stage so that the rolling credits at the beginning and end are combined with the duplicate negative image.

FINANCING A FILM. There is no standard way to finance a film. With the many methods available to cover production costs—private limited partnerships, public partnerships, and bank loans—the deals can be as varied as the films themselves. An understanding of film financing may be served by the following hypothetical situation.

Wickford Films, a major studio, has agreed to buy a film from independent producer Wade Jenkins for $5 million for world rights, upon delivery of the completed motion picture. The studio's decision was based upon Jenkins's track record, the script, and the casting. Jenkins has determined that it will cost approximately $4 million to make the film, excluding his fee. Jenkins will take $500,000 as his fee and the remaining half a million dollars will go to pay the completion bond (*see* **Completion guarantor**) and interest accruing on the loan.

Jenkins approaches Country Bank for a loan, presenting his idea, credentials, and a **deal memo** from Wickford. Country Bank looks at the presentation and immediately declines the loan because they do not deal in motion picture financing, a realm of financing handled by only a handful of banks due to the risky nature of film production.

So Jenkins goes to Los Angeles, where most motion picture financing is done. He approaches United Movie Bank, which specializes in financing independently made films.

In evaluating whether to make the loan, United Movie Bank examines Jenkins's budget, his projected cash needs during the production period, and his track record as a producer. United Movie Bank also does an analysis of Scrutiny Bond Company, the company that Jenkins has chosen to be his completion guarantor. They investigate both Scrutiny's credit history (examining who they reinsure with) as well as their ability to come up with completion funding. In addition, the bank checks out the film industry's experience with Scrutiny, to see if Scrutiny has come through on past obligations. United Movie Bank also does a credit analysis of Wickford Films to make sure that Wickford has adequate financial strength to pay for the film when it is completed and delivered. The analysis is as complete as if Wickford had come to United Film Bank for a loan directly and the loan was approved.

Often the companies that buy distribution rights from independent filmmakers are private companies and refuse to release financial information to institutions like United Film Bank. A solution to this problem is to have Wickford obtain a Standby Letter of Credit through its bank in Wade Jenkins's behalf, guaranteeing payment by Wickford's bank of the $5 million upon successful completion and delivery of the film. This arrangement will most likely be acceptable to United Movie Bank, and if all the other information is compiled to the bank's satisfaction, it will approve a production loan for Jenkins. The bank, in evaluating the production cash flows, figures in interest for a period which includes contractual delivery and payment of the loan, plus a ninety-day force majeure contingency period.

United Movie Bank deposits the loan into Jenkins's account as the funds are needed for production, and the producer sends weekly reports to the bank and to the Scrutiny Bond Company, to prove that the film is progressing on time and on budget.

Ten months later Jenkins completes his film and delivers it to Wickford, which screens it and finds that it is satisfactory, meaning it is of a professional quality and follows the original script. Wickford sends a check to United Movie Bank, paying off the loan and interest. Now all parties—studio, the producer, the bank, and the bond company—have complied with their obligations.

Sometimes loans are made with a floating interest rate, which changes with the prime interest rate or base rate that is set. If a producer is paying 1 percent over prime, the loan's interest rate will change with fluctuations in the prime interest rate. For a fee the producer can obtain a fixed-rate loan or a rate-cap, which will limit his interest expense.

A completion guarantor may, in effect, help a bank decide whether or not to go ahead with a loan, though if a guarantor is not willing to bond a producer, the chances are that the bank will not be willing to finance the project.

Typically it is the producer who will approach a bank for a loan, but a request can be made by other parties also. The studio or the attorney representing the producer, for example, may approach the bank. Sometimes another bank makes a request if it is involved in the project. If a bank will not lend the full amount necessary, additional financing must be obtained from another lender, or the producer may put in his own money.

After a bank is repaid in full, it has no further contractual obligations to the picture.

FINGERS. *See* **Grip Equipment.**

FIRST CUT. The first cut refers to a film after the first edit. A first cut is also called a *rough cut*.

See also **Final Cut.**

FIRST-RUN FILM. *See* **Release.**

FIRST-RUN SYNDICATION. *See* **Independent Television Station; Syndication.**

FIXED WORK. The Copyright Act of 1976 provides protection for an original work when it is "fixed," or embodied in a "tangible medium of expression" by the authority of the author. A screenplay, for example, is a fixed work and is protected under the law. Works consisting of sounds, images, or both that are broadcast live, such as television news broadcasts, are fixed if "a fixation of the work is being made simultaneously with its transmission." The material of a stand-up comedian improvising in a nightclub would not be eligible for statutory copyright protection if his performance is not being recorded and has not been set down in writing.

FLEX ARM. *See* **Grip Equipment.**

FOLEY ARTIST. Certain sounds such as footsteps, fabric tearings, and chair scrapes are not recorded as the actors go through the motions on the set but are recorded in postproduction by synchronization specialists called Foley artists, named after Jack Foley, a sound editor. A Foley artist can walk or run in dead synchronization with an actor, tripping or jumping just as the actor makes these movements. The Foley artist physically makes noises in a sound studio while a microphone records them. This is done while the picture is running, so the Foley artist can watch the actors on the film while mimicking the appropriate sounds.

Consider, for example, a chase scene in which an actor runs over mud and jumps on a porch. The Foley artist runs over wet rags to simulate the sound of shoes hitting mud and jumps on a piece of wood to recreate a porch sound. Other sounds, such as panting, coughing, or wheezing, may be overdubbed at the same time. If a sound turns out to be slightly out of synchronization with the action, it can be corrected manually with an editing machine.

Foley artists experiment to get the most realistic sounds. To get a good sound of hitting someone over the head, the Foley artist might hit a stick or a hammer against different surfaces until a desired sound is achieved. The Foley artist will plunk down a coffee cup, strike metal chains with an object, shuffle his feet, put plates down on a table, flick a cigarette lighter—whatever the action on the screen dictates. The sounds made by a Foley artist are usually recorded on 35-mm magnetic film by the *Foley editor*.

FORMULAS. Formulas are action sequences, plot developments, shticks, and any other conventions used repeatedly in motion pictures and television programs to garner audience attention. Formulas are used primarily out of convenience. Drama, science fiction, comedy, and other genres can be reduced to formulas. Good examples of formulas are car chases, physical transformations, steamy love scenes, and cliffhangers. Music can be formulaic, also. A driving, thumping bass line, for example, is often used to underscore the tension of a scene. Formulas are often criticized as being unimaginative and hackneyed.

FORMULAS, PROGRAMMING. A programming formula is a method, hook, or slant—an undiscovered angle that will make a television show work. Network producers who strongly believe a program is a ratings failure try to bring it to life with a formula that will differentiate it from competition in the same time slot on other networks.

FRANCHISED AGENT. A franchised agent is a signatory to a union agreement that outlines the terms under which an agent may do business with a union member. The Screen Actors Guild and the American Federation of Television and Radio Artists (as well as the American Guild of Variety Artists and American Federation of Musicians) franchise agents and require members to be represented only by agents franchised by the unions. The unions franchise agencies to prevent unfair dealings with respect to their members. Franchising regulates the commissions an agent may charge. Franchised AFTRA agents may not charge more than 10 percent commission or impose a fee that will reduce a performer's gross earnings to less than scale.

GAFFER (ELECTRICIAN). A gaffer is the chief electrical lighting technician for a production, although the term can be applied to any lighting technician on the set. *Gaffer* is a British term meaning foreman.

Hired by the unit production manager, the gaffer joins a production early on. After reading the script, the gaffer participates in meetings with the director, script supervisor, producer, and unit production manager. They discuss which scenes will be shot in a studio and which on location, which will be shot in daylight and which at night, which will be shot inside and which outside, the scope of the shots, lighting strategies, and potential problems.

After acquiring a basic understanding of what the project will entail, the gaffer and other key crew members survey the studio and locations to be used. The director's intentions must be explained to the director of photography and to the gaffer so they can discuss together how to achieve the desired effects.

Some of the decisions made by the gaffer include the amount of power necessary for lighting, the type and size of generator to be used, and whether the necessary amount of power can be obtained at each location. An estimate of lighting required is drafted and then is broken down into a day-by-day schedule.

The gaffer oversees the stocking of an electrical truck for location work. This truck must be rigged for maximum efficiency. For longer productions, more than one truck is used. If shooting takes place in a studio, no electrical truck is needed. For location work, the gaffer may hire electricians and generator operators from a local union. The gaffer also works with a **best boy** (second electrician), a steady assistant; and a **third electrician**.

Because of the large amount of time needed to set up the lighting during production, a gaffer must plan ahead. A good gaffer constantly sets up the lighting one scene ahead of the shooting crew. This way, when the film crew is ready to shoot on the next set, the lighting is already set up, saving time and money. The director of photography only needs to fine-tune the lighting environment.

For lighting electricians, the main difference between a motion picture and television production is one of time. A one-hour television show takes anywhere from two to four weeks to produce. Shooting on a feature film runs ten or more weeks.

The electric safety manual of the National Association of Broadcast Employees and Technicians (NABET) local 15 in New York states the responsibilities of gaffers are "to know the duties of the second electrician and the third electrician; to know film ASA; to know light meters and their uses; to manage all subordinate electrical personnel (seconds and thirds); to coordinate and execute orders of the lighting director or the director of photography; to determine sources of necessary power; to understand location scouting as it pertains to electric work; to be the final authority on the set on electrical safety; and to know how to order electrical equipment."

There are no educational or licensing requirements for a gaffer. *See also* **Grip**.

GALLEYS. A galley is a typeset manuscript of a book before it is published. The galley is read by proofreaders and the author for corrections to be made. It may consist of loose sheets or be bound together. Publishers and agents send galleys to television and motion picture story editors and producers to interest them in buying the rights to adapt the book into a movie.

GAME SHOW. *See* **Television Programming Genres.**

GELS. *See* **Grip Equipment.**

GENERAL MANAGER, TELEVISION STATION. *See* **Independent Television Stations.**

GENERATOR. Generators are used to supply electrical power to remote shooting locations. A generator is usually mounted on a truck or a trailer. Generators may range from a single unit of 10 amps to a three-phase unit up to 3,000 amps A.C. or D.C. They are used to operate lights, machinery, and anything else that can run on portable electrical power. Generators are either gas- or diesel-powered.

GOBO. *See* **Grip Equipment.**

GREENS PERSON. A greens person is anyone who works with live or imitation plants on an interior or exterior set. The International Alliance of Theatrical State Employees and Moving-Picture Machine Operators of the United States and Canada (IATSE) Local 44 of Hollywood lists the kinds of materials greens persons work with as flowers, plants, gardens, hedges, trees, brush, woods, shrubbery, etc., lawns or other nursing equipment."

Basically, greens persons tend to or maintain the greenery on the set, as well as bring in and install pots, plants, and small trees, and remove and store materials for future use. They may also carry out related work such as sodding an area or constructing and erecting fake trees.

GRIFFOLYN BUTTERFLY. *See* **Grip Equipment.**

GRIP. A grip is a worker on a television or motion picture production responsible for erecting sets and rigging equipment for shooting. A grip's functions include:

- Assembling sets and exteriors (*see* **Shop Craftsman**).
- Mounting lights.
- Diffusing, blocking, reflecting, and scaffolding lighting on the shooting set.
- Determining which equipment is best to use in individual circumstances and when to use it.
- Laying the dolly track on the terrain with pipe, plank, or other materials (*see* **Grip Equipment**).
- Setting a dolly rigged with a camera on a dolly track or setting the camera on a tripod.
- Moving the camera by use of a dolly, crane, or other kind of equipment.

- Making and assembling mounts and rigs to hold cameras both inside and outside of cars.
- Making safety provisions for the camera crew for shooting stunts.

The origin of the term *grip* is unknown, although it is most likely a bit of old theater lingo. Sometimes grips are titled by the equipment they handle (dolly grip or construction grip). In California grips are sometimes known as *best boys*. Assistants can also be referred to by number (*second man* or *third man*). Historically, *key grip* has referred to the head grip, but some screen credits list all grips on a production as key grips.

Grips begin working on a film or TV project during preproduction. After reading the script, the grips tour the shooting locations along with the director, cameraman, and other members of the production crew. Such surveys enable them to work out the logistics of a dolly or crane shot, for example. Based on their preliminary work, the grips can order the proper equipment. The key grip oversees the rigging of a grip truck for location shooting.

During principal photography, grips are at least one day ahead of the shooting schedule. While the film crew is shooting one scene, some of the grips are preparing for the next. The grips follow the script closely and communicate with the assistant director so they can stay ahead of the shooting.

Factors such as budget, location, and cast size dictate the number of grips hired. During shooting, some grips monitor the film crew's work, watching for defects or crises, and assisting the director of photography. The others prepare for the next scene.

When cranes are used, they are operated by the grips. The grips handle the booming, dollying, moving, and driving of cranes. Grips also rig cars with cameras. A mount is placed on a car to hold a camera for interior shots. Once a car is rigged, an additional car is used to tow the rigged car, provide the lights, record the sound, and seat the director and the script supervisor.

See also **Gaffer (Electrician); Grip Equipment.**

GRIP EQUIPMENT. A grip production truck carries the tools and equipment needed by the grips on the shooting set. The following materials are the necessary equipment for a professional film production.

Diffusion Materials. Diffusion materials are used in motion picture photography to create lighting effects.

Barn Door. A barn door is a metal object mounted on an incandescent lamp used to decrease the amount of light emitted. A barn door has four doors, one on top, one on the bottom, and one on each of the sides.

Bounce Card. A bounce card has a white or shiny surface used to reflect light from a source to an area. Bounce cards are used primarily to fill in the shadows of a shot for an even lighting effect. A bounce card is mounted on a grip stand unless it is very small. Bounce cards range in size from a few square inches to more than ten square feet. Smaller ones are used for faces and small objects.

Butterfly. A butterfly is a frame with a covering that is usually four to six square feet but can be more than twenty square feet, used to diffuse, reflect, or drop light. Silks and griffolyns are materials often used to make butterflies.

White silk is used for diffusing light, thereby eliminating harsh shadows. Griffolyn is made of opaque nylon and is used either to block light or to reflect it. It may be white, black-and-white, or black.

Butterfly shades are made in different thicknesses. A single net is used to reduce the amount of light hitting the set. It is placed over the area being shot, out of the view of the camera. A double net is used similarly to reduce the level of light twice as much as a single net. A solid black butterfly may be used indoors or outdoors to block the light coming through a window so that light may be used inside. A typical butterfly consists of two single nets—one silk and one solid.

Century Stand (C-Stand). A C-stand is a universal stand with a three-legged base and a telescoping stem used in conjunction with a gobo arm, which holds a flag, net, or another object, and a gobo head, which holds the gobo arm (*see* **Cutter**). C-stands come in different sizes and are also known as *grip stands*.

Clip Board. A clip board extends the front of a barn door to block light without putting a flag in front of the light. A clip board is a space-saving device.

Cucoloris. A cucoloris is a fiberglass insert with irregular-shaped holes that is put in front of a light to project a pattern. Many effects can be created, such as wheels, and striations. Cucolorises are also known as *cookies*. There are also solid cucolorises, which are made out of plywood or bass wood. Cucolorises commonly range in size from eighteen by twenty-four inches to forty-eight by forty-eight inches.

Cutter. A cutter is a metal frame covered by duvetyn, a soft, wooly textile, that is put on top of a light to block the shadow of a microphone on a set. Cutters are normally two by six feet. A solid black cutter is called a *gobo*.

Dot. A dot is a circular piece of material enclosed by a rim with a holder that is used to reduce a light's level of intensity, to add texture and color to light, to diffuse light, and sometimes to change the pattern of a light. A dot looks like a target on a stem and comes in different sizes, including three-inch, six-inch, and nine-inch diameters. The different intensities available are single, double, solid, silk, and lavender. A dot is mounted on a century stand.

Finger. A finger is an oblong piece of material in a frame used to alter thin sections of light hitting an area by blocking, softening, diffusing, or changing the texture of the light. Fingers may be solid or made of a mesh material, and are usually black, white, or lavender. A finger differs from a dot only in shape.

Flex Arm. A flex arm is a metal gooseneck arm for holding flags, dots, or other accessories during shooting.

Gels. Gels are transparent plastic filters used for light diffusion or color. They come in rolls and sheets. A gel is mounted in a frame directly in front of a light.

Grip Net. A grip net consists of gauzy fabric stretched over a frame used to diminish the intensity of a light. Grip nets come in different thicknesses. A single will darken twenty-five-foot candles; a double, fifty-foot candles; a triple, seventy-five-foot candles. A grip net is also referred to as, simply, a *net*.

Overhead Stand. An overhead stand is used to mount accessories or lights. Overheads, also called *high boys*, reach a maximum of eighteen feet. A medium high boy reaches a maximum of twelve to fourteen feet. Overheads usually have a three-wheeled tripod base.

Camera Movement and Mounting Equipment

Boom Track. A boom track is a series of large timbers about twenty feet long and twelve inches wide laid like a train track and used for cranes to run on. A boom track is also called a *camera boom track* or a *camera crane track*.

Car Mounts. Car mounts are hood and door mounts that attach directly onto a car and are used to hold cameras and lights for scenes involving actors in moving cars. A car mount enables a vehicle to be a self-contained mobile shooting location.

Crane. A crane is a large-sized dolly with an arm that pivots 360 degrees and pans up and down. It is set on four wheels and can be pushed or driven on a boom track. Small cranes can be pushed by one grip, but large ones require as many as three or four grips to operate them. There is a protrusion on the front of the movable arm called the *tongue* on which the camera is mounted. There is also room on the tongue for the cinematographer and an assistant to sit.

Motion picture cranes must be counterbalanced with lead weights. Other methods used for counterbalancing include mercury (internally) or hydraulics.

Cranes are used for most major shots in film and television productions. Depending on the crane's angle and height, the camera can shoot from above, close-up, or far away.

Dolly. A dolly is a device with wheels on which a camera is mounted to follow the action on the set. A dolly sometimes moves on a track. The camera operator and the camera assistant sit on the dolly while it is pushed manually by the grip, using a lever or handle. Many dollies can move the camera up and down with a hydraulic system. A crab dolly moves sideways. Commonly used dollies include the Elemack Spider, Moviola Crab, Chapman Pee-wee, Chapman Hustler, and the Stint.

Dolly Track. A dolly track is a set of rails on which a dolly is placed to smoothly follow the action of a shooting on irregular ground without shaking the camera. Before tracks are laid, it must be decided where the camera should begin moving and where it should stop. Then the grip lays dolly tracks down, making sure that the path is level. Finally, the dolly is put on the tracks.

Parallel. A parallel is a multipurpose metal framework, usually six feet by six feet, with two platforms. Parallels are also known as *scaffolds*.

Sandbag. A sandbag is a weight filled with sand and used for holding a light or reflector on a stand so it does not tip over. Sandbags usually range in weight from twenty to thirty-five pounds each.

GRIP NET. *See* **Grip Equipment.**

GRIP STAND. *See* **Grip Equipment.**

HAIRSTYLIST. Along with costume and makeup, hair is an important component of an actor's physical appearance on the screen. A hairstylist contributes to the mien of a character and to the ambience of the film or television program. Hairdos are frequently taken for granted by audiences, but unkempt tresses (unless intentional) and anachronistic coiffures stand out immediately. Hairstylists are responsible for the hairdos of actors in motion pictures, television shows, and commercials, as well as anchors and on-camera reporters on newscasts. When many actors are involved, there may be a chief hairstylist and assistants.

In motion pictures, the hairstylist's work begins during preproduction. The hairstylist does a script breakdown to help decide on the coiffures needed, how the hairstyles will look in each scene, how many assistant hairstylists are necessary, and to schedule time on the daily call sheet when performers must have their hair done. Supplies are ordered, actors are scheduled for wig fittings, and other preparations are made. Special hair effects may fall under the jurisdiction of makeup.

During production, hairstylists work long days. They are among the first to arrive on the set. Depending on the needs of stars in the cast and the types of characters in the production, it may take hours to prepare the performers. Hairstylists may have to wash, cut, and set an actor's hair, as well as design a coiffure. Hairstylists usually crisscross their work with the makeup people. They do the hair of certain actors while makeup begins working on others.

On the set, the hairstylist, equipment in hand, follows the actors around for touch-ups. Since a scene may be shot several times, hairstyles must be maintained for consistency. Because scenes are often shot out of sequence, an actor's hairstyle at the start of each scene must match the style at the end of the previous one. To facilitate continuity, photographs (usually Polaroids) are taken of the heads of the actors (all four sides) as they finish their scenes.

Hairstylists may become involved in postproduction when it is necessary to reshoot a scene. In such cases, photographs and records remind the stylists how the actors look at certain points.

If there is a large cast and assistant hairstylists are needed, the chief stylist does the hiring. The chief stylist supervises the assistants but is ultimately responsible for the coiffures of the entire cast. Usually the chief stylist works personally on the principal performer. Screen credit is given to the chief stylist and, sometimes, to the assistant.

It is important for the stylist to know how the major performers will be dressed before working on their hair. The hair should complement the costume and frame the face. The overall visual appearance requires the collective efforts of the costume designer, hairstylist, and makeup artist.

Many hairstylists employed in television and motion pictures broke into the business by working in Broadway productions or in regional theater. Theater offers stylists the opportunity to cultivate their craft, and the ability to coif actors' hair quickly. There may be union requirements such as a cosmetology license to work in film and television.

HIGH CONCEPT. A high concept is a brief plot summary of a script for the purpose of a studio or producer assessing its commercial potential.

HIT MOVIE. *Hit movie* is a term used in the motion picture industry to denote films that are profitable. *Winner* and *blockbuster* are two other frequently used terms. A winner is simply a picture that has earned more than the sum of its production, marketing, and advertising costs. A hit is a movie that is very profitable, doing perhaps $60 million to $80 million in film rentals. A blockbuster is one that not only perched on the weekly box-office lists but ultimately earns more than $100 million.

New releases generally do their best box-office business in the first few weeks they open. A hit movie will earn at least $3 million or $4 million in its first week.

Of course, the terms winner, hit, and blockbuster are all relative to the costs spent to bring a film to the public. A low-budget movie, which costs under $4 million to produce and market, that earns $30 million in film rentals is much more of a hit than a $30 million picture that earns $50 million at the box office.

See also **Film, Sources of Income.**

HOME VIDEO. In the 1970s the home videocassette tape recorder and player, long a goal of electronics manufacturers around the world, became a reality. Some companies introduced systems in the early 1970s but, with Sony's Betamax VCR in late 1975, a practical machine gained public acceptance. By the end of the decade several different brand-name videocassette recorders (VCRs) were on the market and software product was increasing. A new entertainment medium had not only been born but was growing quickly.

It was envisioned before home video's actual birth that theatrical motion pictures would be its major software programming constituent, but the question concerning the film industry was whether movies on video would cut into box-office receipts or would be a significant source of revenue in addition to box-office receipts. Through the years meaningful data has been accumulated but the answer to that question still remains open.

Home video has surpassed the film industry in terms of revenue. In 1990 American consumers spent approximately $11.7 billion on renting and purchasing home videos, while spending only some $4.6 billion at the box office. Indeed, VCR penetration rivals television penetration. In 1990, 75 percent of TV homes had VCRs, and 18 percent to 20 percent had more than one VCR.

Motion picture studios do not participate in rental receipts of the video dealer. Other than earning income for sales of videos to dealers (and consumers), manufacturers are forbidden by law from enforcing a royalty participation in video rentals from entities that have purchased the videos.

The reasons consumers rent videocassettes rather than go to the theater are sundry and salient, but primary among them is being able to enjoy a film, chosen from a wide selection, in the confines of one's home, and with the lower rental price. But theaters offer the opportunity for people to enjoy a few hours away from home and also afford a higher-quality viewing experience. Indeed, there are advantages and disadvantages to both, and each year the number of people attending the theater decreases or increases. Noticeably, a sizable portion of box-office receipts is produced by only a relatively small percentage of films.

Home videos opened up essentially a whole new industry comprising manufacturers and licensors, retailers, wholesalers, distributors, videotape duplicators, film-to-video transferers, and many other types of companies. From the beginning, creative participants in films and television immediately recognized the potential of the new medium in which their work may be sold and contracts of stars, writers, directors, producers, composers and others specifically accounted for home video sales. Union and guild agreements reflected this, and stars are usually able to negotiate even better terms.

Programming fare of home video embraces many areas outside of theatrical motion pictures. Indeed, practically anything that lends itself to video and has the potential to be marketed profitably has become a software commodity. Among the programming genres of home video are exercise, music, sports, instruction, adult, and children. Videos specially made for release to the home market in these and other areas have enjoyed some substantial sales.

Undoubtedly, as the price of software decreases with time and the number of VCRs increases, more people will be renting and purchasing more videos. But since the advent of video the film industry has enjoyed record years, and it is doubtful that videos will ever have a detrimental effect on theatrical motion pictures. Rather, it is a case of parent and offspring existing side by side, one nurturing the other.

HORROR MOVIE. *See* **Film Genres.**

IF-COME DEAL. An if-come deal is a contractual arrangement between a creative talent and a producer that is contingent upon the producer selling the project to a network or other television broadcaster (such as a cable network). There are forms of it that deal with scriptwriters and forms that deal with other talents such as actors and authors. An example of a writer if-come deal would involve a writer who interests a television producer in an idea for a series. The two parties would negotiate the writer's fee and profit participation over the next several years, but the terms would not become effective unless and until the producer makes a deal with a network. Likewise, an actor's fees for a series may be negotiated when testing for a part. In this way if the network wants to hire the actor, the actor cannot hold up the series with a demanding negotiation. A production company may sign a book on an if-come deal, paying the author only when it sells the project to a network. In an if-come deal, if a deal is struck, the terms of the arrangement are locked in.

There is usually no money paid up front on an if-come deal, which may not give the producer an incentive to vigorously shop the project. With an option, money is paid to tie up a property for a particular period of time, and there may be more incentive to pursue it.

If-come deals are in a sense the opposite of *pay or play* deals. A pay or play deal, usually done with big-time actors and directors, is where a person is engaged for a project and he or she gets paid whether or not the project is produced (this protects the person who has committed his or her time from losing out on passing up other, viable opportunities). In an if-come deal, one does not get paid unless there is a deal. With a pay or play arrangement one gets paid whether or not there is a deal.

ILLUSTRATOR. The illustrator sketches scenes from a production's script under the guidance of the director, producer, or art director. These drawings help the art director design the sets and create a look for the production.

The illustrator drafts continuity sketches (also called *storyboards*) to help the director visualize a scene before shooting. A continuity sketch is not drawn for every scene, only the more complicated ones. The artist sometimes must improvise a few different drawings of a scene, which the director then uses to block the shot. A director might even ask the illustrator to place the actors into position for the actual shot.

Continuity sketches usually are drawn to a small scale so they may be blueprinted or photocopied. They are drawn in black-and-white with ink, charcoal, or pencil. Key scenes, such as establishing shots, are often done in full color. Continuity sketches are unique to high-budget feature films. Low-budget films can rarely afford the cost of an illustrator.

INDEPENDENT TELEVISION STATION. An independent television station is a regional commercial television station that is not affiliated with a **network**. An independent television station solely maintains its own programming schedule. The income for most independent TV stations is derived solely from the sale of advertising time. Some also earn revenue from programming distribution. Many "indies" are divisions of large newspaper chains or entertainment conglomerates. In 1990 there were 339 independent TV stations in 137 U.S. markets (37 were VHF stations).

A station's salespersons usually approach advertising agencies to interest them in purchasing commercial time for their clients. Deals can be made for a month, a week, or perhaps even one movie, although specific titles are seldom sold. Primarily, the movie/time period average is used in deciding to make the purchase. Independent television stations also use the services of a **rep firm** for selling advertising.

The size of the market, annual income, and the parent corporation's intentions determine a station's structure. An indie station in New York, Los Angeles, or Chicago employs a much larger staff than stations in smaller markets, but there are standard administrative positions common to all independent stations.

General Manager. The general manager is in charge of supervising operations and overseeing the station's financial matters. Every department head reports to the general manager. The general manager also remains involved with programming. In small stations, the general manager actually purchases programming. Because the general manager determines a station's programming philosophy, the overall success or failure of the station rests primarily on the general manager's shoulders.

Programming Department. The programming department selects and schedules programming for the station. It evaluates movie packages, shows created for syndication, and off-network programming, making programming decisions based on such factors as ratings, budgets, and competition in the market. Information provided by the research and sales departments is also taken into consideration. The programming department works directly with syndicators and distributors. Many program managers negotiate contracts and close deals.

Programming on independent TV stations generally consists of the following:

- Off-network syndication (reruns of prime-time series that were once on the networks or are still running).
- First-run syndication (shows produced for non-network broadcast).
- Live sporting events, including games of home teams.
- Theatrical or made-for-television motion pictures ranging from old to recent.
- Reruns of old cartoons.
- Original programming (a limited amount of shows produced by the station).
- Public- or community-affairs programs.
- Newscasts (for national news, many indies use the transmissions of TV news services).
- Reruns of network miniseries.
- Commercial programs in which money is solicited from viewers for products, services, or causes (airtime is paid for by the sponsors).
- Original miniseries (such as those produced through a con-

173

sortium of major independent groups known as Operation Prime Time).

Most indie programming is purchased at annual conventions such as those sponsored by the Association of Independent Television Stations (INTV) and the **National Association of Television Program Executives (NATPE)**. These conventions are attended by indie representatives from both small and major markets.

First-Run Syndication. Production of first-run programming exclusively for independent stations is a new trend in television. Selling the rights to first-run programming is often done in group deals. Many indies, for example, are part of a corporation that owns a group of stations. A distributor approaches the corporate parent to convince all the stations it owns to take the show.

The distributors of first-run programming usually keep about half the commercial airtime and give the remainder to the groups. This is known as *barter syndication*. Although barter syndication limits the revenues the stations take in, it also cuts the stations' costs by eliminating license fees. In larger markets such as Los Angeles, Chicago, and New York, distributors tour the stations and sell first-run shows through bidding (*see* **Syndication**).

Original Programming. With the profits made from advertising, some independent TV stations generate their own programming. This practice is an attractive alternative to purchasing expensive syndicated shows. Sometimes indies, or their corporate parents, form partnerships with one another to offset production expenses. Indies that produce original programs often license them to other independent stations.

Off-Network Syndication. Reruns of network programs are an integral part of an independent television station's programming schedule. License fees may run from a few hundred dollars per episode for older shows, to tens of thousands for recent prime-time hits.

Counter-Programming. Independent television stations often air entertainment shows when network affiliates are broadcasting news programs, and broadcast other types of programs when the affiliates are airing sitcoms, dramas, and nighttime serials. This is called *counter-programming*. The theory behind counter-programming is that when affiliates are broadcasting news shows, a sizable portion of the viewing audience wants to watch entertainment programs, and when affiliates are airing national prime-time shows, there is a large audience who would rather watch movies, live sporting events, or newscasts.

News Department. Headed by a news director, the news department produces the station's news broadcasts. While it is economically impossible for many independent television stations to produce their own daily national news programs, in order to remain competitive with other stations in a local market, they must carry news programs. Consequently, many indies broadcast the news productions of television news services. These news shows are broadcast any time the independent station desires. Most stations use individual stories from these news productions rather than the entire shows. Other services prepare related specialized programming such as public-service spots, ethnic news, sports news, investigative series, and editorial segments.

News services transmit their newscasts via satellite. Some news services transmit information by teletype for use by local reporters.

A news service earns income from advertising fees. For each newscast, the service sells a certain amount of airtime to national advertisers and gives the remainder to the local stations. Satellite costs are usually split by the service and the indies. One of the largest TV news services is the Independent Network News (INN).

Research Department. The research department studies and reports on local Nielsen, AGB, and Arbitron ratings of audience preferences toward programming. They also collect information on the demographics and spending habits of the local viewing public, to help the sales department increase the station's advertising revenue.

Sales Department. The sales department sells commercial airtime to advertising agencies, companies, and other clients. The staff is typically made up of a general sales manager, a local sales manager, and account executives, commissioned salespersons who sell time locally. Many stations also have a national sales manager who, with the station's **rep firm**, acquires national accounts.

Promotion Department. The promotion department generates advertising for the station, prepares press releases on the station's activities for the general media and trade publications, creates on-air promos for particular programs, creates sales promotions, and runs sales parties.

Public Relations. Usually only large independent television stations have a public-relations director. This person handles media relations and serves as the spokesperson for the station. In the absence of such a position, public-relations duties are handled by the promotion department. At some stations, the public-relations director also serves as the public-affairs director.

Production Department. The production department produces original programs for the station such as on-air promos and public-affairs programs. The production department also produces commercials for clients wishing to advertise on the station.

Engineering Department. In charge of the technical operations of the station, the engineering department also makes sure the station complies with FCC regulations and makes recommendations for new equipment purchases.

Operations Department. Some larger stations have an operations department which oversees the scheduling and logging of commercials, promotional announcements, and editorials.

Accounting Department. The financial affairs of the station are overseen by the business manager. Payroll and bill-paying are handled by the accounting department.

INFORMATION TELEVISION SHOW. *See* **Television Programming Genres.**

INTERIOR SET. *See* **Set.**

INTERNATIONAL ALLIANCE OF THEATRICAL STATE EMPLOYEES AND MOVING-PICTURE MACHINE OPERA-TORS OF THE UNITED STATES AND CANADA (IATSE). IATSE is a union affiliated with the AFL-CIO whose members are craftspersons and technicians working in film production, video production, television, dramatic theaters, movie theaters, and industry shows. IATSE comprises more than eight hundred local branches in the United States and Canada. Each local branch is autonomous as long as it remains consistent with the bylaws of the international alliance. The locals draft their own constitutions, negotiate contracts for their members, and pay quarterly per capita dues to the international alliance.

The elected officers of the international alliance are the president, eleven vice-presidents, a general secretary-treasurer, delegates to the AFL-CIO and Canadian Labour Congress, and a three-member board of trustees. A regular convention is held every two years to review the progress of IATSE and to amend policies. Special conventions may be called by referendum and unanimous vote of the general executive board (the president, vice-president, and general secretary-treasurer). Each local is represented by one delegate for its charter and one additional delegate, elected from the membership, for every one hundred members.

KEY GRIP. *See* **Grip.**

LAVALIERE. *See* **Sound Recording, Production.**

LAYOUT ARTIST. *See* **Animation.**

LEAD-IN. A lead-in is a popular television show that benefits the program that follows it because a percentage of the popular show's audience stays tuned to the same channel after the show ends. In scheduling prime-time shows, network executives often place new or promising programs that have yet to find their audience after well-received lead-ins.
See **Television Programming.**

LEVELING. *See* **Animation.**

LITERARY AUCTION. *See* **Adaptations.**

LOCATION MANAGER. The location manager scouts places for shooting that bring to life the environment evoked by a film script. This person recommends a number of potential sites and submits photographs or videos to the director, who narrows down the choices with key crew members. Once a site has been selected, the location manager negotiates an agreement with the owner or manager of the premises. To use government-owned properties, clearances, permits, or licenses must be obtained. The location manager serves as the liaison between the production company and the proprietor or proper authorities, and makes sure that the cast and crew can function without encumberances during the production.

The location manager is hired to find sites that fit the requirements of the script and will present minimal problems during production. Sometimes this means finding a site in New York that looks like Boston or providing a village in California that resembles a quaint New England town. The location manager does a **script breakdown** to analyze the kinds of locations where the scenes might be filmed.

The selection of locations is made with various factors taken into consideration: budget, technical logistics, availability, whether clearances may be secured, and the script. Budget restrictions dictate filming locations to a large extent. It sometimes costs substantially less to simulate a particular location than to send a cast and film crew there. The interiors for a film might be shot locally, for example, while a portion of the exteriors are filmed on location.

Cinematographic quality is also a primary concern. The location must be able to accommodate lighting and crew facilities. Some directors determine themselves whether a location is sound, others rely on their director of photography.

The location manager will canvas a number of areas and submit photographs or videos of locations considered most suitable. There may be as many as ten or twenty or more, which will be narrowed down to a handful by the director and production designer who will scout the locations with the location manager. The selected locations will then be scouted on a technical survey with important crew members who usually include the director of photography, production designer, key grip, gaffer, construction coordinator, transportation captain, stunt coordinator, soundman, and location manager. These parties examine the sites to determine the feasibility of filming there as it relates to their own departments as well as the whole project.

Sometimes the script has to be modified to accommodate the technical limitations of a location. For example, a script may describe a five-story walk-up with small rooms with low ceilings. If the five stories and narrow dimensions of the rooms present problems for the film crew, the location might be changed to a five-story warehouse with a freight elevator. Alterations in a script are made in accordance with the logistics of shooting, but the location manager tries to minimize these by realizing a balance between the concept of the script and any practical considerations.

The location manager attempts to negotiate as much flexibility and leeway as possible. This is important for maintaining the budget and accommodating the schedules of the cast and crew. It is also imperative that the location manager establish a trust with the location owner. He or she will discuss with the owner when and how shooting will be done on the property and serve as the liaison between the proprietor and the producer.

Often a flat fee is paid for the use of a location during filming, though sometimes an hourly, daily, or weekly rate is charged. If a place of business is used, hourly arrangements must take into account the amount of business lost. Therefore, most production companies prefer to pay a flat fee for extended filming stints. The promotional value of an establishment's appearance in a motion picture is often incentive enough for proprietors.

Location managers usually have files of locations they can draw on. These might include hotels, parks, houses, apartments, offices, and scenic views. Location managers keep notes on locations where they have worked as well as those they know of or come across that might be suitable for a future project.

If more than one geographic location appears prominently in a film, there is usually more than one location manager. A movie shot in London, Paris, New York, and Los Angeles would need one location manager for Europe, another for New York, and a third for Los Angeles. Each would work autonomously with guidelines provided by the producer, director, production designer, or any combination of these.

Usually there is only one key location manager who oversees the entire production with the help of assistant location managers, known as *scouts*. A scout may be used to prepare a second production site while the location manager is working at the first with the film crew. If the bulk of a shooting is to take place in a particular area such as a large city, with several days of production scheduled at a separate, remote site, a local coordinator may be retained there and a temporary office even set up.

In addition to dealing with property owners, location managers also work with municipal film agencies and authorities. These agencies provide a legal, expeditious route toward production. For example, a permit is required to film anywhere in New York City. The Mayor's Office for Television and Film provides this permit if certain conditions are fulfilled. A representative of the New York City Police Department's Movie and Television Unit may also discuss what is and what is not legally permissible at a public location. The cooperation of other municipal agencies such as the Department of Buildings or the Department of Parks may also be needed. When permission for using a public facility or property is granted, a list of terms delineating restrictions is given to the production company. An agreement may stipulate acceptable hours for filming and whether emergency vehicles must be permitted to pass through at any time.

Ideally, the location manager secures permits for all the locations for a movie before shooting begins. Then, during production, he or she sees to details such as parking, toilets, eating facilities, and holding areas. The location manager works closely with the unit production manager and the transportation captain, making sure the cast and crew are as comfortable as possible on location.

The location manager must attend to the requirements of each department involved in the making of the film. For example, the sound department may need the elevators or central air-conditioning controlled. The set dressing department may want to move furnishings from one location to another. The prop department may need a permit for rain and smoke effects. The location department is one of the few departments involved with so many facets of the production.

A location manager's job involves two very different areas of production. On the one hand, finding locations is a creative process, where the location manager works with the production designer and the director. The production requirements of the job, however, demand business and organizational skills. Often the location manager is considered an assistant unit production manager.

The location manager may also serve as an unofficial public-relations representative for the film crew. After shooting has been completed, the location manager oversees the restoration of a property to its original condition. During postproduction he or she may be responsible for providing a final cost summary.

The location manager is sometimes involved in production at the studio. Duties might include helping the art department with the reproduction of a location by providing them with access to a particular site for measurements.

Location managers are hired less often in television work than in films. Sitcoms and soap operas are shot primarily in studios. However, when outdoor locations are used, as in a drama series, a location manager is needed. In television, the location manager's schedule is more hectic than in films because more script pages are shot per day.

See also **Television Commercials, Production of.**

LOW-BUDGET MOVIE. The cost of a 35-mm feature film production, with major stars, a renowned director, a creditable screenwriter, a union crew, unsparing sets, and remote locations, usually runs from $10 million to $30 million. When producers cannot raise huge sums of money or get the backing of a major studio, they may make what is referred to as a *low-budget movie*. A low-budget film is relatively inexpensive to make because everything in the production—from salaries to sets and stunts to publicity—is economically scaled down.

Low-budget movies are made possible because some dedicated actors and technical people are willing to work for less money if they believe in a project. Stars, who often command $1 million or more per film, may be inclined to drastically reduce their fees (in exchange for a percentage of the film's earnings) if they want a particular film to get made or relish a certain role in a low-budget production. In addition, low-budget movies are stepping stones for career professionals. A low-budget film, for example, is a way for an actor to break into the business, or a director of commercials to gain experience with motion pictures, or a cosmetician to break into films as a makeup artist.

Low-budget movies originally were referred to as *B-movies*, or *budget movies*. The major studios produced a number of B-movies each year that ran as secondary features on double bills. Today they are a common medium for up-and-coming directors and producers.

The term low-budget is relative. Some people classify a $5 million film as low-budget. There are a number of differences between low-budget movies and feature films, as shown in the following table.

Comparison of Low-Budget Movies to Feature Films

Element	Low-Budget Movies	Feature Films
film used	16-mm (some are later transformed into 35-mm for theaters)	35-mm
quality of prints	16-mm prints are grainy	35-mm prints are high quality
salaries to cast and crew	union minimums or less; fees for stars are largely reduced	union minimums or more
crew size	typically 20 to 50	over 75
production costs	$100,000 to 6 million, though most often categorized in the $1 million to $6 million range	at least $6 million
time of production	average of 10 to 60 days	average of 2 months to one year
advertising and promotion budget	typically small; can range from nothing to several hundred thousands of dollars	typically large; can be several million dollars
producer	independent	major studios and producers with track records

Continued on next page

Continued from previous page

distribution	national or selected cities; selected theaters (such as art houses); with occasional exceptions, nowhere near as extensive as features	national
ancillary markets	cable, video, foreign	television, cable, video, foreign, merchandising

MAGAZINE FORMAT TV SHOW. The TV magazine show is a cross between a news program and a documentary. Presented by coanchors and correspondents, a magazine show consists of a series of stories on controversies, people, issues, and events. The goal is to entertain viewers while informing them.

A magazine show differs from a news program in that its stories are more of an investigative than a newsworthy nature. Each story is presented from a specific journalistic angle. A magazine show differs from a documentary in that it is devoted to more than one theme, and is perhaps not as pedagogic. Producers of magazine shows strive to give their shows a glossy look and a journalistic air. But they are sometimes criticized for being full of hype and lacking in substance—that is, not asking key questions and getting to the root of issues.

Magazine shows have become increasingly popular through the 1980s including "60 Minutes," "20/20," "Primetime Live," "Fast Copy," "American Almanac," and "West 57th."

MAKEUP ARTIST. A makeup artist is responsible for the cosmetic appearance of actors and actresses in motion picture and television productions. There are a great number of techniques used in makeup, ranging from beauty applications, which include using colored pigments in different values and hues to enhance the actor, to special makeup effects, such as the fabrication of monster guises or the cutting of someone's throat. The makeup artist uses these techniques to prepare a visual look for actors as called for by the script and envisioned by the director.

The makeup artist for a film may be hired a few weeks to a few months before shooting. If special makeup effects are required, the makeup artist is hired even earlier. Often, there is one makeup artist hired for a film, who hires assistants for busy days. For some films, makeup artists who specialize in prosthetics or special makeup effects are taken on.

The makeup artist first reads the script to get an idea of the look the characters should have, and then meets with the director and/or producer. About a week or two before shooting begins, the lead actors in the film are called in for a makeup and hair test, where different looks are tested for each actor.

The general look of a character is retained throughout the entire production, although there may be modifications of makeup with respect to changes in the color of the wardrobe, story location, time of day of shooting, lighting, and other special situations. For example, if a character is in a swimming pool, makeup is needed that doesn't run in water. If a character is to appear sweaty or slovenly, makeup will be applied accordingly. The makeup artist uses his judgment in preparing the actors the way they should look according to the script, and on the set additional instructions may be given.

The makeup artist is responsible for cosmetic continuity throughout a film. Continuity sheets which outline the chronology of the movie are given to the makeup artist, who must be prepared to make the actors look exactly as they should in any scene regardless of the shooting order.

During shooting the hairdresser usually works on the actors first, followed by the makeup artist. The makeup artist decides who gets made up and to what extent, but must always be open to ideas from the actors or director. Extras rarely get makeup, unless the film is a period piece, in which case the whole cast gets makeup, hair, and costumes. The makeup artist remains on the set throughout shooting, making sure that the actors' makeup looks fresh.

Since makeup artists are among the last persons whom leading performers spend time with before going on the set, their personality is important. They work on a one-to-one basis with the actors, and some of them not only prepare the actors physically, but also help set their moods.

Today makeup is used as little as possible, mostly around the eyes and lips. Usually, at least, corrective makeup is applied to the face to emphasize the actor's most desirable features.

Character makeup is used when an actor must distort physical characteristics to portray a character with different physical attributes. Common kinds of character makeup include wigs and artificial facial hair. Another common form of character makeup is used to help with the simulation of old age. Artificial wrinkles are created with a technique known as *stretch and stipple*. The skin is stretched, latex is stippled on, powder is applied over the latex, and the face is blow-dried. When the skin is released, natural-looking wrinkles form.

When a makeup artist determines that basic techniques such as highlighting and shading or stretch and stipple will not sufficiently alter a character's features, then he or she will make a prosthetic mask with the desired features. To do this, a negative mold of the face is taken by applying alginate ormoulage on the face. Plaster of Paris bandages are then put over this mold to hold it in shape. Once this is set, the bandages and mold are removed and a hard plaster (Ultra Cal 30) is poured into the resulting mold to make a positive impression of the actor's face. Working from this positive impression, the makeup artist can make a latex mask with any features desired that will fit the actor's face perfectly. This technique can be used to create any part of the face or body, as well as full-face masks or body casts.

See also **Special Effects**.

MASTER SCRIPT. *See* **Script**.

MASTER TIME. *See* **Script Supervisor**.

MATTE ARTIST. A matte artist paints photographic-quality backdrops to create the illusion of a specific background setting. Matte paintings are usually done on glass or masonite. A script, for example, may have a scene in which knights ride on horses up a hill and into a castle. The castle door is built on the hill. A matte artist paints the castle on a sheet of glass, leaving empty space where the door is located in the live-action footage. The live action and the matte painting are shot separately. Then the matte shot is laid over the live footage. If the shots are lined up accurately, the final shot will depict a convincing facsimile of the knights entering a castle.

MECHANICAL SPECIAL EFFECTS. *See* **Special Effects**.

MERCHANDISE LICENSING. The licensing of commercial rights to motion picture and television personalities, characters, and productions is an important source of income for rights owners. Merchandise licensing firms, retailers, and manufacturers also reap large profits from merchandise licensing.

A variety of products based on film and TV properties are licensed, and these are essentially limited only to the imaginations of the principals involved. These products are primarily intended for (but not limited to) infants, toddlers, children, and teenagers. Merchandise commonly tied in with movie and TV properties includes toys, dolls, games, T-shirts and other apparel, school supplies, books, novelizations, records, and hundreds of other products. The summer 1989 release of *Batman* is a superb example of creative merchandising with shirts, masks, badges, books, and much else on sale long before and after the movie's release.

What criteria are used to determine if a character, personality, or production has the potential to succeed in various licensed incarnations? First, of course, there is the necessity for mass appeal, which means simply that the property must be popular with a wide segment of consumers. But widespread popularity doesn't always translate into licensing success. Prognosticating potential can be risky business, as deals are often made before a product or property has had a chance to prove itself.

Exposure is crucial but not always a barometer of a property's licensing potential. There are many hit television shows, for example, that are not licensable. A cop show that begins at 10 P.M., for instance, has little or no marketing potential. First, it would have adult themes and adults are not big consumers of licensed goods. Second, since the characters are modeled after real-life people, they may be attractive but not "knockouts" or very novel. It's difficult to license real life. Moreover, the show is on too late for children (the prime licensing audience) to watch, so consequently there would be no juvenile market to go after.

In order to be marketable for merchandise tie-ins, a TV show

190

must appeal to a young audience, air during the daytime or early evening, and have characters who are popular, trendy, and memorable, or who have unique physical characteristics, personality traits, or expressions.

Cartoons generally lend themselves well to merchandising. They are essentially action-adventure comic strips with good guys and bad guys—an assortment of characters with the necessary superheroes, who translate nicely to toys and other products. Kids get to know all the characters in a cartoon and there's repeated exposure, which is vital for merchandising success.

For television shows, the characters and content dictate the kinds of merchandise that may be tied in. Action characters have a natural market in action figures. Elements of kiddie shows may be transformed into a variety of pre-school products. Programs popular with teenagers have the potential to be licensed for a wide range of products.

The timing for movie merchandising is more critical than for television. TV shows are likely to continue at a high level of popularity for a long period, but most movies have a relatively brief theatrical life. Once a film is pulled from the theaters, interest in products related to it dwindles to almost nothing.

Motion pictures with an R or NC-17 rating are often difficult to license, as retailers may not take products associated with a sexual or violent nature. There are exceptions to this, however, such as the movie *Rambo*, which had a successful licensing history.

There are three groups that have to accept a TV show or movie property for products based on it to be made and successful: manufacturers (licensees), retailers, and consumers. When entering into a licensing agreement, manufacturers must consider the property's projected popularity for the two years following the product's release, the target audience, retail cost, projected marketing and advertising expenses, and competition.

The licensing of consumer products based on popular motion picture and television personalities, characters, and productions has created an industry in which merchandise licensing companies license properties to manufacturers for the purpose of designing, producing, selling, distributing, and marketing products based on these properties. Agents represent rights owners in licensing the name, trademark, likeness of characters, personalities, motion pictures, TV series, cartoons, corporate entities, and anything else that can be stripped for merchandising revenue.

Merchandise licensing companies are either independent firms or in-house divisions of large corporations. In-house divisions license merchandising rights only for properties owned by their companies. In corporations, merchandise licensing is handled by the advertising, marketing, or research and development department.

Licensing agents often have to pay guaranteed minimums to the rights owners which are recoupable against earnings. Since agreements between the agent and rights owner are often negotiated before a deal can be consummated with a manufacturer, paying minimums is risky. The agent's income comes from nonrefundable license fees (advances) and royalties that may accrue from sales of the products. Some agents also provide consulting services to rights owners.

While a new property is being produced, merchandise agents may contact the rights owner or the rights owner may contact the agency. Agents are constantly on the lookout for new properties that have licensing potential. They read trade publications and utilize other sources to acquire information about new properties, and contact owners about licensing rights.

The most desirable client for a licensing agent is a major master-toy licensee, a large manufacturer who makes a substantial commitment to making and marketing products based on a property. For a successful master-toy property, dozens of licenses are obtained for the manufacture, distribution, and marketing of many different consumer products.

Merchandise agents also may be involved in creating or co-developing properties. A firm, for example, might create a concept for a new character. The creative director creates a logo and develops different characters. The company, in turn, tries to sell this property to a producer to create animated cartoons based on it. The producer further develops the marketing concept by attaching story lines, themes, plots, and greater character depth.

The merchandise licensing agent negotiates contracts with manufacturers for the properties it represents. The agent usually uses a basic form consisting of two parts: an agreement of general conditions, which outlines terms relating to payment, delivery date, approval of manufactured goods, copyright and trademark notices, representations, warranties, insurance, indemnities, and defaults; and a rider that specifies negotiated provisions such as the guaranteed payment schedule, the royalty rate, the licensed territory, the term of the license, the copyright or trademark notice, and the initial on-sale date. Terms are limited to a specific period and are often automatically renewable for an additional term if a certain amount of product is sold.

Licensing arrangements provide for licensees to pay minimum guaranteed payments and royalties based on their net wholesale revenues. The guaranteed payments are nonrefundable but recoupable against earnings based on sales. Fees received by the merchandise licensing agent are divided with the rights owner.

Royalty rates normally range from 5 percent to 12 percent of the net wholesale revenues. Royalties are usually paid to the licensing agent but sometimes are remitted directly to the rights owner, who in turn pays the agent.

METHOD ACTING. *See* **Actor.**

MICROPHONES. *See* **Sound Recording, Production.**

MID-SEASON REPLACEMENT. A series that debuts in television's mid-season, which begins around January, in place of another that was dropped because of low ratings is called a *mid-season replacement*. In December network executives announce which shows will be taken off the air and what new ones will be added. Mid-season replacements are usually, but not always, pilots that did not make it into the fall lineup. Since time slots are changed in mid-season (sometimes called *second season*), the new series does not necessarily air in the displaced series' previous time period.

See also **Television Season**.

MINOR. The motion picture and television industries hire many people who are minors, or under the age of majority. Indeed, in any era it is easy to name a number of child stars from either medium.

Laws relating to minors are important to understand, as they may differ from laws affecting adults. There is no federal law regulating the business dealings of minors; jurisdiction is at the state or local level. The age at which a person is still considered a minor varies from state to state, and is sometimes different for males and females in the same state. Ages eighteen through twenty-one are usually the years that states no longer consider a person a minor, but one should check his or her state law to determine the applicable year.

A minor who has created an original work may register that work in the Copyright Office under his or her name and with his or her signature.

MISE-EN-SCENE. This French term refers to the arrangement of the actors and the set design within each frame of film. It refers to a fixed element, since once something is on film it cannot be changed. An editor might have wanted to see something else, but he cannot do anything about the *mise-en-scène*. The unfixed or variable part is the length of a shot. How long the audience will see a mise-en-scène is determined by editing.

MIXER. *See* **Sound Recording, Production**.

MIXING. *See* **Sound, Postproduction**.

MODEL MAKER. Model makers prepare architectural renderings of buildings or objects that need to be built for a film's production. There are also model makers who work in the prop department and make scale models of objects that are seen on the screen and which appear to be life-size and part of the action. In the former case, the model maker works in the art department and functions as a set designer or draftsperson, and the model, usually done in one-quarter-inch scale, shows how camera blocking may be done on the set. In the latter case, the propmaker prepares a scale model of an object because it is too expensive to build at full size. Great detail goes into the construction so as to make the object look real when filmed.

MONSTER MOVIE. *See* **Film Genres.**

MOTION PICTURE ASSOCIATION OF AMERICA INC. (MPAA). The MPAA is a trade association representing the U.S. motion picture and television production and distribution industries. Membership is open to any company actively involved in the production and distribution of TV programs and movies. Some members of the MPAA are Paramount Pictures, Warner Bros., Orion Pictures, Walt Disney, Universal City Studios, MGM/UA, and Twentieth Century-Fox Film Corp.

The MPAA serves to advance and promote the film and television industries. One of its best-known programs if the **film rating system.** The association also represents program suppliers before the Copyright Royalty Tribunal, works to curtail piracy on both national and international levels, and maintains a Title Registration Bureau.

The Motion Picture Export Association of America (MPEAA) is a subsidiary of the MPAA that functions to represent the American motion picture business in countries outside the United States. The MPEAA serves to further the distribution and rights of the U.S. film industry by working with foreign agencies, movie distributors, and television stations in the areas of copyright, piracy, taxation, trade, marketing, syndication, and distribution.

MOTION PICTURE DISTRIBUTOR. There are two types of distributors of theatrical motion pictures: studio and independent. A studio distributor is a division of a film studio or its corporate parent and it will have branch offices in every major region of the United

States—northeast, southeast, midwest, southwest, and far west. Some studios have branch offices in two or more cities of a particular region, others operate out of a single office in that region. A studio distribution operation might comprise anywhere from seven to fifteen or more branch offices. An independent distributor, on the other hand, is privately owned or not affiliated with a movie studio. Some not only distribute films for independent producers, but produce their own films or financially back those of independent producers.

Distributors function to get films into theaters through bidding or other arrangements and provide prints and advertising materials, such as posters. A major new film will generally open in at least a thousand or more theaters nationwide. Branch distributors deal with chains and independent theaters in their local territory. Distributors earn percentages of the box-office grosses of the films they handle, usually thirty percent or more. Distributor costs, such as advertising and prints, are also deducted, and these can be substantial.

MOTION PICTURE RATINGS. *See* **Film Rating System**.

MOTION PICTURE, STAGES OF A. The route from script to finished film is a lengthy obstacle course with hurdles called script acceptance, budgeting, financing, hiring a director, finding stars, casting, employing a capable crew, scouting and clearing locations, building sets, designing or buying costumes, rehearsing, shooting, working on schedule, getting along, inclement weather, coming in on budget, editing, scoring, re-recording, and obtaining a satisfactory final answer print. Much money is committed to the process, and each step must be calculated and executed accordingly. There are four basic stages in the making of a motion picture: development, preproduction, production, and postproduction. Once a film is completed it faces other challenges: distribution, box-office sales, and selling to ancillary markets. See the separate entries for each of these terms for a full picture of what goes into making—and making money from—a motion picture.

MOTION PICTURE STUDIO. A motion picture studio is a company that functions to produce and distribute movies for theatrical exhibition, or to finance or purchase them for distribution, or to distribute independently produced films for a percentage of their box-office revenues. The eight major motion picture studios also distribute films (via corporate arms) to theaters around the country. These studios are Columbia, Walt Disney, MGM/UA, Orion, Paramount, Twentieth Century-Fox, Universal, and Warner Bros., and together they account for more than 85 percent of all domestic box-office receipts.

As a producer of movies, a motion picture studio develops ideas and scripts and assembles a cast and crew for those given the green light for production (*see* **Development, motion pictures**).

A studio may also enter into various types of arrangements for the acquisition or distribution of product. It may purchase for a negotiated sum and royalty or invest in an independently made film. It may sign important or hot stars, directors, and producers to exclusive or non-exclusive deals providing for these people to develop and produce movies. It may acquire independently made films as a negative pickup, an arrangement in which the studio guarantees to pay the producer a specified amount after the movie is completed, delivered, and approved (*see* **Financing a film**). It may be a partial investor in a film, with the remainder of the financing coming from a limited partnership or other corporate entity. Another arrangement is a pure distribution deal, in which the studio generally retains anywhere from 15 percent to 30 percent of the box-office receipts it collects for its services, and turns the balance over to the production company directly responsible for the film. Essentially, a studio is a financier and distributor of films, although some tend to get closely involved in production.

Because there are many areas in which a motion picture generates revenue, studios' income is not limited to box-office receipts. Ancillary sources of income include home videocassettes and cable TV and pay-television services (*see* **Film, sources of income**). Many studios are also affiliated with television production companies through corporate parents. The parent company, in addition, may have interests in other areas, such as broadcasting stations, theater chains, record companies, game manufacturers, and hotels.

Tens or hundreds of millions of dollars are needed to keep a movie studio operating. A single film, for example, may cost $10 million or more in production costs alone. Several millions more are incurred for making prints and for television and print advertising. Then there are costs for operating the studio and its distribution branches. Movie studios release usually at least a dozen films per year and hope to have at least one blockbuster, to make up for losses of its other movies and to make the company solvent and profitable.

MOVIE OF THE WEEK. *See* **Television Programming Genres.**

MOVIE TIME. *See* **Script Supervisor.**

MUSEUM OF BROADCASTING. The Museum of Broadcasting is a nonprofit institution located in New York City that was established by CBS founder William Paley in 1975 to house radio and television programs for archival purposes and for access by the general public. In addition to making available tens of thousands of audio- and videotapes spanning most of radio and television history that may be listened to or viewed at private consoles, the museum regularly sponsors seminars conducted by creative people from the world of broadcasting. Screenings are held there as well.

MUSIC DEPARTMENT, NETWORK. Television networks maintain music departments to handle music clearance, music supply, in-house publishing, and American Federation of Musicians (AFM) residuals administration for musicians who record for the networks. Music clearance is a music department's largest responsibility. Television networks must constantly determine whether they have the proper license to air specific musical compositions. The performing rights organizations are bulk licensors of music performing rights and pay performance royalties to composers, lyricists, and publishers for music played on television. In order for the organizations to calculate credits and make payments, they must know what compositions have been performed when.

The producers of shows submit music cue sheets to the music department that contain the name of the produced program, air date, time, music played on the show, uses of the music (theme, background, feature), name of the composer (and lyricist, where applicable), name of the publisher(s), and the performing rights affiliations (*see* **Performing Rights Organization**). The music department ensures that all this information is rendered properly and on a periodic basis, usually monthly; and it, in turn, reports the information to the performing rights organizations, who in turn make the royalty payments to the rights owners.

The music editor or music supervisor of a show submits the cue sheets to the network music department, but the producer is ultimately responsible. Occasionally, a producer is unable to obtain the credits for music played on a program. In these instances, the cue sheets do not reflect what is broadcast and no payments are made. ASCAP has a department continually monitoring broadcast tapes, though. If music is recognized, payment is given for the performance even though it was not reported by the network.

How music is used, when it is played, and how long it plays determine the amount of money awarded by performing rights organizations. ASCAP, BMI, and SESAC each have their own payment systems.

The music department is also responsible for music played during news, sports, and talk shows produced by a network. A music department has a record library from which appropriate music is selected with in-house producers for shows. Composers also can be commissioned by the music department to write music specifically for shows.

Network music departments compute music payments in accordance with AFM guidelines. The music department must submit checks along with each completed contract to AFM for distribution.

MUSIC EDITOR. The work of the music editor differs with the nature or genre of each project. For features in which original music is scored, the music editor works with the composer to provide timings of spots for which the composer will be writing music, and perhaps even do research for him. Later he or she edits the music and may insert music originally written for certain sections of the film into other spots.

For documentaries and industrials, the music editor usually serves to select music from background music libraries that fit various sequences and edits it in. Music in background libraries is diverse and of arbitrary lengths. The music editor listens to selections and decides whether they are appropriate and if they can fit well into a particular spot with editing. If a prerecorded selection, for example, is two minutes but only one minute of music is needed, the editor must be able to edit the piece gracefully to fit the spot. The music editor picks background music by character and tempo and then edits to the desired length. Prerecorded music should sound like it was composed exclusively for a particular scene.

A music editor has an excellent knowledge of various kinds of musical repertoires and a good feel as to what would be appropriate for a particular scene. Also depending on the freedom given by the director, the music director will stylize the production to an extent.

MUSIC LICENSING, FILM. Under the law, an owner of copyright has the exclusive right to reproduce or authorize the reproduction of the copyrighted work in motion pictures. Consequently, any producer who wishes to use a musical composition in a film must obtain a **synchronization license** (which for U.S. theatrical exhibitions must include a performance license) from the copyright owner.

In commercial reality, music publishers are the owners of copyrights. Even songs whose ownership is retained by the writers will be vested in publishing companies formed by the writers.

If a production company or studio is interested in using a song in a motion picture, it will contact the publisher of that song or its agent and negotiate a license. Many music publishers are represented by a music reproduction licensing organization for the licensing of film synchronization rights to producers. If a licensing organization receives an inquiry from a producer or its agent, it will contact the publisher to get a quote (price) and terms for use of the song. The organization in turn brings this back to the producer and acts as an intermediary as negotiations are carried on.

There are various criteria considered in establishing a fee for using music in a film:

- size of the budget
- popularity of the composition
- how the song is to be used:
      over opening titles
      over end credits
      intermittently throughout the film
      as a theme song
      as background music
      whether an artist is seen performing the song
      whether used as a vocal or an instrumental
- length of the song (for each use) in the picture
- exclusivity
- scope of license (outside of film)
      free television
      cable television
      satellite television
      home videocassette
      public television
      in-flight
      territorial versus worldwide

Of course a producer will seek as broad a license as possible. A worldwide synchronization license for a flat fee is ideal for producers, but, on the other hand, perhaps not in the best interest of publishers, who may seek to limit the scope of the license.

There are many different forms of film synchronization licenses for theatrical release. The Harry Fox Agency, the largest U.S. mechanical and synchronization rights organization, issues a *theatric broad rights* film synchronization license which provides for use of a song in a motion picture that may be exhibited in theaters; broadcast on free, cable, and pay television; and reproduced on home videocassettes. Video rights, which today are important, may be negotiated as a separate appendage to the synchronization fee. These may be licensed as a *video buyout*, in which the rights are granted for a one-time flat fee, or as a *video rollover*, in which the publisher will license the song on a penny rate based on units sold. The rate has historically ranged from $.04 to $.08 and has been based on 50,000 units. For example, if the rate was $.06 based on 50,000 units, the producer would advance the publisher $3,000 on the first 50,000 units.

As an example of a fee for a synchronization license, there might be $5,000 for the synchronization use of the song and $5,000 for a video buyout, for a total fee of $10,000. Fees for use of a single song in a motion picture range from a few thousand dollars to $50,000 or more.

In a theatrical synchronization license the performing right of the song for U.S. performances should be included. This is because ASCAP is prohibited by its consent decree from licensing performing rights to music contained in motion pictures when they are shown in movie theaters in the United States, pursuant to a 1948 court decision, *Alden-Rochelle v. ASCAP*. The other performing rights organizations have not sought to enter the area. This is not the case in many foreign countries, however, and local performing rights societies in such countries collect performance royalties and transmit these moneys to American copyright owners via U.S. performing rights organizations, with which they have reciprocal relations.

The producer must be sure to obtain the rights to distribute and exhibit copies of the film containing the musical composition. These rights are normally granted as part of the synchronization license.

MUSIC LICENSING, TELEVISION. To use a musical composition in a taped or film television show requires the authorization of the copyright owner. Two rights are involved here: the right to perform the work publicly and the right to reproduce it in copies (videotape or film). In practice, the nondramatic right to perform a work on television is granted automatically by virtue of stations and networks having blanket licenses or other arrangements with the performing rights organizations (which license on behalf of copyright owners).* Consequently, the stations and networks—not the producers—pay for the performing right. The right of synchronization, however, must be obtained by the producer. Negotiations are conducted between the producer and the copyright owner (or his or her agent) and, if an agreement is reached, permission to use a musical composition on television is granted in the form of a **synchronization license**.

The acquisition of a television synchronization license commonly works in the following way: Someone from the production company, usually the music coordinator, contacts the publisher of the song desired. Most publishers are represented by a music reproduction licensing organization and, if this is the case, the inquiry would be directed to this agent. The licensing organization in turn contacts the publisher, which advises on the terms it would like. This information is reported by the licensing organization to the production company and a negotiation may continue with regard to fees and the length of the license. Of course, a publisher may not have an agent, in which case negotiations would be carried on directly between the publisher and the production company.

Synchronization licenses are issued in various ways: *flat buyouts* and *term licenses*. A flat buyout provides for the transfer of rights to a composition perpetually. While a flat buyout is in the interest of producers, most publishers wish to limit the length of their licenses. Most common are term licenses, which provide for unlimited use of a song in a television program or episode for a specific length of time; five-year term licenses are used quite often. If the production company wishes to use the program or episode after the license expires, it must acquire a *renewal license*. Renewal licenses commonly run for the same term as the initial license. The Harry Fox

*If the music is to be used for a dramatic performance such as an opera, a grand rights performance license is needed. This is obtained directly from the copyright owner, not from a performing rights organization.

203

Agency, which represents many U.S. publishers, automatically sends letters to production companies on behalf of its publisher affiliates when licenses are due to expire.

Television synchronization licenses normally grant the rights to use a composition in a show that will be aired on free or cable television, or will be released on a videocassette, and is worldwide in scope. The rates established by the publisher for TV synchronization licenses are negotiable although a five-year term license for one song commonly runs from $500 to $750.

Music reproduction licensing organizations report that most initial inquiries to use compositions in television shows are very preliminary in nature and rarely materialize. Inquiries are made pursuant to creative ideas being considered but which may ultimately change. When it has been definitely decided that a particular song is wanted for a show, then serious negotiation begins.

It is not necessary to obtain a synchronization license to use a composition in a show that is broadcast live and will not be rerun such as an award show that is broadcast live.

MUSIC PUBLISHING COMPANY. A music publishing company is a firm that owns rights to musical compositions and administers and exploits them in an endeavor to have the copyrights derive income. Motion picture and television production companies and television networks often own music publishing companies to collect on copyrights acquired or commissioned by the company.

In terms of copyright ownership, original music for film or television is created either as **work-for-hire**, in which case the producer owns the rights, or on an assignment basis where the composer retains the publishing rights. The latter case is rare, as only a handful of the top film and TV composers are able to negotiate this. Sometimes, however, a co-publishing arrangement is entered into where the producer or network and the composer split the publishing rights. Either each of the firms will administer their share of the copyright or, more commonly, one firm will, usually the producer's or the network's. An administering publisher takes a percentage of the revenues of a composition, commonly 10 percent of the gross income. Administering a composition refers to performing various tasks in three main areas: copyright administration, financial administration, and contractual administration.

To use a preexisting musical composition such as a former hit pop tune in a film, a license is needed from the publisher. Under the compulsory license of the copyright statute, anyone may record a song once that song has been recorded with owner's permission, by complying with procedures set forth in the law and paying royalties on a monthly basis. Because the compulsory license requirements are regarded as too rigorous by the music business industry, compulsory licenses are rarely used. However, they do establish the basis for artists and companies to use any published song, and therefore new users negotiate mechanical licenses that provide for quarterly payments and statements, and revoke the need to serve a notice of intention on the copyright owner within thirty days of distributing audio recordings of the composition or for filing notice in the Copyright Office if the owner's name and address cannot be identified in the Office's registration or other public records.

There is no compulsory license for using a preexisting composition in a commercial motion picture, however, and if studios and producers wish to use a published song, they must seek permission from the copyright owner and negotiate a synchronization and performance license. Of course a fee will be negotiated and this could stand as the stumbling block in consummating a contractual arrangement. Such factors as the importance of a song to a movie, and whether the singer can be seen or the song is heard in the background, how many times it is used and for how long, and the budget of the movie will be considered in establishing a fee. Naturally, studios and producers desire unrestricted use of the composition—that is, for cable, videocassette, and other areas, as well as for worldwide rights—and these factors are considered in establishing a license fee.

Income from a musical composition is normally split fifty-fifty between the publisher and the songwriter, except with regard to print income, which has traditionally been in the favor of the publisher. If two or more songwriters are involved, such as a composer and a lyricist, their share is split on the net 50 percent of income received. Composers and lyricists usually divide their income on the basis of half the songwriter's revenues going to the composer(s) and half to the lyricist(s), but sometimes creative contributions overlap, so this division is not sacrosanct but rather subject to negotiation.

A **sound track** issued from a motion picture will result in mechanical royalties for the publisher and writer, and perhaps performance royalties for airplay on the radio and print royalties from distribution of sheet music and folios and fakebooks containing the song. (A *fakebook* is a printed edition containing the melodies, chords, and lyrics to hundreds of songs.) The publisher tries to exploit the composition in other ways, such as interesting other artists in recording it, getting it used in commercials, and arranging for items such as toys or gift wrap to be based on it. Ingenuity, creativity, enterprise, and industriousness dictate the extent of exploitation and the ultimate income of a musical copyright.

Because it would be an administrative burden, if not a practical impossibility, for a publisher to negotiate performance licenses with radio stations throughout the country (and world), performing-rights organizations exist that serve as central clearinghouses for the licensing of music to radio stations, as well as television stations, discos, restaurants, ballparks, bars, and other users of music. Publishers in the United States belong to ASCAP, BMI, and/or SESAC. The reason for multiple affiliation (usually through different corporate entities) is that a publisher and writer must be affiliates of the same organization; this enables the publisher to register the song with the same performing-rights organization with which the writer is affiliated. The performing-rights organizations pay royalties for performances of U.S. songs in many countries throughout the world because they have reciprocal relations with similar foreign societies.

Likewise, there exist music reproduction licensing organizations that negotiate recording and synchronization rights on behalf of publishers with record companies that wish to issue recordings of preexisting songs or producers that want to use music in a new motion picture or commercial. The majority of U.S. music publishers are represented by the Harry Fox Agency (a subsidiary of the

National Music Publishers' Association) for the disposition of recording and synchronization rights. The Fox Agency, like other music reproduction licensing organizations, negotiates terms and fees of licenses under the instruction of its affiliated publishers.

MUSIC REPRODUCTION LICENSING ORGANIZATION. A music reproduction licensing organization acts as a licensing agent for music publishers with respect to recordings (tape, CDs, vinyl), film, videotape, and television commercials. Publishers often have so many songs in their catalog that to entertain all inquiries for use of compositions would be impossible. So instead of negotiating directly with the publisher of a song for its use on a recording or in a movie or TV program, a manufacturer or producer will negotiate with the music reproduction licensing organization representing the publishers. For its service, the music licensing organization would keep a percentage of the fee negotiated or royalty received.

The largest music reproduction licensing organization in the United States is the Harry Fox Agency (a subsidiary of the National Music Publishers' Association), which in 1990 represented 7,500 music publishers. Affiliation with a music licensing organization is voluntary. Some music publishers license their own recording and synchronization rights.

MUSIC VIDEOS. *See* **Television Programming Genres**.

MYSTERY. *See* **Film Genres**.

NATIONAL ASSOCIATION OF BROADCAST EMPLOYEES AND TECHNICIANS (NABET). NABET is an international union (affiliated with the AFL-CIO) that represents news writers, camera operators, news producers, editors, audio mixers, and technicians at the ABC and NBC television networks and certain local television and cable stations in the United States and Canada. NABET also represents free-lance technicians and craftspersons working in motion pictures. NABET has two film locals, Local 15 in New York and Local 531 in Los Angeles.

See also **Unions.**

NATIONAL ASSOCIATION OF BROADCASTERS (NAB). The NAB is a trade association representing the U.S. television and radio broadcasting industry. Its members are television and radio networks and stations. Membership in the NAB is open to any FCC-licensed television or radio station in the United States. Regular associate membership is available to record and film companies and distributors, law firms, consultants, advertising agencies, research films, station representatives, and other companies that are associated with the broadcasting industry. Another category of associate membership is open to licensees of lower-power television broadcast service. International associate membership is for private and government broadcasting stations and networks, equipment manufacturers, and broadcasting service organizations outside the United States.

To advance and promote the interests of the broadcasting industry, the NAB comprises various departments and committees that work for this common goal. The government relations department acts as a liaison between the broadcasting industry and government agencies; the public-affairs and communications department explains to people and the media how television and radio stations serve the public interest; the science and technology department provides technical comments to the FCC, as well as technical advice and help to broadcasters, and fosters new broadcast technology such as high-definition television; the legal department interprets technical and judicial rulings and conveys these to TV and radio stations, and represents the broadcasting industry to the courts and at the Federal Communications Commission; the television department assists broadcast personnel in increasing their stations' revenues. Other departments include radio, station services, research and planning, minority and special services, and conventions and meetings. (The NAB's annual convention, with about fifty thousand registrants, is the world's largest broadcast industry trade show.)

Thirty-five committees serve to counsel the NAB's board of directors (a joint board of television and radio members) and these include: children's television, local television audience measurement, hundred-plus markets TV, copyright, and broadcast marketing task force.

The National Association of Broadcasters was formed in 1922 to "foster and promote the development of the arts of aural and visual broadcasting in all its forms." As of 1990 there were approximately 950 television and 9,000 radio station members in the association.

NATIONAL ASSOCIATION OF TELEVISION PROGRAM EXECUTIVES (NATPE). NATPE is a professional association for program managers and buyers of TV stations, networks, cable systems, and satellite networks. NATPE sponsors various activities but is best known for its annual program conference, when television-program buyers from around the country gather to buy programming from syndicators, producers, and rights owners. NATPE presents the Iris Awards each year to honor local TV stations for programming production.

NATIONAL ASSOCIATION OF THEATER OWNERS (NATO). NATO is a trade association whose members are theater owners, operators, and chains throughout the United States. NATO represents its members with respect to legislation, practices, marketing, technological developments, and government agencies and other industries. A number of state and technical theater owner associations are affiliated with NATO. Theater owners from several foreign countries are members of NATO, which itself is affiliated with the Union Internationale Des Cinemas, located in France. NATO was founded in 1924 as the Motion Picture Theater Association of America.

NATIONAL CAPTIONING INSTITUTE. *See* **Closed-Captioning.**

NBC. NBC is a television **network**. In 1919 the Radio Corporation of America was founded as a manufacturer of electronic components and products. Seven years later, in 1926, a subsidiary, the National Broadcasting Company, was organized to broadcast radio programs. The radio network expanded through the years and, with David Sarnoff as chairman of RCA, NBC's first commercial television station, WNBT, began to broadcast out of New York City in 1941. In 1986, RCA merged with the General Electric Company, a major stockholder in RCA when it was formed in 1919. The purchase price was $6.4 billion.

Experimental television broadcasting began in 1928, when WGY in Schenectady, New York, aired a drama, and continued for more than a decade. On April 30, 1941, the FCC began issuing licenses for commercial television operations (following approval of a technological standard of 525 lines and 30 frames per second), and NBC's New York City station, WNBT, soon was the first TV station to broadcast commercially, albeit very limitedly. Within a decade, television experienced phenomenal growth in the United States, both fueled by and compelling the networks to innovate creative programming.

Historically, NBC has been strong in certain programming genres, although some have been marked with inconsistency. In its early years, the network was a leader in comedy, with such successful shows as "Texaco Star Theater" and "The Colgate Comedy Hour." CBS and ABC dominated comedy in the 1960s and 1970s, but in the mid-80s, such successful sitcoms as "The Cosby Show," "Cheers," "The Golden Girls," and "Family Ties" made NBC the number-one network.

In the area of late-evening talk shows, the network has continuously been on top with its "Tonight Show," first slotted in that period in 1954. In the late 1950s and 1960s, NBC led the Western genre with such fare as "Wagon Train" and "Bonanza." It has also had several successful one-hour dramas, from "Dr. Kildare," "The Man From U.N.C.L.E.," "I Spy," and "Star Trek" in the '60s to "Miami Vice," "Hill Street Blues," "St. Elsewhere," and "L.A. Law" in the '80s.

NBC is also known for certain innovations. On September 26, 1960, as John F. Kennedy and Richard Nixon faced each other at lecterns yards apart at a TV station in Chicago, the network transmitted the first Presidential debate in history on national television. It has had innovative programming, such as "Rowan & Martin's Laugh-In," first broadcast in 1968, and "Saturday Night Live," which debuted in 1975. In 1985 NBC began broadcasting programs to affiliates in stereo, the first network to do so. Also that year, NBC was the first network to implement Ku-band satellite technology to distribute programming, eliminating its dependence on interconnection facilities on land.

NEGATIVE PICKUP. A negative pickup is an arrangement made prior to the production of a motion picture in which a distributor agrees to pay a producer a specified amount of money upon completion of the film and delivery of the negative. A negative pickup gives a producer or filmmaker the credibility to obtain a loan from a lender to defray production costs. The negative pickup is a guarantee and the loan is made against the guaranteed receipt of that money. Most banks require a **completion guarantor** to be secured to protect their investment. The producer presents a **deal memo** to the bank to prove that a studio has agreed to buy the film and bring it to the marketplace. The deal memo also is used by completion guarantors to file completion guarantees. When the producer receives the money from the distributor, the loan is paid off. The distributor makes prints of the negative and distributes them to theaters.

See also **Pickup.**

NET. *See* **Grip Equipment.**

NET PROFITS, FILMS. Under the accounting system traditionally used by many large Hollywood motion picture studios, few films show a profit though their earnings may be substantial. A film may have various sources of income (*see* **Film, sources of income**) with domestic box-office receipts generally the highest. But the system provides for major stars, producers, and directors to take percentages off the film's gross. Then the studios deduct the cost to make the picture (*see* **Budget, motion pictures**), with interest on financing the film, overhead, distribution percentage, distribution expenditures (for example, advertising and film prints) also taken off the top. Consequently, a screenwriter or a lower-level star, director, or independent producer whose contract provides for a percentage of a film's net profits, may not, despite the film's box-office success, enjoy any such earnings.

NETWORK. A network is a company that broadcasts programs on a daily basis to markets throughout the country via affiliates and owned stations during the broadcast day. The Federal Communications Commission (FCC) defines a network as "any person, entity, or corporation which offers an interconnected program service on a regular basis for 15 or more hours per week to at least 25 affiliated television licensees in 10 or more states."

The three traditional major television networks are ABC, CBS, and NBC. A few attempts to start other networks have been ultimately unsuccessful. The success of the most recent attempt, by the Fox Broadcasting Company, which in the fall of 1986 began broadcasting limited prime-time programming on dozens of independent stations, remains to be seen. Cable networks, public television networks, and ad hoc independent TV networks, created for the purpose of producing and airing programs such as miniseries, also compete for viewers.

ABC, CBS, and NBC each have more than two hundred affiliate stations across the United States and its possessions. The networks pay fees to their affiliates and derive their income from selling commercial airtime to advertisers. The networks also own several TV stations each, but the number of stations a network may own is restricted by the FCC. This number has changed through the years and currently is limited to twelve TV stations, provided that the network does not reach more than 25 percent of the U.S. television audience, as determined by Arbitron's ADI (Area of Dominant Influence) market rankings.

A network programs for a national audience and must satisfy a very broad range of interests to achieve maximum profits. The network's offices typically are made up of many departments, whose names reflect the network's many concerns: research, market planning, strategic planning, affiliate relations, business affairs, broadcast standards and practices, ad sales, national, daytime, news, sports, early morning, prime time, special projects, spot sales, theatrical motion pictures, movies for television, comedy series development, dramatic series development, variety series development, prime-time series development, children's programming, daytime programs, casting, program administration, music licensing, and on-air promotion.

Networks acquire programming through a combination of buying programs, licensing, and producing their own.

The FCC prescribes various rules pertaining to contracts between networks and affiliates and the program practices of the networks. Among other terms, FCC rules provide that a contract or arrangement between an affiliate and a network may not: endure for more than two years; prohibit the affiliate from refusing to broadcast network programs "which the station reasonably believes to be unsatisfactory or unsuitable or contrary to the public interest," or to substitute a show that the station believes "is of greater local or national importance;" prevent the affiliate from broadcasting shows of another network; hinder another station in the same geographic area from airing shows not taken by the primary affiliate; penalize the affiliate for fixing its commercial airtime rates for nonnetwork shows.

The networks are currently prohibited by the FCC from syndicating shows in the United States and from owning any part of a

Network Programming

Type of Show	How Obtained by Network
Prime-time series	Purchased from independent producers and limited amount of network-produced programming. (The networks are restricted by law to produce a certain number of hours of shows per week, but the law provides for that number to increase over time.)
Sports events	License fees paid to rights owners and usually produced in-house.
Morning shows	Produced in-house.
Game shows	Produced in-house and purchased from independent producers.
Newscasts	Produced in-house.
Daytime soaps	Produced in-house although some produced by independent producers.
Talk shows	Purchased from independent producers.
Feature films	License fees paid to rights owners.
Movies of the week	Produced in-house and purchased from independent producers.
Miniseries	Produced in-house and purchased from independent producers.
Award shows	License fees paid to rights owners although sometimes produced in-house.
Specials	Produced in-house and purchased from independent producers.

program produced by someone else. A network is allowed, however, to sell or distribute programs of which it is the sole producer for broadcast in foreign countries, and it is also allowed to sell U.S. syndication rights to programs not acquired from another entity provided that the network itself does not engage in U.S. distribution or share in derived revenues.

The FCC also restricts affiliates in the fifty largest television markets from devoting more than three hours in prime time to network shows or shows formerly broadcast by a network (reruns), except for theatrical motion pictures. There are, however, certain programs excluded from the three-hour limitation, including special news programs, children's shows, public-affairs programs (other than on Saturday evenings), and sporting events such as Olympic games.

NEWS SHOWS. *See* **Television Programming Genres.**

NIELSEN COMPANY, A. C. *See* **Audience Measurement Service.**

NO-BUDGET MOVIE. Filmmakers are by nature a determined and resourceful lot. Since low-budget movies have become increasingly expensive to produce, it has become more difficult for those without track records or financial backing to make commercial motion pictures. Rather than trying to get a studio to purchase a film as a **negative pickup,** or to interest a bank in committing a large amount of money, some filmmakers produce professional movies for under $100,000 each, a minuscule sum in the world of motion picture production. Movies made with next to no capital are sometimes referred to as *low-low budget* or *no-budget* films.

The no-budget filmmaker is often a screenwriter or director who has an idea and is committed to its realization.

Obviously, a no-budget script must lend itself to a very, very low budget. Period pieces, aerial shots, car chases, and elaborate special effects are not possible. Sets and sound stages are also out of the question. Real-life locations are used.

Everyone involved in a no-budget film is hired on a deferred-payment basis. Payment is made only if the film sells and shows a profit. While the cast and crew realize that it is unlikely that they will ever be paid for their work, working on a no-budget movie gives exposure to actors and experience to the crew. A director of commercials might welcome the opportunity to make a no-budget film to use as a stepping stone. Makeup people and hairstylists working in other fields work on no-budgets to break into the entertainment industry.

Of course, a system of deferred payments undermines the goals of the entertainment unions, which have contracts providing for minimum wages and working conditions, but the cast and crew are not likely to be a signatory to any union agreement.

To find actors and crew members, the filmmaker advertises in various trade publications. *Backstage* in New York and *The Hollywood Reporter* in California are two popular trade publications.

In hiring people, there are certain qualities and elements a filmmaker looks for other than talent. Commitment and enthusiasm are the most important.

There are two primary hard costs necessary to make a no-budget film: film and developing. There is no way to avoid paying for these and they compose the bulk of the budget. There may also be camera and lighting costs, but often the crew hired has access to equipment.

Since there is no costume designer or prop master, wardrobe and props are often obtained by the cast and crew. Soliciting companies to use their products for screen credits is an excellent approach to obtain better-quality props, equipment, or materials.

Often the money to make a no-budget film comes from the producer's own pocket as well as from family and friends. Production usually takes place during the weekends, when people have time off from their jobs.

Because no-budget films are made without certain crew members, there are additional responsibilities for those involved. For example, without a unit production manager, the filmmaker or some assistant will have to make the crew calls. Without a script supervisor, someone or a few people will have to keep track of continuity. Indeed, it is essential that the film be cuttable, and continuity is one of the major concerns.

A no-budget film typically takes several years to make—years for principal photography and years for editing and postproduction.

During production or postproduction, attempts may be made to raise capital to pay off bills and complete the film unsparingly. Ads may be taken out in the trade press and screenings of rushes or a rough cut held to interest potential investors.

When a no-budget film is finally completed, the filmmaker must obtain a distributor for the film. However, a distributor with exclusive rights, who does not back a film with enthusiasm, can ground it. If a distributor cannot be found, there are alternatives to bring a film to industry and public attention: It can be exhibited at film festivals, sold to foreign markets, or shown at benefits and charitable functions.

Making and promoting a no-budget film is indeed an uphill battle. It requires innovation, perseverance, and dedication. For the people involved, however, the end may justify the means.

NUDITY. The basic agreement between the Screen Actors Guild and the Alliance of Motion Picture and Television Producers provides the following conditions with respect to nudity:

> The Producer's representative will notify the performer (or his or her representative) of any nudity or sex acts expected in the role (if known by management at the time) prior to the first interview or audition. The performer shall also have prior notification of any interview or audition requiring nudity, and shall have the absolute right to have a person of the performer's choice present at that audition.
>
> During any production involving nudity or sex scenes the set shall be closed to all persons having no business purpose in connection with the production.
>
> No still photography of nudity or sex acts will be authorized by the Producer to be made without the prior written consent of the performer.
>
> The appearance of a performer in a nude or sex scene or the

doubling of a performer in such a scene shall be conditioned upon his or her prior written consent. Such consent may be obtained by letter or other writing prior to a commitment or written contract being made or executed. Such consent must include a general description as to the extent of the nudity and the type of physical contact required in the scene. If a performer has agreed to appear in such scenes and then withdraws his or her consent, Producer shall have the right to double, but consent may not be withdrawn as to film already photographed. Producer shall also have the right to double children of tender years (infants) in nude scenes (but not in sex scenes).

OFF-NETWORK PROGRAMMING. This term refers to reruns of previous or current prime-time network shows that air on independent television stations and affiliates. A series must have amassed at least sixty or more shows before it can be sold for **syndication**, although there are rare exceptions as, for example, "The Honeymooners."

See also **Independent Television Station.**

OFF-NETWORK SYNDICATION. *See* **Independent Television Station.**

OPERATIONS DEPARTMENT, TELEVISION STATION. *See* **Independent Television Station.**

OPTION. An option is the exclusive right to produce a property (book, script, treatment, or synopsis) within a certain time period. The term is negotiable but it commonly ranges from six months to two years. Writers (or their representatives) try to negotiate brief option periods to encourage action on their properties. Depending on the contract, the option may be considered part of the purchase price. The option period can sometimes be extended by the fulfillment of stipulated minimum provisions.

See also **Adaptations.**

OSCAR. The Oscar is the name of the golden statuette given to winners of **Academy Awards**. An Oscar is thirteen-and-a-half-inches tall, weighs eight-and-a-half pounds, and costs a few hundred dollars to make. The figure is a man standing erect and holding a long crusader's sword downward, with its point between his feet. His arms press his sides, elbows bent at the hips, with his hands, right on top of left, grasping the hilt at the sternum level. The figure stands on a reel of film with five spokes indicating the five original branches of the Academy (acting, producing, directing, writing, and technical), which is mounted on a short, wide, circular pedestal. The statuette is based on a sketch made by

Hollywood art director Cedric Gibbons and a model by sculptor George Stanley.

In 1931 Margaret Herrick, the librarian of the Academy of Motion Picture Arts and Sciences, remarked that the figure reminded her of her uncle Oscar. A journalist heard the comment and wrote, "Academy employees have affectionately dubbed their famous gold statuette Oscar." The name caught on and remains to this day.

After each Academy Awards ceremony, the winners return their Oscars to the Academy for engraving. The Academy mandates by written agreement that if any winner wants to dispose of his Oscar, it must first be offered back to the organization for a few dollars.

An Academy Award is meant to commemorate artistic excellence. It is, more realistically, an industry award which generates revenue for its recipients.

OVERHEAD STAND. *See* **Grip Equipment.**

PACKAGE. A package consists of a screenplay or an idea for a movie along with the commitment of one or more integral people (such as a renowned director or a star) to make the movie, that is submitted to a studio or an investor. The combination of these elements makes it more attractive and commercial than if a single element, such as the script, were submitted alone. Large talent agencies, which represent a cross-section of established actors, screenwriters and directors, as well as independent producers, stars, and others commonly package projects.

PARALLEL. *See* **Grip Equipment.**

PEGGING. *See* **Animation.**

PENCIL TESTING. *See* **Animation.**

PENSION, HEALTH, AND WELFARE PLANS. Unions and guilds negotiate industry-wide agreements with producers on behalf of their members for minimum working conditions. These contracts contain provisions for pension, health, and welfare plans. In essence, employers make contributions to these unions' and guilds' plans based on formulas involving percentages of salaries and other remuneration paid to employees covered by their contract. Members are given credit for qualification to receive benefits from these plans in accordance with their employment.

PEOPLE METER. *See* **Audience Measurement Service.**

PERFORMING-RIGHTS ORGANIZATION. A performing-rights organization pays composers, lyricists, and music publishers who are members or affiliates royalties for public performances of their compositions. Public performance of a song includes a rendition, live or recorded, on radio or television (network, local, and cable), or at concert halls, stadiums, restaurants, or nightclubs. Performance royalties are distributed under methods devised by the organization.

There are three performing-rights organizations in the United States: the **American Society of Composers, Authors and Publishers (ASCAP)**, **Broadcast Music Incorporated (BMI)**, and SESAC, INC. (formerly the Society of European Stage Authors and Composers). In addition, there are performing-rights organizations throughout the world with whom the U.S. organizations have reciprocal relations.

It is a practical necessity for composers and lyricists to be members of the performing-rights organizations, and virtually all professionals are. Often, songs from motion picture sound tracks are released as singles and enjoy substantial airplay on radio stations around the country (or world). Movie and TV theme music is often played on the radio. As bulk clearinghouses, the performing-rights organizations license music users on behalf of the copyright owners and collect license fees, which are apportioned to the songwriters, lyricists, composers, and publishers of the performed compositions under systems that reflect performance frequency.

PERSONAL MANAGER. A personal manager is one who oversees and guides all aspects of an entertainment career. Not only does the personal manager make sure that the client's other representatives—which may include an agent, attorney, business manager, and publicist—are serving the client's best interest, but the personal manager also carries on whatever other functions are necessary to establish and maximize the longevity and renown of the client. He or she is there to advise the client on a daily basis and may represent the client on virtually any matter, including the selection of roles and proceedings with unions. Personal managers generally earn from 10 percent to 25 percent of their client's income.

PHYSICAL SPECIAL EFFECTS. *See* **Special Effects.**

PICKUP. A pickup is the acquisition of a completed film. The term is used in reference to movies made by small independent producers or foreign films acquired by a distributor. A straight pickup is made when a picture has been completed under the financing and operation of another party, without collaborating with the distributor.

See also **Negative Pickup.**

PILOT. A pilot is an introductory episode of a planned television series. Sometimes network executives are confident enough in a series to order a number of episodes without seeing a pilot. But generally a pilot is made for network executives to determine whether to schedule the series and order additional episodes. If the network picks up the series, the pilot often becomes the premiere show.

A pilot introduces the premise, the major characters, the setting, and the tone. These elements are discussed with network executives prior to the production of the pilot (*see* **Development, Network Television**).

Dozens of pilots are commissioned by the networks each year, but very few become regularly scheduled series. The networks conduct research tests in which viewers are invited to screenings of new pilots and then asked to evaluate the shows on questionnaires. Based on the response to the screenings, network executives make their decisions. Pilots are also tested on cable channels.

About five to ten new shows per network debut each fall. If a new series is given a green light, a specific number of episodes is ordered. When a small number of shows is ordered, the network uses ratings to decide whether to order more. Producers of dramas and action-adventure shows prefer to make two-hour pilots so that if a series is not picked up by a network they can try to sell it as a movie to other markets. The decision as to whether a pilot gets made into a series is made by upper management in the programming department as well as upper management in the corporate network.

Pilots that do not get made into series often get broadcast during the summer.

PORNOGRAPHY. *See* **Film Genres.**

POSTPRODUCTION. Postproduction is the phase in the making of a film that takes place after **principal photography**, when a film is prepared for commercial release. The steps included in postproduction are

- editing
- addition of sound effects
- addition of special visual effects
- addition of computer-generated graphics
- sound dubbing
- scene reshoots
- music synchronization
- addition of titles
- negative matching
- production of answer prints

PREEMPTION. Preemption is the substitution of a network broadcast with other programming. Though affiliates sometimes preempt a network series when its ratings are low, the networks deplore this practice and try to offer the affiliates incentives (such as advertising time) to keep them from using other programming. Preemption also occurs because of special telecasts, such as Presidential speeches.

PREMIERE/SHOWCASE RUN. A premiere run is the theatrical exhibition of a film in its first release. In its premiere run, a film will usually play at theaters whose ticket prices are full-priced. A showcase run is the exhibition of a movie in its second major release. In this run it will play at reduced prices. Showcase theaters are more often found in suburbs or small towns than in large cities.

PREMIERE, TELEVISION. A television premiere is the first episode of a new series. A premiere is often the **pilot** episode. Television premieres often run longer than a series' average episode and are introduced in popular time slots. This practice helps attract viewers whom the program might not reach in its regularly scheduled time period.

PREPRODUCTION. In the making of a film, preproduction is the phase after packaging or financing and prior to **principal photography**. Preproduction includes all the technical planning necessary to make filming as smooth and cost-effective as possible. During preproduction:

- A production office is set up.
- Crew members are hired.
- Department heads determine budgets for their departments.
- Parts are cast.
- Locations are scouted and clearances obtained.
- Continuity sketches are prepared (*see* **illustrator**).
- The production designer works with the director on the look of the film.
- Sets are designed.
- The shooting schedule is made up.
- Contacts are negotiated and signed.
- Props are ordered.
- Costumes are obtained.
- Script changes are made.
- Actors rehearse.
- Stunts are planned.
- Special effects are constructed.

Prior to preproduction, when there is only a script, a budget for the project is estimated and a **stripboard** is made.
See also **Development, Motion Pictures.**

PREQUEL. A prequel is a film whose storyline precedes that of a previously released motion picture. The main characters often are present. A prequel serves to explain how or why events in the original film transpired. Prequels are made only if the original film is highly successful and the writer or director wants to make a follow-up.

PRERELEASE. Prerelease refers to the period before a film is officially released when it is shown to selected audiences. Based on the responses of these audiences, changes may be made in the movie before its official release.

See also **Preview; Screening.**

PREVIEW. A preview is the exhibition of a film before its official release date. Previews are used for test purposes or to generate advance hype.

PREVIEW AUDIENCE. An audience that is used to judge the quality of a motion picture before it is released to the general public. At the end of the movie the audience will usually evaluate different aspects of it on a card or sheet of paper.

PRIME TIME. Prime time is the period of television programming from 8 P.M. to 11 P.M. Monday through Saturday and 7 P.M. to 11 P.M. on Sunday. Viewing audiences are the largest and advertising rates the highest during this period. Consequently, prime time is a network's major programming priority.

The staples of network prime-time television are sitcoms, action-adventure programs, dramas, variety shows, magazine-format programs, sports games, miniseries, made-for-TV movies, and feature films.

The popularity of program genres in prime-time network sometimes runs in cycles. In the late 1970s, some people predicted the demise of the sitcom. By the late 1980s, many popular nighttime series (soap operas) seem to have run their course. Hit shows spawn other series of the same genre, and, after a number of years, repeated exposure to the genre often causes audiences to grow tired of the format and seek out new types of programming.

Under FCC regulations, prime time refers to the hours between 7 P.M. and 11 P.M. Eastern and Pacific time, and from 6 P.M. to 10 P.M. Central and Mountain time. The networks are restricted by the FCC from broadcasting in-house productions for more than three hours during this period.

PRINCIPAL PHOTOGRAPHY. Principal photography is the shooting of photography that becomes a motion picture. Principal photography marks the beginning of production.

PRODUCER, MOTION PICTURE. The film producer generally may be described as one who conceives an original story or selects an existing property on which the film is to be based, and then initiates the process by which a film may be made; overseeing the making of the film from inception to finish in both creative and managerial capacities.

There are basically two types of producers—the studio and the independent. The studio producer gets the studio to do the buying. For example, if there is a particular book for which the producer wants to obtain the rights, the studio pays for the rights. Not only does the producer not put up his or her own money but, having the clout of the studio behind the producer, might make him or her more attractive to the author than other producers who are interested in the book. The studio producer, invariably a producer with a good track record, is not financially at risk but is rather, in a sense, an agent for the studio. The studio pays production costs as well as costs for film prints and advertising.

The independent producer, on the other hand, has to put up his or her own money or the money of a consortium of people or entities who are backing the producer to get the project moving. Sometimes the independent producer is more attractive to a rights owner as he or she can pledge that the project will have his or her full concern, time, and commitment. In a sense the studio producer is to the independent producer as the big chain store is to the mom-and-pop operation.

Some independent producers take options on properties and try to sell them to studios, making a profit on the turnaround, or they develop properties themselves. They are in at risk because they lay out money for a property and may not be able to sell it to a studio. If they get studio backing, the studio usually pays for a portion of the production costs, leaving the rest to be raised by the producer.

Actually, producers are as varied as the individuals they are.

Some are essentially businesspersons; others are talented filmmakers who immerse themselves in the creative process. There are producers who get movies made because they have arrangements with certain stars they can deliver. There are producers who get movies made because of their dedication and perseverance. And there are the infamous producers who bring to the motion picture and financial arenas their talents of glibness. They will talk about arrangements they have with stars, distribution deals they have made, money they have already secured—when in fact they don't have anything. For example, one might approach a famous female star and say he has a famous male star signed, and vice-versa. Certainly, there is no morality code for producers nor any educational or licensing requirements to be one. It's an attractive career or endeavor because it need not require much more than option money and taste—the latter something most people believe they have.

Virtually every deal is different for the independent producer. A producer might go to a studio and ask for $12 million to make a particular movie. The studio might give $6 million for North American distribution rights, leaving the producer $6 million short. The producer then seeks money from other sources—loans from banks, private investors, perhaps even mortgage the house to raise money—as well as try to get vendors, such as a film lab, to defer fees. A producer might also obtain money by selling off various rights, including pay television, home video, and foreign rights. Some producers attend film festivals such as the Cannes Film Festival to sell some of these rights. Or they might try to sell distribution rights to a movie there just on the basis of a concept or title ("Would you be interested in a movie called _____"), perhaps saying they already have a script or the commitment of a star. Once they get the commitment of money it is certainly no problem to get a script written; a script can be written within a matter of weeks. In fact, why invest money in a script if the distribution rights to the movie cannot be sold? This in return is what may be needed to pay for the script and the production of the film. Movies are usually not made on the basis that there is a story that must be told. Rather, the concern is can the film be made? Does the marketing department think it can sell the movie? How much money has already been invested into the project? The issue of whether a movie is good or not sometimes becomes secondary if it is even considered. People in the industry work not on the basis of the quality of projects but on the basis of whether movies get made.

After a film is released, the producer works to maximize its success by being involved with distribution, marketing, and publicity.

Perseverance is a key requisite for producers without a substantial track record. The projects pitched may be rejected or projects in development may be dropped; in either case the producers may want to take their projects to another studio or obtain the needed financing themselves.

Hot producers having deals with studios may collect salaries in addition to their normal production fees and financial participations. They may even be given offices at the studio with staff salaries and overhead paid for by the studio.

PRODUCTION. Production is the stage of filmmaking from the start of principal photography to its completion. A shooting schedule maps out the dates, times, and places for production, and in order to meet the budget, the cast and crew must work as efficiently as possible. Call sheets tell actors and crew members where to report each morning—whether a sound stage in a studio or a remote location—and typically, shooting starts early. While various members of the crew are setting up for shooting, actors (outside of extras) are having their makeup applied, their hair done, and their wardrobe laid out. Before the actual shooting begins, the actors may go through rehearsals. On the set are the crew—director, assistant directors, cinematographer, grips, gaffers, sound mixer, boom operator, and extras—the props, and the camera and lighting equipment, including dollies, cranes, dolly and boom tracks, carbon arc lamps, HMI lights, butterflies, scrims, barn doors, bounce cards, and C-stands. When all is ready to begin, the cast and crew will take their places and the director will call "Action." The clapstick, with the scene and take number noted on it, will hit and the script comes to life. The master, or establishing, shot is made first and this is followed by different coverage. The director observes the dailies each day to monitor the quality of shooting, and the editor, in consultation with the director, begins cutting during production. Production reports summarizing the progress of each day's shooting are prepared by an assistant director, analyzed by the unit production manager, and sent to the studio or completion guarantor. Shooting may take several weeks or months, and if all goes well, the script will be shot on or in close proximity to both the schedule and budget.

Who is involved in making a motion picture? The members of a crew, and their responsbilities vary from picture to picture and depend upon such factors as budget, special needs, and the work habits of the director. A comparison of the credits of any two movies will reveal different size crews and job titles, although there are many functions that are common to all films. The following list contains the titles of people who contribute to the making of films from development to final cut. As titles may vary from production to production, however, the list should not be considered definitive. There are always movies with special production or postproduction needs, and credits may sometimes use variations or other names for these titles.

MEMBERS OF A PRODUCTION CREW

actor

bit part

cameo role

day player

extra

leading man/lady

  (stars)

   minor role

   supporting actor

animator

associate producer

best boy

boom operator

cameraman

carpenter

casting director

cinematographer

commercial coordinator

completion guarantor

construction coordinator

costume designer

cue card operator

dancer

dialogue coach

dialogue editor

director

director, first assistant
director, second assistant
director of photography
dolly grip
electrician
executive producer
film editor
film loader
Foley artist
Foley editor
gaffer
greens person
grip
grip best boy
hairstylist
illustrator
line producer
makeup artist
matte artist
mixer
model maker
music editor
music supervisor
musician
optical-effects specialist
orchestrator
producer
production accountant
production designer
production manager
production office coordinator
property master

property person
publicist
reader
re-recording mixer
scenic artist
screenwriter
script supervisor
set decorator
set designer
set dresser
set painter
shop craftsperson
singer
sound editor
sound-effects editor
sound mixer
special-effects coordinator
still photographer
story analyst
story editor
stunt coordinator
stuntperson
supervising producer
swing gang
technical advisor
title artist
transportation captain
transportation coordinator
unit production manager
visual consultant
wardrobe supervisor
wrangler

PRODUCTION ACCOUNTANT. The production accountant is in charge of the accounting department, which is responsible for the day-to-day financial affairs of a motion picture. Film productions are self-contained financial entities operating under the auspices of a corporate parent. Therefore, the production accountant (sometimes called production auditor) must set up a bank account for the project and, under the direction of the **unit production manager** or the producer, handle the project's financial affairs. Charge accounts must be established at companies where purchases and rentals of significant sums will be necessary.

Although a lump sum of money is contracted for a production, that money is rarely available all at once. Rather, it is received on a prearranged payment schedule from the **completion guarantor**. Sums are regularly deposited into a checking account from which the production accountant issues checks. The various departments of a production are assigned separate account numbers, and each expenditure is credited to the appropriate department.

Essentially the responsibilities of the production accountant fit into five categories: payroll, petty cash, bills (accounts payable), living/location expenses, and cost reports.

The salaries of the cast and crew are established under union guidelines. (**Above-the-line** employees such as the stars and the director, however, often negotiate individual contracts with the producer.) Payroll companies are often employed to pay salaries. When the payroll is handled by a production company's accounting department, payroll assistants work under the supervision of the production accountant.

The production accountant also pays for daily expenses, which include production office and location site rentals, office equipment, supplies, telephones, airfares, hotel rooms, vehicle rentals, gas, technical equipment purchase/rental, catering, film, film developing, printing, editing expenses, costumes, set dressing, and film projection.

Films made on location require funds for housing, meals, transportation, and allowances for daily expenses. All bills are paid upon approval from the unit production manager.

The production accountant prepares weekly cost reports which summarize how much money has been spent to date in each budgeted category and projects the amount of money necessary to complete the project. A cost report enables the unit production manager to keep track of which departments are over budget, which are saving money, overall expenditures, and the general financial health of the production. This report is submitted to the producer and financial investors.

The production accountant monitors day-to-day production costs and assists in revising the budget if necessary. When a production company shoots at a location for an extended period of time, an account is opened at a local bank for payments to local vendors and employees.

Production accounts are often freelance employees, hired a few weeks prior to principal photography by the unit production manager. If assigned to a production by the completion guarantor, the accountant is responsible to the guarantor and not to the unit production manager.

The accounting department pays bills incurred during the production of a film by the producer, director, unit production manager, and department heads. The unit production manager reviews the bills, and once approved, checks are remitted by the production accountant.

PRODUCTION COMPANY, TELEVISION COMMERCIALS. *See* **Television Commercials, Production of.**

PRODUCTION DEPARTMENT, TELEVISION STATION. *See* **Independent Television Station.**

PRODUCTION DESIGNER. A production designer develops, plans, and coordinates the visual appearance of a motion picture.

Production design is a highly creative job in which the designer is responsible for the visual interpretation and reinforcement of a story in cinematic terms. It requires a knowledge of art, interior design, lighting, photography, and history. A production designer must be able to reproduce, build, or create whatever is needed, whether an ancient village, a nineteenth-century American living room, or a park of the future.

Most film scripts are written with little description of background and scenery, yet each setting must be designed to complement and advance the story and convey a mood. The production designer works in conjunction with the director in mapping out the visual direction. The production designer reads the script and discusses with the director such elements as setting, locations, and the tone of the story. The director gives his or her ideas for visual approaches and the production designer interprets them into workable sets, often extending them conceptually to the enrichment of the film. Some directors rely solely on production designers for visual approaches.

The challenge for the production designer is to develop with the director a vision and carry it out in a practical and cost-efficient manner. The production designer helps select locations for shooting, design the sets, choose the props, and perform many other relevant tasks. The decisions of where to shoot are normally made early in preproduction and determine a great deal of what will happen later. For example, the production designer may say, "This picture needs to take place in the Amazon jungle," and if the location is approved, this would influence financial, creative, and other aspects of the film.

The production designer may also suggest how filming can be done at a local studio rather than in locations where expenses may be high. With drawings, photographs, and other illustrative materials, the production designer will show how the shooting can be accomplished and offer solutions to ostensible problems. He might recommend that a second unit film necessary on-location shots while the basic unit shoots in the studio. On the other hand, the production designer might convince the frugal director or producer that it is absolutely necessary to shoot on location to maintain the integrity and convey the beauty of the story. In the ideal situation, the cinematographer, production designer, director, and producer will jointly be involved in discussions, but the final decision is made by the director (or in some cases, the producer).

Even the simplest scenes will require a number of decisions from the production designer, who will base them on the circumstances of the story. Consider, for example, a scene in which a woman comes into a room, sits down at a table, and drinks a cup of coffee. Is the door she opens in the style of early American, Dutch or Venetian, or is it arched? Is the table Gothic, French, English, or just box-like? Is the coffee cup an Italian glass or a tin can? Is the sugar brown, granular, or in lump form? The moviegoer may not give any thought to these elements, but they subtly reinforce the credibility of the story. The story suggests the settings and the production designer creates them to their best advantage. While the settings mentioned in the script are sometimes palpable in a general sense, the production designer must determine the specific ambience the director wants to convey. For example, for a jungle story the production designer would assist in selecting forestland for the setting. But is it a frightening jungle or is it lyrical and exotic? Is it dappled with rays from the sun or do the tall trees create a pall of sinister darkness? Are there wild animals roaming in pursuit of prey or is wildlife nonexistent?

The production designer confers with key crew members involved in the visual aspects of the movie—the art director, location manager, set decorator, property master, construction coordinator, transportation captain, special-effects coordinator, and costume designer. For example, the costume designer will show sketches and fabrics to the production designer for an opinion. The transportation captain will obtain approval for any vehicles used. The cinematographer will discuss how lighting can be done to achieve certain effects. The production designer might also make recommendations regarding such elements as wallpaper, molding, fixtures, and lamps.

Production designers usually start out in a studio art department, ascending the ranks until they finally get assignments for production design. Some production designers and art directors from television cross over into theatrical films. Training or experience can be gained in art, theater, or film school.

PRODUCTION DESIGNER, TELEVISION. *See* **Art Director, Television.**

PRODUCTION MANAGER. *See* **Unit Production Manager.**

PRODUCTION OFFICE. A production office is the workplace of the **unit production manager, production office coordinator (POC),** and **production accountant.** When a film is in production, this office serves as headquarters for the cast and crew. During principal photography, a temporary production office may be set up at a particular location, staffed by some employees of the main production office. After all the paperwork has been completed following principal photography, the production office is shut down and records are stored.

PRODUCTION OFFICE COORDINATOR (POC). A POC is a liaison between the employer (producer), unit production manager, assistant director, and script supervisor. The POC is responsible for the efficient operation of the production office in the preparatory, filming, and production wrap-up stages.

POC responsibilities include:

- Distributing staff and crew lists, cast lists, contact lists, shooting schedules, etc. These lists/schedules are constantly revised.
- Distributing scripts and revised script pages to cast members, crew members, editorial staff, and studio personnel.
- Distributing call sheets. (The call sheet is prepared by the first or second assistant director.)
- Getting price quotes from vendors for all aspects of the production for the unit production manager.
- Preparing actor contracts.
- Preparing location contracts.
- Filling out union forms and workers' compensation forms.
- Keeping production files.
- Preparing a production report each day of filming from information provided by various departments.
- Setting up travel arrangements and hotel accommodations for all personnel involved in the production.

- Working with municipal or government agencies to secure permits for location shooting.
- Dealing with performance unions (SAG, AFTRA, etc.).

It is not unusual during principal photography for a POC to work more than twelve hours each day. The POC usually opens the production office at the time of the crew call.

PRODUCTION REPORT. A production report is a progress report prepared each day of filming by the second assistant director compiled from information provided by the various departments. The production report includes the number of hours each crew member worked. It is reviewed by the unit production manager and is sent to the studio or completion guarantor monitoring the production.

The production report is an important means of keeping track of a film during production. It communicates the advancement of the picture on a day-to-day basis. While the **call sheet** tells what should happen, the production report tells what actually did happen.

PROGRAMMING DEPARTMENT, TELEVISION STATION. *See* **Independent Television Station.**

PROMOTION DEPARTMENT, TELEVISION STATION. *See* **Independent Television Station.**

PROMOTIONAL CONSIDERATION. A promotional consideration is an arrangement in which a manufacturer provides merchandise, at no cost, to a television game show for use as a prize in exchange for a promotional announcement for the product on the show. The cost of the product is invariably less than the price of an advertising spot, and the game shows acquire prizes for free, resulting in lower production costs.

PROP. Props (an abbreviation for "properties") are divided into three general categories: hand props (objects that can be held, such as a glass or a pen), set props (which are used to decorate a set), and vehicle props. Depending on such factors as budget and the availability of needed items, props are rented, bought, or constructed.

Commercial products are sometimes deliberately used as props in films under arrangements in which manufacturers are charged for advertising. Specialized promotional firms represent companies in getting their products placed in movies. If a product's brand or trademark is displayed without an advertising arrangement, permission must be obtained from the manufacturer or rights owner. Indeed, there may be legal repercussions if authorization is not obtained.

PROP HOUSE. Prop houses serve the special prop requirements of entertainment productions. Today there are a number of companies that rent, sell, or custom-build props for film and television productions as well as other areas such as theater, TV and print advertising, and publishing.

Prop houses carry items that would be difficult to obtain elsewhere, such as telephone booths, old firearms, barbershop poles, pushcarts, and World War II army tanks. Some specialize in such areas as dishes, furniture, accessories, flowers, vehicles, jewelry, hand props, robots, or antiques. Others carry general props but specialize in one or more areas, while still others are completely general.

During preproduction the set designer or prop person of a film or TV production goes to a prop house with a list of items needed. The terms of rental vary from prop house to prop house. Props are rented for an initial period such as three days or seven days. There are additional charges for extended uses. Commonly, rental prices are based on 10 percent of the list price of the item. Some prop houses allow certain props to be painted or altered in some way.

PROPERTY MASTER. A property master acquires, sets up, and maintains the props for a film or television program. While duties vary from production to production, the property master may do or oversee any of the following: determine what props are needed, based on the script and the input of key crew members; rent, have built, or purchase props; deliver or ensure that the props are on the set when needed; oversee the setting up of props during shooting;

restore props to their original position for retakes and coverage from different angles and ranges; prepare and operate cards to cue actors' lines during production; care for and store props during production; return rented props or sell those owned by the production company when they are no longer needed.

In feature films the property master handles action props used by the actors, such as a gun, watch, pair of scissors, or cane. (The responsibility for set props belongs to the **set decorator**.) Working under the property master is one or more assistants, prop persons who put the props on the set. To prepare for shooting the property master does a script breakdown and discusses ideas with the director and production designer.

The property master often must investigate numerous sources to find the necessary props. **Prop houses** are primary sources, but because scripts sometimes call for the unusual, the property master may have to pursue other markets as well: advertising in newspapers and specialty magazines, contacting clubs and organizations, browsing at antiques shows and flea markets.

During shooting the property master makes sure the props are restored to their original positions in repeated takes. Consider a scene of an actor drinking beer, for example. There may be several takes of the master shot, so for each shot the beer must be restored to its original level (if any props were moved, they also have to be returned to their original position). This practice applies also to scenes shot from different angles and ranges. This is for matching purposes. The film editor might decide to cut back and forth from different angles and ranges, but if the level of beer varies with each cut (when the character supposedly has not sipped it), the edit will not be possible. Overseeing continuity is the **script supervisor**.

The property master's job is sometimes complicated by last minute changes or additions requested by the director or other crew members. For example, a gun instead of a rifle may be requested, or another bicycle may be needed. When production falls behind schedule the property master may have to postpone orders. Rental fees can be high and to pay for props while waiting for production to catch up is an unnecessary expenditure of funds. The property

241

master consequently coordinates rentals with the up-to-the-minute schedule of shooting.

PUBLIC RELATIONS. Outside of births, weddings, deaths, and other newsworthy events, most media coverage of the movie and television industries results from concerted public-relations programs. Public-relations (PR) firms employ methods and activities to promote favorable relationships with the public for the industry. Most entertainment PR firms operate out of either Los Angeles or New York. The larger firms have international branch offices. Major film studios and the networks have their own publicity departments, but today in-house staffs are equipped for only a limited amount of PR activities. Independent public-relations firms are hired for the rest.

An entertainment public-relations firm caters to each client's specific publicity objectives. PR firms represent a wide assortment of entities in the television and motion picture fields. Included are actors, studios, independent production companies, directors, producers, scriptwriters, executives, and syndicators.

A public-relations firm can either be hired for a specific project or maintain an ongoing relationship with a client. When involved in a continuing relationship, a PR firm must promote the client's long-range goals as well as the client's latest project.

In obtaining publicity for a client, PR firms will flood a variety of media outlets with favorable biased information on their clients. Common outlets are talk shows, radio programs, magazines, newspapers, trade publications, wire services, and fanzines. Other forums in which clients may be promoted include trade exhibits, film festivals, film classes, commercials, conventions, and contests. Trade exhibits such as those put on by the American Film Market, the National Association of Theater Owners, or ShoWest are also forums for exposing new releases to distributors, exhibitors, theater managers, and other industry people. Occasionally, a PR firm might arrange a commercial endorsement and paid speaking engagements for a client. Fan magazines are approached to run contests for a date with a star, radio stations are given tickets to the premiere of a new movie to give away on the air, and trade fairs are given "dream vacations" to give away to visitors of the sponsoring studio's suite.

In the early years of Hollywood, studios staged dramatic publicity stunts and apocryphal love affairs, and exploited their stars in many other ways as well. Today image-making primarily consists of increasing an actor's visibility. Image-making establishes an actor in the public's mind.

The most desired medium in which to promote a client is television, because television reaches more people than any other medium. Publicity campaigns often are launched with TV appearances in the top twenty major markets. Frequently, talk-show representatives approach PR firms for the bookings. Public-relations employees spend years developing and maintaining contacts with people in the media. They get to know TV show talent coordinators, newspaper and magazine editors, and prominent writers and photographers.

To promote a client, a PR firm sends out press releases and press kits. A press release is a one- or two-page typewritten announcement of an upcoming event or newsworthy story. A press release would promote a world premiere of a film, for example, by giving the details of the happening as well as listing celebrities expected to attend.

A press kit contains a number of items designed to promote a film or client. A movie press kit may contain bios for each of the major stars and the director, information about the music sound track, a production booklet giving detailed information on the movie, and photographs of the principal actors and filmmakers.

Because theatrical motion pictures generally cost a minimum of several million dollars to make, it is important that substantial and well-orchestrated public-relations campaigns be devised and implemented to create a public awareness about the films and motivate people to see them. Each film will dictate to an extent the kinds and amounts of efforts that will be needed. The subject matter, the stars, the director, the scriptwriter, the studio—all these and more will guide the direction and intensity of the PR campaign.

The stars are not always the focal point of attention in a publicity campaign. Sometimes an actor's or actresses's image is so well established—as in the case of a Sylvester Stallone or a Jane Fonda— that the PR firm will concentrate on other people or elements such as the lesser-known but important cast members or the director or the film in its entirety. Efforts are often concentrated on films themselves when they are considered to have blockbuster potential.

The PR firm tries to be creative in obtaining publicity. It might arrange a profile of a well-known star in a publication that would ordinarily not devote much space to that person, or a piece on an industry trend that the movie is part of, or it might publicize the extraordinary special effects of the film. There are many ways to obtain media interest without perfunctory mailings of press releases about a movie and its stars to the usual publications.

The publicity wheel for a motion picture is often set in motion during preproduction. At that time the producer or director calls on a PR firm to plan a campaign. During this stage the firm might advise the producer on the selection of a unit publicist and unit photographer, who will supply the agency with vital publicity materials. While the movie is in production, the unit publicist and photographer are in close contact with the PR firm.

The unit publicist writes bios of important cast and crew members, production notes, and brief features for wire services and newspapers. The unit photographer is there to take still photos of the production. The PR firm may hire a special-assignment photographer also. Special-assignment photographers do one-day shoots and are often celebrities in their own right. Their fees are high, but the publicity that may result from their work is extremely valuable.

During principal photography the PR firm might invite entertainment writers from popular and important magazines to the set. Interviews take place during the production to allow publications to cover a film at the time it is released. Occasionally a set will be closed for the entire production, but even then the PR firm might open it up to a key journalist if it believes the film will get a lot of publicity from the writer's story or syndicated article.

Correspondents from network morning programs are sometimes invited to sets to tape interviews which may ultimately become multi-part pieces. One part may air while the picture is in production, the others when the movie is about to be released. Sometimes arrangements are made for those TV shows on the set during principal photography to get first rights to booking the stars as live studio guests when the movie comes out.

During postproduction the PR firm begins to circulate preliminary information about the film to newspaper columnists and editors. The period during which the PR firm wants to create the most excitement about a film is the few weeks prior to release. The firm makes its heaviest promotional push at this time. Press kits are sent out to appropriate journalists and editors, and arrangements are made to have the stars and principal filmmakers appear as guests on talk shows. The momentum should build in the two-week period prior to release, peaking in the last few days before the film opens. This momentum must be sustained during the initial two weeks after release to help the movie succeed.

Anywhere from a few days to weeks prior to the release of the film, the PR company holds screenings for movie reviewers and journalists. "All media" screenings are not held for all new releases. Sometimes it is more desirable to build excitement about a film with promotional articles.

Once a film opens, PR firms also serve as spokespersons to the media for their clients. If a newsworthy event occurs, they issue statements on their clients' behalf.

A large entertainment-oriented PR firm might have film, television, music, and corporate divisions. PR firms obtain new clients mostly because of successful past ventures. Firms are always on the lookout for companies that advertise a lot. A new or expanding company might be convinced that money invested in public relations would be well spent. PR firms charge flat fees for a minimum period of time when retained temporarily.

PUBLIC-RELATIONS DEPARTMENT, TELEVISION STATION. *See* **Independent Television Station.**

RATINGS, MOTION PICTURES. *See* **Film Rating System.**

RATINGS SERVICE. *See* **Audience Measurement Services.**

RATINGS AND SHARES, TELEVISION. Commercial television is a business, and profit is the bottom line. Because commercial television earns its income from advertisers, shows that draw the largest audiences are the most profitable.

Audience measurement services such as A. C. Nielsen and Arbitron measure audience size in ratings and shares. On a national scale, a rating is the percentage of all TV households in the United States viewing a particular program. On the local scale, a rating is the percentage of all TV households in a broadcasting area viewing a program.

In calculating either rating, it is necessary to know the approximate number of TV households in the area. In 1990 there were approximately 92.1 million TV households in the United States. A 20 rating meant that 20 percent of 92,100,000 TV households, or 18,420,000 homes, were actually tuned in to that specific show. Each rating point represented 921,000 TV households. In measuring the percentage of houses using television (HUT), a home is counted only once, regardless of how many TV sets there are there.

A share is the percentage of homes that have television sets turned on that are turned to a specific program.

For the week ending April 29, 1990, the top show had a national rating of 22 and a share of 34. This meant that 22 percent of all TV households in the United States were viewing that show. Of all the homes in which the sets were on, 34 percent were tuned in to that show at 8 P.M. on Sunday, April 29, 1990.

Ratings and shares are quantitative measurements and are not meant to evaluate the artistic merit of a show. Also, low ratings do not always guarantee that a program will be pulled off the air. Dinnertime news programs of network affiliates are often topped in the ratings by local independent fare. The programming philosophy of a station usually encourages a variety of shows, and the station tries to reach different audiences at different times. An advertiser may buy commercial time on a particular program understanding that the number of viewers is going to be low but realizing it will reach a specific audience.

See also **Audience Measurement Service.**

READER. A reader evaluates the commercial potential of scripts, treatments, proposals, and ideas for development into motion pictures, miniseries, television movies, television series, or television programs. Readers are employed by motion picture studios, independent filmmakers, television production companies, and networks.

A reader, or story analyst, represents the first hurdle that submitted material must clear to be considered for development. The reader serves to ease the burden of the story editor, who must sift through the huge quantity of material received by producers. The reader submits reports on incoming proposals to the story editor.

Some areas of the country have unions for story analysts. To become a member of the IATSE Local 854 in California, one must work for at least thirty days for a company that is a signatory to the union's contract.

See also **Story Department.**

RELEASE. A release is a distribution of a film for theatrical exhibition or video consumption. A first-run release is a film that is playing in theaters and has never been released before. A second-run release has been released previously and is again being distributed to theaters.

RELEASE FORM. A release form is a document signed by a screenwriter promising not to bring legal action against the party reading a script or proposal. It is common practice for firms that produce movies, miniseries, and TV programs—motion picture studios, television production companies, and the networks—to refuse to read a script, treatment, synopsis, or proposal without an accompanying signed release form (unless it is submitted by a reputable agent or writer). This serves to protect the company from any copyright infringement lawsuits. Often writers submit scripts or proposals that are similar to projects that a company has in production or development.

RELEASE PRINT. A release print is a copy of a film that is distributed to theaters for exhibition. A release print is made from the **final cut.**

REMAKE. A remake is a new, reworked version of a film previously produced. Remakes are usually characterized by updated dialogue, characters, setting, design, and themes. Classic motion pictures are prime candidates for remakes.

Motion picture studios produce remakes primarily to cash in on old film ideas already proven successful, while spending as little money as possible on development.

Some old TV series are redone as one- or two-hour specials several years after their initial run. These try to be as faithful as possible to the original production, using the same ensemble of leading actors, with the exceptions of those who are deceased. People who saw the series in its first run may not only feel a wave of nostalgia in seeing a show that ran ten or twenty or more years ago but may tune in just out of curiosity—to see how the original actors and actresses look at the present. These factors are duly considered by television executives in approving an updated special, or revival.

REP FIRM. A rep firm is a company that sells commercial airtime to advertising agencies on behalf of television stations. Rep firms are retained by both network affiliates and independent TV stations. As a matter of practice, rep firms represent only one station per market. Most rep firms have ten or more offices located in major United States cities, which try to sell airtime to local advertising agencies.

National advertisers generally reach consumers by either buying time on network stations or buying spots in individual markets around the United States.

When an advertising agency calls a rep firm and expresses interest in one or more of the rep firm's markets, the agency stipulates the criteria by which it wants to buy, which correspond to demographics and ratings points. Ratings reports provide the ad agencies with the demographics of a show's audience. A rep-firm salesperson finds the best spots for a commercial in the requested market. This information is presented to the agency, which most likely will consult other rep firms selling station time in the market. Business rarely goes completely to one rep firm. After an order is placed and a price settled upon, the rep firm reports to the station for confirmation. For their services, rep firms earn commissions.

See also **Ratings and Shares, Television.**

RE-RECORDING MIXER. A re-recording mixer does the final mix-down of a film's sound track during postproduction. He or she electronically fixes the audio by equalizing and filtering out bad or unwanted noise and blends the dialogue, sound effects, and music sound tracks. The re-recording mixer works in a recording studio on a mixing console.

After the editors cut the **dailies** and synchronize them with the picture, the separate sound tracks for each film reel are put on playback machines (35-mm or 16-mm) in the dubbing room and run interlocked with the picture. The editor gives the re-recording mixer a cue sheet which lets the engineer know where each track should be heard. The mixer must consult the cue sheet to make sure the sound tracks appear on cue. Volume levels are determined by the director and the mixer together.

RERUN. A rerun is a television show aired after its initial broadcast. Reruns earn residuals for the leading actors. Reruns of network programs constitute a substantial part of programming on independent television stations. Networks often show reruns of continuing series during the summer months, to stabilize the show's audience until the new fall season. Dramas that were hits during the regular season frequently fail to attract significant numbers of viewers in reruns. Sitcoms, on the other hand, generally draw large audiences in reruns.

See also Independent Television Station; Off-Network Programming; Residuals; Television Season.

RESEARCH DEPARTMENT, TELEVISION STATION. *See* Independent Television Station.

RESIDUALS. Residuals are payments to contributing actors, directors, and writers of motion pictures, television shows, and commercials that are reused in supplemental markets (television, videocassettes, etc.). Residual formulas are complex and vary according to the market. Residuals are covered by the contracts of the Screen Actors Guild, the Directors Guild of America, and the Writers Guild of America.

REVENGE MOVIE. *See* Film Genres.

REVIVAL. *See* Remake.

REVIVAL HOUSE. A revival house is a movie theater that exclusively plays vintage films. Prior to the advent of videocassettes, revival houses flourished, but with many classic films available now on videocassette, the number of revival houses has dwindled. Unlike first-run theaters, revival houses must pay for their own advertising.

ROMANCE MOVIE. *See* Film Genres.

ROTOSCOPE. *See* Animation.

ROUGH CUT. *See* First Cut.

RUNNING TIME. The running time is the length of a film (usually measured in minutes). Feature motion pictures commonly range in length from 70 minutes to 120 minutes.

RUSHES. *See* Dailies.

SAFETY STANDARDS. Filmmaking is an artistic endeavor, the success of which is predicated on many factors. But achieving a genuine sense of realism on the screen with respect to action and setting is absolutely vital. Both the integrity and credibility of motion pictures are based to a large extent on how well action events are simulated and, to this end, actors and crew alike engage in real-life derring-do: filming in the air, underwater, on mountains, on top of tall buildings, on remote islands, and in jungles; employing breathtaking stunts on land, water, and air; shooting with special effects such as bombings and simulated atmospheric conditions. To accomplish these shots vehicles, equipment and materials such as airplanes, helicopters, boats, trains, racing cars, parachutes, cranes, and dynamite are often used.

It is the concern of the motion picture and television industries to prevent the reckless endangerment of casts and crews for productions to adhere to reasonable standards of safety. The Industrywide Labor Management Committee, consisting of officials from the Alliance of Motion Picture and Television Producers, the Screen Actors Guild, the Directors Guild of America, and the Screen Extras Guild, was formed in the early 1980s to issue rules, standards, and safety procedures regarding the use of dangerous materials, the preparation and use of equipment, and the execution of stunts. The first bulletin was issued on January 20, 1983.

State laws and union contractual provisions govern certain aspects of filmmaking such as employment of minors and stunt work. Depending on the nature of shooting, other law-enforcement or government agencies may have jurisdiction regarding the use of airplanes, boats, or trains. Perhaps the most important barometer of reckless endangerment is common sense. The director, who usually bears the ultimate responsibility for safety on the set, should put the welfare of the cast and crew above all.

SALES DEPARTMENT, TELEVISION STATION. *See* **Independent Television Station.**

SANDBAG. *See* **Grip Equipment.**

SCENIC ARTIST. A scenic artist creates backdrops and other background paintings for a motion picture or television set.

Usually exteriors are shot on location and interiors in a studio on a sound stage. The scenic artist paints the scenery of the location to ensure a realistic view through a window or out an open door.

Enlarged photographs of an actual location also may be used as background scenery, in which case a cameraman photographs a location and the picture is blown up on translucent film and pieced together. But because locations called for in scripts do not necessarily exist, scenic artists are very much needed.

SCIENCE-FICTION MOVIE. *See* **Film Genres.**

SCREEN ACTORS GUILD (SAG). The Screen Actors Guild is a labor union that represents actors, stunt players, singers, and airplane pilots employed in making motion pictures, filmed television programs, and filmed commercials. SAG has industry-wide agreements with the Alliance of Motion Picture and Television Producers providing for minimum working conditions for members who are employed by producers represented by the Alliance.

The Screen Actors Guild was founded in June 1933 as a result of austere employment conditions in the motion picture industry. Work days were long; there was often an insufficient number of hours separating the end of one work day and the beginning of another; and actors worked long hours without breaks for meals. In addition, there was no industry establishment of overtime compensation or premium payment for weekend or holiday work. Compensation for travel time for location work was at the producer's discretion. It was common for actors to work six-day weeks and earn less than seventy dollars. This wasn't the first attempt of film actors to band together to create a union, but it was the first successful one. Two years after forming, SAG affiliated with the American Federation of Labor.

Through the years, SAG has collectively bargained for better contractual terms for actors in motion pictures and television. In commercial television's infancy, SAG successfully negotiated for residuals for actors for reruns of television films in the United States, and later, for actors to earn compensation for theatrical motion pictures aired on television and for theatrical and television motion pictures released in ancillary forms such as pay television and videocassette. SAG also regularly conducts audits of production companies. The union offers qualified members a comprehensive program of pension and health and welfare benefits.

There are two ways to join SAG: by doing an on-camera speaking line in a movie or commercial under SAG's jurisdiction, or by being a member of a sister entertainment union (such as AFTRA, Equity, AGMA, or AGVA) for at least one year or longer and having done principal work under that union's jurisdiction. There is an initiation fee and semiannual dues.

SCREEN TEST. A screen test is a short film shot taken of an actor to determine whether the actor has the screen presence that a director is looking for. Only actors contending for substantial roles are given screen tests. Screen tests are also done to observe how costumes, wigs, makeup, and special effects will look on film.

SCREENING. A screening is the showing of a film or part of a film, usually for a professional or nonpaying audience. There are different types of screenings. Dailies are screened by the director to observe a day's shooting. Pre-release versions of films are screened by studios to determine whether any fine-tuning is needed before the films are commercially distributed. An audience screening is one in which people in test markets watch new films and give written feedback (*see* **Preview Audience**). Screenings are also held for testing pilot television shows. The feedback of audiences is used by network executives in determining which new programs to air and which not to.

SCREENWRITER. The screenwriter may be described as one who writes, in dialogue form and with limited screen directions, stories that lend themselves to cinematic depiction. Screenplays are essentially blueprints for a cast and crew to transform the written words and ideas of the screenwriter into cinematic life. A script is, in fact, a master plan that goes through a development process in the studio system, is broken down by the cast and crew during preproduction, and becomes the basis for shooting during production. Because making a movie is a collaborative process, everybody reads the **script** and uses it as a launching pad for injecting their own creativity.

For the screenwriter, it starts with an idea. Some writers convert the idea into an outline or treatment to gauge the interest of studios, producers, directors, and others before creating a full-blown screenplay, others proceed directly to penning the screenplay. For neophyte writers, the latter is often necessary to open the doors. A screenplay should generally envelope a fresh story line (or workable approach if based on an actual event), plots and subplots, interesting characters, and engaging dialogue.

Screenwriters basically work in several ways. Some are under contract to studios in an arrangement called an overall deal. In this situation all the writer's output—ideas and scripts—goes to the studios. The screenwriters do not present their ideas elsewhere except in possible turnaround deals, where the writers are free to pursue their ideas or scripts elsewhere if rejected by their studios. In this arrangement the studios have a certain degree of exclusivity over the writers.

Another way screenwriters work is to write a script on *spec* and have their agent sell it. A studio could option the script—pay a sum of money to secure the rights to a property for a limited period of time against payment in full if it exercises its option—or make a complete buyout. Buyout prices are higher than option prices, and where multiple studios are interested the agent could sell the script to the highest bidder.

A third way screenwriters work is by going to a producer or studio and pitching an idea for a project. The writer presents the idea to be as exciting as possible to interest the producer or studio in developing it. Conversely, ideas are sometimes generated by studios for development by writers. A studio, for example, might circulate a note to agents saying they are looking for a writer to develop a particular concept. It could initially sound bland but be one the studio thinks it could market successfully if developed creatively. The agents present the studio's concept to their writers and those interested in pursuing it cook up ideas and make appointments for presenting their ideas to the studios.

SCRIPT. A script is the text of a television broadcast or motion picture and is the blueprint for shooting a production. The director and actors use the script as the basis for their own interpretation of the material.

The script the writer delivers is called the *master-scene script* and usually goes through many revisions. The master-scene script contains no descriptions for camera angles or types of shots. The director inserts these directions. The final script that is released to the cast and crew is called the **shooting script.**

SCRIPT BREAKDOWN. A script breakdown is the analysis of a script to determine what is needed for shooting each scene. Because scenes are often shot out of sequence, script breakdowns enable the cast and crew to be prepared to shoot any scene at any time. A script breakdown is used to determine the shooting schedule, the sequence of scenes, and what props and equipment are needed. Script breakdowns are made by the director, the leading actors, the unit production manager, the script supervisor, the production designer, the property master, the costume designer, the wardrobe supervisor, the location manager, the key grip, the gaffer, the stunt coordinator, the sound effects specialist, and all other department heads. Breaking down a script is an essential means for preparing for a role or job and is one of the first tasks done by actors and crew members after being hired.

SCRIPT RESEARCHER. A script researcher verifies the accuracy of material in a script, and also checks for potential copyright infringement or defamation.

SCRIPT SUPERVISOR. A script supervisor is responsible for keeping track of details for continuity in a film or television production. In the labyrinthine process of making films, television, movies, and miniseries, it is potentially easy to lose sight of any of the innumerable details and their consistency from one scene to the next. Wardrobe, hair, makeup, set design, and prop people attend to their areas of responsibility, but the script supervisor devotes last-resort attention to all of these areas. The script supervisor also monitors the action and dialogue for continuity and accuracy.

Consider, for example, a wide shot of an actor holding a glass of water in his right hand. In the close-up shot of the scene (filmed later), does the actor forget to hold up the glass of water or is he holding it in his left hand? Is the water at the same level in the close-up as in the wide shot? Are the actor's fingers holding the glass in the same position as in the wide shot? Is the actress who is walking out of a scene moving camera left to camera right, then walking into the next scene also camera left to camera right (correct), or is she coming into the next scene camera right to camera left (wrong)? Working closely with the director, the script supervisor breaks down the script, prepares print logs during production, times the scenes that are shot, and makes sure the actors get the correct script changes.

During preproduction the script supervisor does a time and continuity breakdown, taking apart the screenplay, scene by scene or day by day, to check the connections between scenes. It is not uncommon for a screenwriter to lose track of where screen days begin in the process of rewriting a screenplay, and the script supervisor must correct any conflicting details at this time. While doing the breakdown, the script supervisor also divides the script into its individual scenes and writes the names of the characters, the props, the wardrobes, the locations, whether shooting is interior or exterior, whether it is day or night, what has to match for the scene, and what day of the movie the scene is in. From this breakdown, a time line for the movie is drafted.

Because scenes are often shot out of sequence, the script supervisor also must ensure continuity between screen days. A character who is badly hurt on one screen day shouldn't appear healed by the next screen day. The script supervisor should be able to look up any scene and find out its screen day and the important continuity details for that scene. Copies of the continuity breakdown and the time line are distributed to key people involved in the production. Some script supervisors break down a screenplay by sets, as well as by consecutive scenes (as the screenplay is written). They list all the scenes that play in each set and whether they are interior or exterior, day or night, and what screen day they are in. This enables a script supervisor to readily determine whether the crew has scheduled all the scenes that are supposed to be shot on a particular set, before the set is torn down or the cast and crew move on to another set, or even to see if all the day scenes on a particular set are done before relighting is done for night. The script supervisor's breakdown is actually a backup check for the **assistant director.**

The script supervisor also must estimate the length of time each scene will play, and calculate an approximate screen time for the film. This is done to ensure that the master time on the script that is shot each day is relatively close to the amount of time desired. Timing is especially important for television because the finished product must be a certain length. When shooting TV movies, directors prefer to have 10 to 15 percent more footage than actually needed. Timing out a production is important because overshooting can cause the production to go over budget, and undershooting can leave the director with unresolved gaps.

The script supervisor will compare the estimated times for the scenes with the master times, and if there is a serious difference between them—for example, twenty minutes more master time halfway through shooting—the script supervisor will confer with the director. Most directors, after two or three weeks of shooting, will ask the script supervisor how the times compare. A producer might request a script supervisor to report when the master time exceeds the estimated times beyond a certain limit, such as fifteen minutes, or the producer might even request a weekly report of master time versus estimated time.

To time out a script, the script supervisor reads and acts out each scene. Action scenes, such as car chases or ones involving riding on horseback, are difficult to get a precise timing on because they have to be imagined. Usually, however, the script supervisor will confer with the director to find out how much screen time is wanted for the various action scenes. Even the opening of the film, when the credits roll, has to be timed out.

The script supervisor tries to determine the approximate length of each scene and the total running time of the film. When scenes are filmed, they run longer than they will appear in the edited film. When shooting a car pulling up to a hotel, for example, the director will hold on it much longer than the amount of time it will probably be shown in the final cut. Most of that footage will end up on the cutting room floor. But this is done for safety purposes. During filming it is not known what part of the footage will be used, so when calculating master time, the script supervisor must estimate this.

The script supervisor will submit a list of the times, broken down scene by scene for the film. This might be typed up as "Estimated Timing of Screenplay," and it will include the date because scripts are constantly rewritten, creating changes in the timings. For a television movie or miniseries, the times will be broken down on an act-by-act basis.

The table on page 261 summarizes the many responsibilities of the script supervisor on the set, during production.

The job of script supervisor requires a good working knowledge of film production and writing. The best preparation is film school, followed by an apprenticeship with a professional script supervisor. Once enough experience is gained through working on non-union projects, the beginning script supervisor might be able to gain union membership.

SECOND-RUN FILM. *See* **Release.**

SEQUEL. Any film produced subsequent to another in which the same leading character (usually played by the same actor) is re-

Script Supervisor's Responsibilities

Responsibilities	Explanation
Monitors coverage.	Informs the director of any portion of the script not covered. On occasion, the script supervisor might suggest added coverage for a scene for the sake of continuity.
Runs through lines with the actors during rehearsals.	Listens to the actors go over their lines in rehearsals before shooting and corrects mistakes.
Follows dialogue during shooting.	Monitors actors' lines on the set while following the script to make sure the dialogue is correct. If actors change lines, they are corrected. If the director approves them, the changes must be noted.
Monitors action for continuity.	Ensures continuity in shooting the script. The script supervisor informs the director of inconsistencies in screen direction.
Times scenes.	Keeps track of master time that has been shot each day to make sure it is relatively close to the amount of time desired. (Each take is timed.)
Takes production notes.	Certain information is compiled at each day's end: how much of the script was covered on a given day, how many minutes of screen time have been shot to date, which scenes were shot, and how many pages of the script were shot. This report is handed in at the end of each shooting day. The assistant director uses it to complete the production report, which is then passed on to the unit production manager, producer, and executive producer.

Continued on next page

Continued from previous page

Responsibilities	**Explanation**
Prepares a print log, or *sync sheet*, for the editor.	Makes a list of every camera shot and every sound recording. Writes a brief description of each shot in the print log. Indicates the desired print takes during the course of photography and verifies these print takes with the camera assistant and with the sound mixer at the end of each day. This information is used by the editor in synchronizing the dailies.
Lines the script.	Indicates to the editor options in cutting. Every shot is diagrammed. If an actor is on camera for a particular scene, a straight line is made through the dialogue. If the person is off-camera, a wavy line is used.
Makes and fills in *opposite pages*.	The script is put in a looseleaf binder (its left margins are punched), and opposite each page the script supervisor inserts a form divided into several columns—remarks, timing of each take, camera roll, sound roll, shot description, screen direction, and lens—and then fills in notes pertaining to each. The opposite page contains continuity information on each shot of the movie. It is important to keep track of the continuity information if shooting of the scene is to be continued the next day, or if reshoots are necessary.

Continued on next page

Continued from previous page

Checks scenes and take numbers for slates.	The second assistant camera person physically changes the numbers, but the script supervisor, who provides this information, much watch to see that the proper slates appear on every take. The script supervisor also listens to make sure that the announcement of each take is correct.
Matches details.	The script supervisor records for the director certain movements of the actors for takes the director wants to print to enable matching in later takes.

prised. A sequel is basically a continuing adventure in the life of that character and is made because of the success of the original movie and any other sequels that may have been made. An audience has been established and a substantial portion of it—usually 50 percent to 70 percent—can be counted on to see the sequel; marketing and word-of-mouth might build onto this base audience.

Blockbusters commonly spawn sequels, which unfortunately often fall artistically short of their predecessors. Sequels often display more flash than substance and fail to exude the energy, creativity, and charisma of the original. Some seem to be made merely for the sake of cashing in on a proven product. Historically, sequels that have stayed faithful to the original concept have fared best at the box office.

Because of the potential financial bonanza it may reap for the studio and various profit participants, a sequel may even dictate the script to an extent, saving the life of a protagonist. (After all, you can't have a sequel if you kill the hero.) Roman numerals may be used to designate a sequel, or there may be a different title altogether, although succeeding titles usually reflect or capture the flavor of the earlier one.

SERIAL TELEVISION SHOW. A television serial is a series with episodes linked by a continuing story line and recurring characters. Both daytime and nighttime soap operas are serials. Episodes of serials end with one or more characters facing difficult or seemingly insurmountable problems (*see* **Cliffhanger**). This is a commercial ploy designed to lure viewers to tune in to the next episode.

SET. A set is a fabricated unit of scenery in a studio or a location where shooting is taking place. A set on location will be dressed up with props, and there may or may not be construction involved. A set in a studio has already been constructed or will be specially constructed, and has to be decorated accordingly. An exterior set is an outdoor set, an interior set is indoors. A set is essentially any area against which the action takes place.

SET DECORATOR. The set decorator is in charge of the dressing of the set. He or she supervises the placement of furniture, chairs, rugs, pictures, and other props so that the set captures the vision of the art director or production designer. The set decorator is responsible for all internal dressings, such as those that make up a living room, a doctor's office, or a hotel room, and those for certain small exteriors such as a porch.

For location shooting requiring only a small amount of set dressing, the contract of IATSE Local 44 in Hollywood stipulates that a property master may handle the duties of the set decorator provided that, prior to shooting, the arrangement is discussed between a representative of the producer and the business manager of the local union.

SET DESIGNER. A set designer prepares layouts and working drawings that are used for building a set. While the art director creates the conceptual look of a set, the set designer executes plans for the actual construction. Set designers are the architectural draftsmen of the motion picture industry.

SET DRESSER. The set dresser takes props acquired by the **set dec-**

orator and places them on the sets. He or she arranges furniture, lays carpeting, hangs drapes and curtains, and puts up lighting fixtures.

One or more set dressers (though not necessarily including the head dresser) will normally be present during shooting. The dressers know how everything is arranged on a set, and when a scene is re-shot, they know where all the props go and what can be moved and what cannot. Consider a scene shot on location at an actual restaurant. A preexisting agreement may stipulate what objects in the restaurant may be moved or handled and what must remain intact. Continuing with the example, the dressers have placed a number of props in the restaurant and a scene is shot from one side. To do the reverse-angle shot, the original side has to be taken apart—that is, all the tables have to come out—so that the camera, dolly, and other equipment can go in there. The other side, then, has to be assembled as the original side was. In such cases, the dressers function to disassemble and reassemble sets exactly as they were. The crew of set dressers is sometimes called the swing gang, and the head of the group is called the lead person.

A lighting unit that is seen in the picture is usually assembled or acquired by the property department, of which the set dresser is a part. (If it is rigged for a special effect, however, it would be built by the special effects people.) Any lighting effect for production (behind-the-scenes) purposes is handled by the electricians.

See also **Property Master.**

SET PAINTER. The set painter paints the sets for a film or television production, as well as performs other tasks such as wood graining and aging and distressing of materials. The set painter often tries to make objects or sets look like what they are not—for example, making wood look like concrete or painting a set to look like a dilapidated tenement.

SETUP. A setup is each new camera position in production and the action to be shot. There may be several setups for one scene.

SHOOTING SCHEDULE. A shooting schedule is a plan of when and where the scenes of a film are to be shot. Important factors in making up a shooting schedule are the budget, availability of the leading actors, and restrictions on filming in certain locations. Customarily, exterior shooting is done first so that if inclement weather prevents filming outdoors, the cast and crew can move indoors and do interior shots.

The shooting schedule is initially mapped out on a **stripboard.** During production the shooting schedule may be revised if the director is not satisfied with the shooting of a scene, or an actor is ill, etc.

SHOOTING SCRIPT. The Directors Guild of America, in its Basic Agreement, defines a "completed shooting script" as "that script (not necessarily the final shooting script) which the employer intends to use for photography of a motion picture, subject to changes such as acting, technical and/or staging problems or those with respect to weather or other emergencies." The Guild's Basic Agreement provides that the employer (producer) of a television series must furnish a completed shooting script to a director at least one day prior to the commencement of the director's preparation period, and that for each day its delivery is delayed there shall be another day added to the director's preparation period. For network primetime shows (excluding pilots), the Basic Agreement provides that directors "shall be afforded actual preparation time of no less than three days for a one-half hour program, seven days for an hour program and fifteen days for a two-hour or longer program."

See also **Script.**

SHOP CRAFTSMAN. Working from blueprints made by the art director, the shop craftsman and assistants construct the set for a television production. Objects they build might include walls, doors, furniture, and signs. The shop craftsmen do not actually erect the set, however, but supervise the grips, who do the actual physical labor.

In filmmaking the building of sets is supervised by a construction coordinator, who is assisted by a construction foreman. On some smaller budgeted films, only a construction foreman is used.

The shop craftsman is hired by the production designer or the art director anywhere from four to eight weeks before principal photography commences.

SHOT/SCENE/SEQUENCE. Shot, scene, and sequence are interrelated terms whose meanings or applications are somewhat nebulous and which depend upon individual interpretations and individual circumstances. Generally, a shot is an uninterrupted filming or taping that starts when the director says, "Action" and ends when the director says "Cut." A series of shots constitute a scene. A series of scenes create a sequence.

If there is action that takes place in a kitchen, living room, and dining room of a house, would that be one scene or one sequence? Some people might call the entire action that takes place in one location a scene. Others might say all the action that takes place in the kitchen is one scene, in the living room another, in the dining room a third, and that the kitchen–living room–dining room scenes collectively form a sequence. The reference or term *shot* may be applicable here also if the action is captured on a single, uninterrupted piece of film or videotape.

Some people do shot breakdowns and consider them to be entire scenes in and of themselves. A shooting script might specify *close-up*, *medium shot*, and *long shot*, and each of these might be construed as a scene. The unit production manager might do a strip on the stripboard for each of these shooting directions.

SHOWCASE RUN. *See* **Premiere/Showcase Run.**

SITCOM. A sitcom, or situation comedy, is a series of half-hour television shows in which the characters get into predicaments which they spend the rest of the show trying to get out of. The situations themselves function as frameworks into which comedic dialogue and actions can be stuffed. Sitcoms in recent years have attempted to deal with more serious and sensitive subject matter than they did in the past.

Some traits common to traditional sitcoms are simple settings, characters to whom large audiences can relate, predicaments which ordinary people find themselves in, an overall tone of cheerfulness, domestic situations where the characters are related or close friends, running gags, expressions and *schtick* repeatedly used, and happy endings.

The sitcom is a staple of American television programming. Though it has suffered an occasional lull (with industry soothsayers even pronouncing it defunct), it has enjoyed greater and more continual popularity as a group than perhaps any other form of programming. Indeed, the television sitcom is indigenous as an American art form, as jazz is in the world of music.

Why is the sitcom embraced so affectionately by the masses? There are many reasons: It is simple, light, and mirthful in content; it pokes fun at ourselves in a good-natured way; it makes us laugh; we enter somebody else's living room; everything turns out fine; comedy is a universally popular form of entertainment; the characters and situations are realistic enough so that people can identify with them but escapist enough so that the sitcom is a flight of fantasy for its audience; the characters are likeable; there is little if any preaching; it is brief enough so as to keep the attention of viewers; it generally appeals to all ages and demographic groups; it may be considered family entertainment. Of course, as with all TV shows, intrinsic qualities such as the appeal of the stars or premise of the series are contributing factors also.

SNEAK PREVIEW. A sneak preview is an exhibition of a new motion picture prior to its official opening. The sneak preview is a marketing device intended to create interest in a film. Studios and distributors use sneak previews to take advantage of word-of-mouth advertising, because if sneak-preview viewers enjoy a film, they will recommend it to others.

Television series also have sneak previews. Prior to debuting in its regular time slot, a show may be aired at a different time in order to introduce viewers to the series and attract those who ordinarily might not tune in at the regularly scheduled time.

SOAP OPERA. *See* **Television Programming Genres.**

SOUND, POSTPRODUCTION. Once principal photography for film is completed, the sound must be transferred onto a sprocketed magnetic film and synchronized to the picture from the quarter-inch reel-to-reel tapes recorded during filming. Then sound effects and music must be re-recorded onto a three-, four- or six-track master. The final mix is then transferred to an optical sound track from which release prints are made.

The quarter-inch audiotapes are delivered to a sound transfer company, where they are run through a playback tape machine linked to a resolver, which matches the synchronization signal on the tape to the speed of sprocketed magnetic film to which the sound must be transferred. Any necessary filtering, equalization, or other processing also may be done at this point.

Next the sprocketed magnetic film is synchronized with the picture by matching it to where the clapstick hits. Then, take by take, a reel of film and its corresponding audio track is made. The reels are then viewed by the director and editor to determine which to use during editing.

Detailed sound track work now begins. The **dialogue editor** listens to the dialogue sound track to determine if the pickup (sound quality) is satisfactory. Actors may need to re-record certain lines in a sound studio if the pickup is not good. The assistant sound editor edits out pops, clicks, director cues, and background noise for sound track consistency. The **sound-effects editor** edits in special effects such as gunshots or cricket chirps. A **Foley artist** records any additional sound effects necessary. And the **music editor** notes scene times for the composer.

Then *interlock* screenings are held where the director, editors, and recording engineers check the separate tracks as they will appear in the mix. Usually, several interlock screenings are required to examine dialogue, music, and effects separately. Then an interlock is held of all the elements together, to see how they blend.

After all the audio tracks—dialogue, effects, and music—are edited to the director's satisfaction, the tracks are ready for mixing.

Production sound is placed on one track, sound effects on another, and music on a third. The remaining tracks are free for other purposes. In documentary films an additional track is allocated for voice-overs. Many features are in stereo and require left, right, center, and surround tracks.

After mixing is completed, another interlock is held to check the sound track before making the **answer print.** The 35-mm full-coat mix (which consists of mixed down tracks) then is transferred to a 35-mm optical sound track, which is developed and sent to a laboratory to be matched with the picture negative.

See also **Film Editing.**

SOUND-EFFECTS EDITOR. The sound-effects editor decides, in conjunction with the editor and director, what sound effects to add to a film sound track, finds the effects, and records and synchronizes them. The kind of sound effects used depends, to a large extent, on the kind of mood the director wants to impart. For example, should a crowd be noisy or quiet? Should there be cricket sounds in a park or not? The sound-effects editor will be consistent in the use of effects. If a motor boat appears on screen, the engine roar will be heard until the boat stops or it is off the screen.

SOUND-EFFECTS LIBRARY. A sound-effects library maintains a collection of prerecorded sounds that can be used for a fee. The sounds are usually available on tape, compact disc, or 35-mm magnetic film.

SOUND RECORDING, PRODUCTION. The recording of sound on a movie set is handled by a small team consisting of a mixer, a boom operator, and, depending on the project, an assistant (a recordist, swing man, or second boom operator). The sound team records dialogue, sound effects, and background noise on a movie set.

Prior to principal photography, the unit production manager hires a mixer, who is in charge of sound on the set. On a set the mixer operates the recording equipment, the boom operator follows the actors with a long maneuverable arm holding the microphone called a boom, and the assistant keeps records and helps the other two with their work.

The mixer receives a **call sheet** each day of shooting and often does not know in advance how a director is going to cover the scenes, but by reading the script ahead of time, he or she is always prepared. Before shooting begins there is a **camera blocking** and then a rehearsal. During the blocking of a scene, the sound crew watches the action and decides how to cover it.

The mixer or recordist operates a portable reel-to-reel machine (a popular model is the Nagra) with quarter-inch-wide tape. A sync pulse, or electronic sprocket, is also recorded to ensure synchronization in postproduction. (In the past, sprocket-driven tape was used.) The sound often is recorded in mono. A mixing board, or console, with multiple microphone input channels is used so that the volume and quality of the sound recorded may be adjusted.

In location recording it is important to record the level and quality of the sound uniformly. The same scene may be covered at various angles (at different times), and if the microphone is a bit off each time, there could be inconsistencies in the sound.

On location the mixer also functions to keep the background levels of scenes consistent, in their various coverages. Background noise is normal to the ear, but if the levels keep changing with various cuts, then it becomes objectionable. Each scene may have different background noise, but because a single scene may be shot over a period of several days, the mixer must keep the level uniform for that scene.

For example, the boom microphone may be used to record close-up coverage of a scene on one day. The microphone will pick up and establish a certain background sound—such as a combination of playground chatter, bird chirpings, and traffic noise. Then a wide-angle shot may be done the next day with a wireless microphone. Since background noise would be lost, a boom would also be used to record background sounds to keep the ambience the same.

The mixer directs the boom operator to make adjustments to

balance the recording, such as bringing up the *gain* to get more background noise. Sometimes the sound on location does not come out well (for example, the ambient noise might be too loud for a successful track), and this will be corrected by dialogue replacement or looping during postproduction (*see* **Sound, Postproduction**). As a rule, however, the sound of any action that the camera sees is recorded.

Ambience is more controllable in a studio set than at an outdoor location. With soundproof walls and other elements reducing extraneous sounds, very little background noise permeates the microphone. The sound quality in a studio, consequently, will be better, though of course not all studios are acoustically well designed.

Sound is checked when the dailies are screened. If certain sounds do not come out right, they can be corrected during postproduction. The mixer is not involved in postproduction sound work.

Microphones must be kept out of the camera frame while remaining close enough to pick up optimal sound levels. The boom operator follows the actors with the boom microphone. A wireless (lavaliere) microphone pinned to the actor contains a transmitter that sends FM radio signals to a receiver. The quality of sound from a wireless microphone is not as good as that obtained from a boom microphone, but wireless microphones are invaluable during long shots. Since a panoramic view is seen during these shots, an overhead boom would be visible on film. Only when the director covers a scene from a close-up angle or with dolly moves can a microphone boom be used.

The mixer also decides which microphones are best for each shot. Commonly, highly directional microphones are used for booms. These microphones pick up sound in a narrow pattern and therefore require the boom operator to follow the scene closely.

Wild track is sound that is recorded during production without the camera rolling. For example, an entire scene can be shot, with all the coverage, and the mixer can find that one line or word did not record properly. He or she will ask to have that line wild from the actor—that is, just to have the actor say the line again without the camera rolling, without any picture. The actor will do the line over, with the same timing as he acted it out. The soundman may play back the original recording of it to help the actor get the tempo. This is all done on location. During postproduction, the editor will lay the line in with the rest of the dialogue. Certain effects such as car door slams, cars passing, light traffic, heavy traffic, water noises—indeed, any ambience seen by the camera—should be recorded wild by the sound crew to aid the postproduction editor.

The sound crew is also responsible for playback. Production scenes with music, dancing, and singing are rarely recorded live by the production mixer. The music is recorded at a sound studio. The pulse track (usually a sixty-cycle neopilot reference signal) is recorded with a transfer of the takes. The production sound crew then sets up a public address system, and the singer or musicians mime to the music and voice being played back. The sound crew records the section of music used in the particular scene on a separate tape machine. They also record clapstick snaps to aid the postproduction editor in lining up the picture with the original tracks.

Major film studios used to have sound departments which employed a staff of full-time soundmen. Today most sound people are freelancers. The best way to become a professional mixer is by getting jobs as a production assistant on low-budget films and making contacts.

SOUND TRACK ALBUM. A sound track album is a record, cassette tape, or CD containing music from a motion picture. For some movies the music is of a dramatic nature and serves to underscore the action. Others incorporate a collection of tunes from a certain era or genre which may be heard in the background or featured prominently over the action. Popular artists frequently are hired to write and perform songs for movies. A hit single or sound track album attracts more people to the theaters. Radio airplay is free advertising, not to mention a source of performance royalties for the writer and publisher. Some large studios are affiliated, through a corporate parent, with a record company, and record sales are simply another source of income for the corporation.

SPECIAL. *See* Television Programming Genres.

SPECIAL EFFECTS. Special effects are the simulation or creation of real and fantastic phenomena, occurrences, and events in motion pictures and television. While in some films special effects play a vital role, almost all motion pictures, dramas, and actions-adventure television shows use them to one extent or another.

Overseeing the planning, building, and execution of special effects is a coordinator. Not only a technician but a designer, the special-effects coordinator makes effects such as rain, fog, snow, or explosions to look many different ways. After being hired, the special-effects coordinator does a **script breakdown** to get a rough idea of the special effects to be used. The script often indicates where special effects are needed but usually offers only general descriptions.

In production meetings, the script is reviewed carefully by the special-effects coordinator, the director, and department heads. When a special effect is called for, the coordinator asks the director what exactly is desired. For example, if someone is shot with a gun, the coordinator will want to know if it is to be a regular bullet hit or a blood hit. If a blood hit, should there be a lot of blood or a little? And how many times should the coordinator be prepared to create the effect? The special-effects coordinator complies with the director's requests during production.

Special effects must be coordinated with other departments. If there are to be six takes of a bullet hit with blood spattering, the wardrobe and prop crews must be prepared to do the scene six times.

Special-effects people build devices in shops and install them on the sets. Construction often involves building breakaways—objects that will easily split, crack, burst, or shatter. For example, a door may be made of balsa wood and have part of its inside cut for a more spectacular effect when somebody crashes through it. An actor or stuntman who smashes into it may wear pads on his arms, elbows, hips, or knees as a safety precaution. Special-effects coordinators also are responsible for devices such as special dollies for moving shots, camera mounts that spin, or rigs that fly overhead from the ceiling of a set, enabling a camera to be suspended in midair.

Rain scenes may be shot when there is a thin drizzle or there is no rain at all by using water that is heavier than natural rain. Long pipes are mounted on stands as high as twenty or thirty feet to create a rain tower that can simulate rain in a large area. Tops of windows are rigged with small pipes to create a raining effect when viewed from the other side of the window. When rain is seen in films and television programs, there is back light or side light.

The illusion of snow is created with various materials depending upon the particular situation. Large rolls of cotton, called snow blankets, may be placed over lawns, bushes, and rooftops to simulate snow. Sprinkling bleached-white plastic flakes in front of the camera can make it seem as if it is snowing. Small fans may be used to blow the "snow" around and add to the realistic effects. Normally, objects are covered with cotton and the backgrounds are sprayed with a sudsy white foam. Fog can be simulated with an oil-cracker fogger, which operates on a bottle of compressed nitrogen mixed with oil.

For fires, a special-effects department can rig a building or house with pipes, pans, and ducts to make fire come out of certain windows and smoke out of others. Special-effects crews usually coordinate these effects by walkie-talkie. The coordinator cues the crew members in a prepared sequence to simulate a fire's deteriorating effects.

A simulated bullet wound may be created by hooking up a tiny explosive to the area where the character appears to get shot. The explosive is attached to a wire running down the leg to a striker board with a battery. When the charge is detonated, it explodes a little sac of fake blood, commonly made of corn syrup and coloring. If an actor is to be hit by several bullets, a number of explosive charges are rigged up to an automated firing board. In scenes involving special effects that are potentially dangerous, a **stuntman** substitutes for the actor.

Usually a special-effects company is contracted to do the work. They are chosen carefully, based on reputation and experience.

With features costing millions of dollars, a producer cannot afford to hire someone (or a company) who is not adept in this complex area.

Liability insurance for a special-effects company is very expensive. Special-effects companies often request that studios add the company onto the studio's umbrella policy (for additional insurance). This practice covers the special-effects house should someone be killed or seriously injured on the set as a result of a special effect.

In certain states a pyrotechnics license is needed to create fires and explosions for films and TV programs. Special-effects people also may need licenses to own guns, even if they are rigged for theatrical purposes. In some jurisdictions, motion picture special-effects licenses covering explosions and smoke effects can be obtained.

Creatures and monsters are designed and fabricated by special makeup effects (FX) artists, who are hired according to their specialties. The chief FX artist employs other specialists to help carry out the work.

The FX artist begins a job by reading a script and meeting with the director to discuss creative possibilities and the amount of pre-production time needed to enact them. The FX artist next submits sketches of the intended effect to the director. The effect is then fine-tuned by the director and FX artist until a compromise is made. At this point, small sculptures are made for size, relation, and detail reference. When a crew is hired sculptors are enlisted first because the actual construction begins with preparing casts and armatures on which sculpting will be done.

When sculpting is completed, the FX artist employs mold makers to make precision molds of the sculptures, sturdy enough to withstand many different types of construction materials. Fiberglass (polyester resin) is used to construct molds for skulls, arms, legs, torsos, and other large models because it is light and durable. Smaller molds are made of stone (Ultra Cal).

When the molds are dried and cleaned, a special release agent such as stearic acid is applied to the inside of the mold to allow the latex foam used for the models to separate without tearing. Foam technicians then run foam through the mold until a usable piece is obtained.

Using cables, a mechanic can rig a molded skull to simulate human expressions. Radio-controlled servomotors are used in situations where it is not practical to use cables.

The foam skin is then painted and hair is inserted. Each strand of hair is punched into the foam skin with an instrument resembling an inverted Y. The finished skin is next glued onto the skull in a manner that ensures unimpeded mechanical movement. Then, before it is brought to the set, a test run of the creature moving is often done on videotape. On the shooting set, technicians assist the FX artist in operating the creature.

SPINOFF. A spinoff is a television series inspired by characters from a preexisting series. The major character of a spinoff is usually a supporting character from the earlier series who was so well received that the television studio has decided to capitalize on the character's popularity. Given the popularity of the character on the show, plus an existing audience, a spinoff has an easier time attracting viewers in a new season than a completely new and original series. Thus, the spinoff is a safe addition to a network lineup, containing few of the risks that accompany new ideas.

In a spinoff, the character has the same name and basic personality, but the show has a different story line than its predecessor. Occasionally a character from the former show (if it is still running) may make a guest appearance or the spinoff character may appear on the former series as a form of cross-promotion.

SPORTS SHOW. *See* **Television Programming Genres.**

SPY MOVIE. *See* **Film Genres.**

STAND-IN. A stand-in is a substitute, usually an **extra,** for an actor. Stand-ins are used during **camera blocking** when lighting adjustments have to be made. In rehearsals, which are observed by the stand-ins, a scene is blocked by the actors. The stand-ins later are called in to run through the scenes for the cameramen, a practice that rescues the actors from the monotony of running through a scene just for the lighting to be set up. Stand-ins are not filmed or videotaped.

See also **Double.**

STAR. *See* **Actor.**

STEP DEAL. A step deal is an arrangement in which a screenwriter is hired to write an outline, treatment, and script for a producer. Each is subject to approval before the next is written. If any of these are rejected by the producer, the writer goes no further on the project. Step deals enable producers to gauge a writer's ability without having to pay up front for a script to be written.

STOCK FOOTAGE LIBRARY. A stock footage library is a company that licenses the film and tape libraries of motion picture studios, networks, television stations, and individual photographers. The inventory of stock footage libraries is catalogued in card catalogues, books, or on computers. When a customer has decided on particular production footage, the library makes a duplicate print on videotape or film.

Licensing fees are based on footage and type of use. Stock footage libraries are also known as film archives.

STOP-MOTION ANIMATION. *See* **Animation.**

STORY ANALYST. *See* **Reader.**

STORY DEPARTMENT. Story departments of independent motion picture production companies screen and consider scripts, treatments, magazine articles, and books for development into motion pictures.

Scripts that are received by an independent production company are first logged in. A reader then evaluates the script and writes a reader's report. If the reader recommends the script, a story editor, development director, or creative-affairs staffer will read it. If approved at each level of hierarchy, the project goes into development. Before reviewing unsolicited materials, most production companies require a writer to sign a **release form.** Story editors prefer to work with screenwriters' agents because agented work is generally of a high caliber, and because agents actively search for new talent.

Because it is desirable to acquire the film rights to books before they are published, story editors regularly meet with writers and literary agents. While production companies are taking a risk by contracting for a book adaptation prior to the book's publication, the fact that the book is under option with a film producer might encourage the publisher to spend more money on marketing, advertising, and publicity (*see* **Adaptations.**).

Independent production companies usually have weekly meetings in which they discuss material recommended within the company for consideration. Attending these meetings are story editors and the director of development or vice-president of business affairs. From these meetings a list of rejected scripts is compiled (these will be returned with rejection letters). Those that have been recommended for consideration will get a second reading. If it is decided to pursue a particular project, the writer or his agent might be called in to negotiate a deal.

Rather than simply acquiring scripts, some independent production companies develop ideas, titles, and concepts in-house, and then hire writers to develop them. Such companies are constantly on the lookout for good screenwriters.

In some cases a company might have merely a title or concept in mind and will hire writers to come up with an outline or treatment based on the concept or title. Whichever writer's outline or treatment is liked best may be given a **step deal.**

At a television network, the story department evaluates new projects for development for television or motion pictures. The story department consists of at least one story editor and a number of readers. The story department receives submissions from production companies, agents, and publishers. For legal reasons, unsolicited material is not accepted for consideration. Story departments of networks either are separated into divisions for television movies, comedy series, and drama series, or else function as a single unit.

A story editor works in the story department of a network, screening treatments, scripts, manuscripts, books, and other materials, as well as initiating projects for development. A good editor must follow current events closely for ideas. Publications that review books in advance of publication, such as *Publishers Weekly* and *Kirkus Review*, are especially helpful.

While television movie projects may be developed either by outside suppliers or by in-house staffs of the networks, networks generally prefer internal development to allow them total control of the project. Sometimes story editors are directly involved in the development of in-house TV movies as well as the editing of scripts.

Submissions received for TV movies usually take several weeks to be evaluated. However, "unofficial and confidential" projects are handled immediately due to the obvious competition. Pitch meetings are sometimes held in which agents, writers, and producers verbally present and discuss new ideas.

STORYBOARD. A storyboard is a series of illustrations, drawn to depict the action of a script. Storyboards are made for commercials, animated cartoons, and motion pictures. Drawings are not made for each frame of a production, only for each key situation.

For commercials, storyboards are used by advertising agencies to show clients the concept of a commercial before it is produced. In the field of animation, storyboards are drawn after the final script is approved to give the artists a visual outline of the cartoon's story line and pacing. For films, storyboards outline the design of each shot and how the scenes are going to work into the film. A storyboard is a graphic presentation of the director's conception of a film. While some directors draw their own storyboards, often the art director (or an assistant) prepares them in consultation with the director. Some directors follow their storyboards loosely, while others make a film precisely as depicted in the storyboards. Storyboards in film are also called "continuity sketches."

STRIPBOARD. A stripboard is a specially designed board on which colored cardboard strips are mounted to graphically depict the shooting schedule of a motion picture. Each of the strips represents one scene. The strips can be moved around to change the shooting schedule.

Each strip provides the scene number, a list of cast members appearing in that scene, the time of day shooting will take place, the scene location, equipment needed, and the length of the scene.

The strips are colored to designate exterior day shooting, interior day shooting, exterior night shooting, and interior night shooting. The color blue, for example, might be used to indicate a night exterior shot.

A stripboard is used to determine the most efficient way to shoot a film. The scene strips can be rearranged to plan the most economical and convenient way of shooting. The stripboard enables whoever calculates the budget to estimate the number of days to be spent shooting on each sound stage and location, the number of cast and crew members working, and props and equipment that will be needed. A stripboard is prepared either during development or preproduction by the unit production manager or the first assistant director.

STUNT COORDINATOR. *See* **Stuntman.**

STUNTMAN. A stuntman is a professional who doubles for an actor in scenes requiring physical prowess or involving physical risk.

Stuntmen work in various mediums including motion pictures, television, documentaries, educational films, industrial films, commercials, music videos, and stage shows. Not all productions require stunts, of course. The key is whether there is action.

Stunts range from simple to elaborate and commonly include precision driving, car spins, car crashes, falls from heights, falls through windows and doors, catching on fire, wrestling, fistfights, stair falls, walking and hopping on to running trains, motorcycle gymnastics, horseback riding, helicopter and airplane maneuvers, freefall and skydiving.

Simple stunts are those that do not require any particular skill but present some physical risk to an actor. Dangerous stunts are considered those that go beyond what is called "safe measure." A freefall from a helicopter into a body of water, for example, would be considered dangerous. The precariousness of virtually any stunt can be increased by making it more elaborate, tricky, or difficult.

Stuntmen are usually hired by the stunt coordinator, who in turn is hired by the unit production manager.

The amount of time in advance that stuntmen are hired depends on the number of stunts and their complexity. Obviously, the greater the number and intricacy of the stunts, the more preparation that will be needed. When the stunts are few or simple, the notice may be short, from a few days to two weeks before production starts. When more complex stunts are involved, the lead time may be several weeks. More stunt work requires more money, and so the budget is also a factor in how many and when the stuntmen will be hired. There could be as many as forty or more stuntmen used on a single feature film.

Most stunt situations do not require the stuntmen to resemble the actors, although they are made to look similar through makeup, hair styling, and costume. Through manipulative camera coverage, the audience can be prevented from getting a close view of the stand-in. The stuntman must look like the actor only when close-ups are desired, and yet directors do welcome a resemblance because it affords more freedom, enabling them to come in closer, to cover the stunt closer, and to shoot it from different angles without the danger of recognition. As a matter of fact, when the resemblance is strong, the director may offer the audience glimpses of the face to fuel the illusion of the original actor doing his own stunt work. Fistfights are examples of stunts where a stuntman may be required to strongly resemble an actor. Indeed, a stuntman having the desired physical appearance may be hired more for his mien than for his ability.

When several stuntmen are to be used on a project that requires choreographed physical action, a stunt coordinator is hired. This person suggests where stunts are needed in the script and what kind or how elaborate they should be; surveys potential locations and advises on their conduciveness for execution of stunts; hires those stuntmen he feels are most capable or best suited to do the work; obtains the necessary equipment; choreographs stunts; coaches the stuntment (as well as the regular actors when doing physical maneuvers); oversees the execution of stunts; and serves to maximize safety on the set at all times.

As a subcontractor of sorts, the stunt coordinator is a "middleman" between the stuntmen and the production company or studio. The stunt coordinator estimates a budget, trying to economize as much as possible, while looking after the interests of the stuntmen. The professional stunt coordinator must maintain a file of experienced stuntmen, logged by skills and physical qualities.

It is up to both the stunt coordinator and the stuntmen to research and approach each stunt as carefully as possible. Stunts must be performed to the satisfaction of the director or producer while adhering to rigid safety standards. Usually only one stuntman per actor is hired, but there are occasions in which multiple stuntmen will be hired for the same actor. Since many stuntmen specialize in a specific skill, such as jumping, falling, or driving, a different stuntman may be hired for each stunt a character must perform. A stuntman who is a precision driver, for instance, may not like to work at high altitudes, and might decline stunts involving heights.

Strategies for stunts must be mapped in advance to allow the coordinator time to acquire the necessary equipment. Take, for example, a scene that calls for a character to fall thirty-five feet from the masthead of a ship and to wind up dangling by a rope around his feet just above the deck. One possible way of accomplishing this stunt would be to insert a metal cable in the rope for reinforcement. Next, the distance of the fall will be measured to ensure that the stuntman will not hit the deck below. The stuntman will be hung upside down at the point of impact and hoisted up to check the length of the cable. Then a body harness will be attached to the rope by elastic cords to minimize body shock. When the cable pulls, the elastic cords will absorb the shock and the stuntman will feel little of the fall's force.

The shooting schedule tells the stunt coordinator and the stuntmen which days they will be working. If on a weekly contract, the stunt coordinator must be on the set even when not needed. Some regular actors like to do their own stunts, and if they are given approval by the director, and the coordinator teaches them how to execute the stunts. Leading actors, however, generally are not permitted to engage in stunts that present even small risks because if they are injured the production schedule will be interrupted, resulting in substantial financial losses.

A stunt is usually rehearsed till the player feels comfortable and confident doing it. Dangerous stunts are practiced only once or twice, so as not to increase the risk of something going wrong. The ideal goal of stuntmen is to satisfactorily execute a stunt on the first take. Sometimes a director will call for a stunt to be repeated to ensure proper coverage, but most stunts are covered from at least two or three different camera angles to avoid having to do them more than once.

Stuntmen may also find employment as safeties. When stunts are executed, safeties are there on the side, ready to jump in if something goes awry.

There are some formal training programs available for those who wish to pursue careers as stuntmen, but being in good physical condition is the only prerequisite. To break in as a stuntman, a candidate should contact active stunt coordinators and stuntplayers and prepare a resumé listing abilities and training. In the beginning, the candidate also might approach casting directors to see about getting work as an extra.

SUBTITLES. For foreign-language films, subtitles are printed translations of the dialogue shown at the bottom of the screen. For silent films, subtitles are printed narration or dialogue flashed on the screen in between scenes. Subtitles are also used to give background information in films and television programs.

SUMMER SEASON, MOTION PICTURES. Extending from Memorial Day to Labor Day, the summer season is traditionally the strongest season for the motion picture industry, although it is not immune to failures. The most obvious reason for the surge in box-office sales is vacations—for both students and many workers. Weather also is a factor. People like to go out on warm summer evenings, and movies are a viable source of entertainment (not to mention the fact that most movie theaters are air-conditioned). To cater to this wide potential audience, studios release major films during this period, particularly ones targeted for teens.

SUSPENSE MOVIE. *See* **Film Genres.**

SWEEPS. A sweep is a four-week local television programming period during which Nielsen sends out approximately 200,000 TV diaries to viewers across the country to measure local audiences. The results inform local stations of how competitive they are in their own markets and are used in setting advertising rates. Sweeps occur four times per year—in November, February, May, and July.
See also **Ratings and Shares, Television.**

SWING GANG. *See* **Set Dresser.**

SWING MAN. *See* **Sound Recording, Production.**

SYNCHRONIZATION LICENSE. A synchronization license is a contract between a music publisher and a film or television producer, providing for a musical composition to be used in a film or videotape. The license specifies the mediums in which the song may be used, the geographical licensed areas, and applicable fees. Film synchronization licenses include the right of performance for the United States only.
See also **Music Licensing, Film; Music Licensing, Television.**

SYNDICATION. Syndication is the distribution of programming to independent television stations and affiliates. Unlike network programs, which affiliates automatically receive and air, syndicated shows are purchased on a market-by-market basis for the best price the distributor can get. Affiliates buy syndicated shows to fill time slots in their schedules when they do not receive network programs. The affiliates compete with independent stations in each specific market for coveted syndicated fare.

There are two basic types of syndication: off-network and first-run. Off-network syndication is the practice of selling broadcasting rights to old network series or episodes of a long-running series that is still on the air. First-run syndication is the practice of selling broadcasting rights to programs produced specifically for non-network broadcast—programs made expressly for purchase by independent stations and network affiliates. First-run programs usually cost less to produce than network prime-time series, and therefore sell for less than off-network shows.

For producers of network television shows, syndication is an important and valuable source of revenue. The high costs of producing network shows exceed the license fees paid by networks. Revenues from foreign sales add some income, but rarely enough to help the shows break even. Syndication not only puts the programs in the black, but is extremely profitable for producers.

Stations in major markets pay from $50,000 to $100,000 per episode for reruns of popular network shows. Stations in secondary markets pay from $7,500 to $20,000 for half-hour reruns. Indeed, the income generated from all markets for a single episode of an off-network series could be well over $1 million.

Producers of prime-time network series own the rights to their shows. When enough episodes of a show have accumulated, a studio's distribution division tries to sell it for syndication. Production companies without distribution divisions arrange for independent syndication companies to distribute their shows. There are two basic ways deals are made: The distributor is paid either a flat fee or a percentage of the gross revenues.

A syndication company typically consists of a sales division, (which makes deals with the stations), a barter sales division (which sells commercial airtime to national advertising agencies), a research division (which conducts studies and provides the sales division with information that will assist it in selling shows), and production representatives. Heading each division are vice-presidents who report either to an executive vice-president or the company president.

For an off-network series to qualify for syndication, it must have enough episodes to avoid excessive repeats. As a rule of thumb, a series needs one hundred episodes for it to be syndicated. Stations will not take a series that cannot run for at least thirteen weeks without a repeat. However, because the syndication market is so lucrative, producers, distributors, and TV stations often enter into agreements under less than optimum circumstances. There are certain series the episodes of which can repeat several times per year and still attract large audiences.

Network prime-time shows are aired once per week. With an average of twenty-two episodes produced each season, a series would have to be on the air for at least four or five years to be eligible to be sold for syndication. Producers therefore try to keep their shows in production and on the air until they can build up a substantial number of episodes.

Syndication contracts provide for stations to carry programs for specified minimum lengths of time. For a first-run show with no track record, the deal usually runs for fifty-two weeks. Off-network series are contracted for longer periods because they are proven commodities. Off-network series are usually sold in deals allowing from four runs over three years to six runs over six years. A deal allowing four runs over three years would permit a station to air each of the episodes in the syndication package four times over the following three years.

If an independent station wants to cancel an off-network series, it asks the distributor to try to sell the program to another station in the market. If this cannot be arranged, the station must continue to pay the license fee, even if the series has been pulled off the air.

First-run programming is often sold via an arrangement called "barter syndication." Under one form of barter syndication, a show is traded to TV stations for commercial airtime. Profits from adver-

287

tising time sold during the show is split between the distributor and the station in approximately equal parts. The station and the distributor agree that the show will be run on a certain day of the week at a specified time.

The distributor sells the advertising time it is allotted much like a network would. If a show is sold, for example, in the top one hundred markets (covering 88 percent of the country), the distributor approaches national advertisers as if it were selling ad time for a network program. The distributor informs potential advertisers of the cities in which the show will run, the time slots, and the predicted ratings. Barter agreements provide that if a station decides not to fulfill its commitment to air a show, it must run the national commercials contracted for by the syndicator in the same or a similar time period.

There is another form of barter syndication, which involves a combination of commercial airtime and cash. Under such an agreement a show is sold for a fee and a small portion of advertising time that is held out for barter. For example, many half-hour game shows in syndication have six and a half minutes of commercial airtime. In taking such a program, a station might pay a fee and keep five and a half minutes of advertising time. One minute goes to the distributor, who sells it to a national advertiser. This arrangement provides the distributor with the potential to earn more money than a straight cash deal. The cash-flow benefits provided by barter syndication are especially attractive to syndicators who produce shows. To produce first-run programming requires substantial capital, and license fees paid by TV stations rarely cover the production costs of shows. Even if a show is not sold in major markets, it can still be produced and syndicated as long as license fees from stations in the rest of the country cover production costs. For example, when "Wheel of Fortune" went on the air it wasn't sold in New York, Los Angeles, or Chicago. It was only after the show became a hit that stations in these major markets bought it. But the syndicator did not need these markets in the beginning because the costs of producing, promoting, and distributing the show were covered by the fees paid by stations in other markets. A first-run barter show would need to be carried by stations in New York, Los Angeles, Chicago, and other major markets to sell it to national advertisers. Generally, a syndicator must place a show in at least 75 percent of U.S. markets to attract national advertisers.

When a show is a hit, or expected to be one, a syndicator might try to sell it through a process called *bidding*, whereby a syndicator tentatively offers a program to a station in a market for a particular price, and if the syndicator gets its price, the company meets with other stations to try to get a better offer. A variation on this procedure is called *blind bidding*. In blind bidding, a distributor sets a base price for a show in a market and auctions it off to interested stations. The distributor may request that each successive bid has to be a certain increment above previous bids. Bidding and blind bidding are done market-by-market. Syndicators approach both independent stations and affiliates and these broadcasters compete against each other.

Not all successful shows in network prime time are good candidates for syndication, even if they have amassed a considerable number of episodes. For example, a hit show that ran at 10 P.M. on a Friday night might air at 5, 6, or 7 P.M. in syndication; during family viewing time. Would it have the same audience? Would it have such elements as drugs, sex, and crime that could reduce the size of the audience? Is the show so stylized that it is outdated in only a few years? Syndicators and TV stations generally prefer timeless shows.

Many shows that are successful in prime-time fail in syndication, even if all the elements are right. People may simply tire of them. This usually hurts the stations more than the producers and distributors. As deals are made in advance, the producers and distributors get guaranteed license fees. The fees are usually large and the deals are made for a number of years, sometimes as many as six. When the ratings are low, the stations suffer, and ultimately, of course, the programs are not renewed.

The Federal Communications Commission prohibits network affiliates from running off-network programming in prime access (7 to 8 P.M. Monday through Friday). This is to prevent the networks from beginning their prime-time programming earlier and monop-olizing the airwaves. Without this restriction, affiliates could air reruns of popular shows at 7:30 P.M. and, in effect, expand their prime-time hours. The FCC ruling, which went into effect in 1971, enables local stations to program shows of a regional nature, if desired. This practice also helps stations comply with the Commu-nications Act of 1939, which requires that broadcasters serve the public interest.

In setting the price for syndicated shows in each market, distrib-utors consider the fees paid in the past for similar shows in the same markets and how these shows fared. Within any given market some stations are able to pay considerably more than others. Affiliates usually can afford to pay more for shows than independents.

The National Association of Television Programming Executives (NATPE) holds a programming convention between January and March of each year. For syndicators, the bulk of their selling is done during the winter months, and the NATPE convention begins the process.

TAKE. A take is the filming of a scene. When a scene has to be re-shot, the takes are consecutively numbered—for example, "Scene 20, Take 1" "Scene 20, Take 2," "Scene 20, Take 3."

TALENT COORDINATOR. A talent coordinator schedules guests for television talk shows. There may be a number of talent coordinators for a single show, since booking anywhere from three to six or more guests per show, five shows a week, requires much organization and scheduling.

To book distinguished guests, talent coordinators usually have to pursue leads. This process entails tracking down a potential guest and convincing the person to appear on the show. If a person in the news who is not normally of media interest is wanted for the show, he or she must be booked quickly because of the topical nature of the event.

An appearance on a popular talk show can translate into widespread recognition or substantially increased sales of a product. Publicity departments of entertainment companies frequently approach talent coordinators to get bookings for their clients so they can promote their latest work.

A good talent coordinator builds up a list of contacts over the years. With a list of phone numbers and addresses, a coordinator can reach many celebrities directly. For other contacts, talent coordinators draw on various publications and trade directories. Talent coordinators must be on top of the print and visual medias to be able to spot potential guests and to act quickly.

TALK SHOW. The talk show is a television format in which a host interviews guests on a simple set, usually before a studio audience. Most talk shows fit into two basic categories: serious issue-oriented forums and entertainment-oriented shows. The latter is more successful and prevalent.

The format of entertainment-oriented talk shows is a well-established one. An announcer introduces the host, who opens the show with a monologue done standing. The monologue consists of topical jokes. The house band tags the end of the monologue, which segues into the first commercial break. After the commercial break, the host, seated now, introduces the first guest. One after another, the guests are summoned forth, and arrive to the applause of the audience. Celebrity guests, whose appearances are arranged by **talent coordinators**, usually entertain before they sit down to plug their latest film, TV show, record, or performing engagement. Part of the entertainment lineup also may be "everyday people" who have an interesting experience to relate or an unusual talent to demonstrate, as well as variety acts such as jugglers or acrobats.

Essential to the energy and enthusiasm of the show is the audience. The audience is warmed up prior to the commencement of the show and instructed to exhibit its zealousness throughout the taping, as well as to respond appropriately to machine cues which may produce such signals as "applaud" and "laugh." Occasionally, the host involves the audience in some routines or entertainment.

Many talk shows are characterized by a *buddy-foil* system. The buddy, a sidekick or the musical conductor, plays foil to the host.

Television talk shows sometimes broadcast telephone conversations. The **Federal Communications Commission (FCC)** promulgates rules regarding this practice. A station must inform a person before the broadcast of the conversation, or prior to its recording for possible later broadcast, of its intention to broadcast the conversation. However, if callers are invited to call in, this restriction does not apply.

TV talk shows are produced by networks, syndicates, cable stations, and independent stations. They appear in all time slots, although the late-night slot from 11:30 P.M. to 1 A.M. is the prime talk-show slot. The shows are taped to occupy thirty, sixty, or ninety minutes of television time. Many TV talk shows have come and gone through the years, and, undoubtedly, more will continue to proliferate as the talk show is an engaging yet relatively inexpensive form of programming to produce.

TECHNICAL ADVISOR. A technical advisor is a person possessing expert knowledge of a specific subject, hired for a motion picture or television show as a consultant in that area of experience. A real policeman, for example, might be hired as technical advisor for a television crime show.

TECHNICAL COORDINATOR. A technical coordinator, according to the Directors Guild of America, is employed by a producer "to assist the director on a multi-camera television motion picture film production photographed continuously, before a live audience, or as though a live audience were present, in planning the placement and movement of each such camera, with the responsibility for coordinating the execution of such placement and movement of each such camera."

TEEN MOVIE. *See* **Film Genres.**

TELEPROMPTER™. A TelePrompTer is a mechanical device with a rolling script, with enlarged print, that is placed next to a television camera to feed lines to an actor or newscaster.

TELETHON. A telethon is an extended, live television show featuring entertainment, talk, and information, usually to benefit charity. Theater Authority Inc., a nonprofit organization, serves to safeguard professional entertainers' rights with respect to performing on telethons and at other charitable functions by checking the legitimacy of such events and establishing certain terms and working conditions that must be provided for the entertainer.

TELEVISION COMMERCIALS, PRODUCTION OF. Television commercials are advertisements produced to sell products and services on commercial television. Sponsors retain advertising agencies to produce commercials, and the advertising agencies contract specialized directors and producers to shoot the commercials. A primary function of commercial television is to produce a format in which television advertisements can be aired to reach a mass audience.

After an advertising agency has been approached by a product sponsor, the agency's creative team is assigned to devise a commercial for an account. This team includes a scriptwriter and an art director, who draws the **storyboards**. Upon completion, the script and storyboards are presented to the client along with an estimated budget. If the client approves, television airtime may be booked. A producer from the ad agency then offers independent production companies the opportunity to bid on the job. In an effort to have the commercial done for the least amount of money possible, it is not unusual for five or more producers to be asked to submit bids.

The executive producer hires the crew, determines what equipment and materials are needed, arranges for shooting locations, and disburses payments. In addition to the director, who is sometimes hired directly by the sponsor, the production crew typically consists of a production coordinator, an art director, a cinematographer, a wardrobe supervisor, a property master, and a location manager.

The director starts by reading the script and studying the storyboards. Sometimes the script and storyboards are so clear that the director simply determines the best way to execute them. Other times the concept is vague, and the director attempts to clarify it. While the director's function is to bring the agency's creative work to life, sometimes his or her artistry and vision causes friction with the agency.

After the director and production company are hired, casting and location scouting begin. The director will confer with the ad agency's creative team to get a consensus of what the actors should be like and will then convey this information to the casting director. Some agencies have in-house casting departments, but independent casting companies are frequently used. If there is to be location shooting, a location manager is hired to scout potential sites, supplying photographs of these. Also at this time the production coordinator is assembling a crew.

Throughout the process the director will meet with the agency's people to show them selected location pictures and scout the sites with them. The director also carries on discussions with the wardrobe supervisor, the property master, the set dresser, and other crew members.

A preproduction meeting might take place with the sponsor, the ad agency, the executive producer, and the director. The agency's people will review what it has promised to do for the client and what the other parties have agreed to do.

A few days before shooting commences final details are wrapped up: script changes may be made, new actors may be hired, and other necessary improvements effected. For location work, a technical scout is done in which the director, cinematographer, property master, gaffer, and key grip visit the location to plan out strategies. Then production is ready to begin.

During shooting, various people associated with the commercial might be present. This would include the ad agency writer, art director, producer, account executive, junior account executive (if any), and a representative of the sponsor, such as the marketing director. Sometimes they offer input during production but the decision of how to creatively proceed on the set ultimately lies with the director.

The agency producer monitors the costs in making a commercial. It is important that the commercial doesn't exceed its budget. Television commercials' production costs commonly range from $75,000 to $250,000, including the fees of the director and producer.

Postproduction work begins with a screening in which the dailies are seen by ad agency people, the film editor, the director, and the client. If the footage is approved, the editor pulls selected takes and makes a rough cut. Often the editor screens the shots again with the agency's creative team and then makes a rough cut based on the team's selection of takes. The result is screened by agency people, resulting in further changes, and the process continues until a satisfactory cut is obtained. During this time, music and effects are added. Finally, the account executive of the agency approves the commercial, and it is shown to the client. If the client requests changes, there will be further editing. Most commercials are shot with 35-mm film and transferred to videotape after being edited. Copies of the finished commercial are shipped to television stations for broadcast.

TELEVISION NEWS SERVICES. *See* **Independent Television Station.**

TELEVISION PRODUCTION COMPANY. Most network prime-time series are produced by outside television production companies. Such firms are divisions of large entertainment corporations or independent companies. The networks pay a television production company a license fee for a program, which initially entitles them to two runs during prime time. When a series lasts into a third or fourth season, and the salaries of the stars increase and production costs rise, producers negotiate higher license fees with the networks.

Network licensing fees are usually less than the costs of producing shows. TV production companies pay the difference "out of pocket" in the hope that their series will run long enough to build up enough episodes for **syndication**. It may cost a company, for example, $1.2 million to produce a one-hour drama. If the network pays it a license fee of $900,000, the deficit is $300,000. If the series does not go into syndication, the producer will not ever recoup its investment. While there are foreign, cable, and overseas markets that offer opportunities to recoup some of the investment, usually a series cannot be profitable unless it is sold for syndication.

TELEVISION PROGRAM DELIVERY SYSTEMS. For years, free television has been the predominant delivery system, but the program delivery marketplace is changing rapidly. Cable television has now reached about 50 percent of U.S. households, compared to television broadcasting's 97 percent.

Program delivery systems are not to be confused with UHF and VHF, which are different parts of the television broadcast band. UHF, or ulta high frequency, refers to any television station that broadcasts over channels 14 through 69. VHF, or very high frequency, refers to any television station that broadcasts from channels 2 through 13. Current TV program delivery systems are summarized in the following table.

Television Program Delivery Systems

Delivery System	Explanation
Cable television	A subscription service that offers the viewer most over-the-air signals in addition to programs from the cable network by way of electric cables. Some cable systems offer more than one hundred channels. A variety of programming is offered, including sporting events, movies, reruns of old television programs, talk shows, home shopping, information shows, financial news, weather, and foreign-language shows. There is a monthly fee for cable television.
Free television	Television signals automatically picked up on a regular receiver without any special arrangements between the viewer and the stations or a service.
Low-power television	Signal delivery in a radius of about five to twenty miles. Stations are a few thousand watts or less, and delivery is primarily designed for small communities. LPTV is a secondary service to full-service TV stations.
Pay-per-view television	Viewer pays on a per-program basis. It is a delivery system in which programming is transmitted in the form of a scrambled signal that can be converted into images by a decoder. This system is used primarily in hotels. Programming on pay-per-view television includes first-run movies and specials. Also called "pay" or "subscription" television.

Continued on next page

Continued from previous page

Delivery System	Explanation
Public television	Public television is delivered free, but because public TV stations have a different support system than commercial broadcasters, it is included in this table. Public television stations are noncommercial broadcasters that are supported by the federal government, businesses, and individuals.

TELEVISION PROGRAMMING. Various philosophies guide television executives in lining up shows and air times, but the strength of a network or station is based on its programming. *Programming* is a general term that refers to selecting shows for broadcast and putting them into the various time slots to attract as wide a viewing audience as possible. It results in a network's or station's entertainment lineup, which ultimately is responsible for the station's or the network's income.

Much of the programming for affiliates is determined by their networks. There are a number of hours that are left for the affiliates to fill themselves, however. Around May of each year the networks announce their fall lineups at affiliate conventions (usually held in Los Angeles). The networks bring on anywhere from five to thirteen new shows each fall season. Ratings determine what gets canceled and what continues: Shows with very low ratings are discontinued, those with high ratings are picked up for the new season, and programs in between can draw either fate.

As it is expensive to create new shows and difficult to build their ratings, some television executives hold the belief that shows with borderline ratings should be renewed in an effort to give them more time to attract more viewers. Major changes may be made, however, to infuse more life into them. Nevertheless, shows—new and old alike—whose ratings are in the cellar may be canceled only a few weeks into the new season. While network executives prefer to give a series a chance to build an audience and replace it after the fall season if necessary, they do keep new programs ready for broadcast, should there be any early casualties.

While every series was new at one time, it is nevertheless difficult for a new one to succeed. A new series must compete against other series, which have established audiences that are loyal, devoted, and resistant to change. Money may be spent in advertising and promoting a new series, but if it is up against a popular show or is noncompetitive in any time slot, no sum will make it a hit. Sometimes all of the new programs of a network will fail. Indeed, it may take three, four, five or more years for a last place network to recover from its slump and overtake the others.

Two important considerations in scheduling a program are competition and the demographics of the audiences in the various time slots. A show with potential scheduled against a hit series may not have a chance to find its audience. Rescheduling it in a different time slot might be advisable. Also one show's cancellation could open up a new time slot for another that is struggling against strong competition. Programmers might also reschedule a successful show if they believe another one in its place could earn even higher ratings. Likewise, a show that could benefit from the higher ratings of another may be scheduled to follow that show.

The demographics of a show's potential audience must be considered. Research describes the demographics of audiences for different shows and enables programmers to decide which shows to schedule and where to schedule them in order to approach or surpass the competition. If a highly rated series that draws a substantial female audience dominates a particular time slot, a new program intended to draw male viewers might be put against it.

Some shows that are holdovers from one season to the next are placed in new time slots. If their ratings could stand improvement, they might be juxtaposed to highly popular programs. Shows with strong ratings may be rescheduled to help the network on a day where it is weak.

Prime time is the television period when advertising rates are at a premium. Shows that begin at 8 P.M. are lead-ins, and the networks strategize what to place there in the hope that these programs will keep audiences tuned to the local affiliate or network-owned station. Sitcoms commonly dominate the 8 P.M. and 8:30 P.M. time slots (with a sprinkling of action-adventure programs), while dramas, cop/detective shows, and similar fare, each one hour long, occupy the 9 P.M. to 11 P.M. period. The networks usually devote one evening a week each to broadcast a theatrical motion picture (usually Sunday) and often air made-for-TV movies and miniseries.

Popular feature films sometimes spawn imitative television series. Network executives look for trends in public taste, and the box-office success of movies is an important barometer of this. A miniseries that achieved high ratings could also inspire a new series.

In a new season, adjustments are made in the lineups as the networks deem necessary. An entire evening's programming may be replaced by new shows and existing shows from other nights, or it may remain intact. Commonly, one or two new shows are inserted.

The networks seem to diverge a bit when it comes to miniseries programming philosophy. One network may schedule one or two for a fall season while another may air as many as seven. Miniseries are expensive to produce and network executives are cautious in deciding if they will be profitable.

What does the networks' prime-time mix look like? Based on 63 prime-time hours per week (three hours per network per evening, 8 P.M. to 11 P.M. for seven days), a recent fall season appeared as this: 32 dramas (soaps, action-adventure, cop/detective) at 32 hours; 29 sitcoms at 14.5 hours; 5 feature films at 10 hours; 2 newsmagazine programs at 2 hours; 2 anthologies at 1.5 hours (the one-hour per week Disney movie is included here); and 1 sports event (football) at 2 hours.

The table that follows is a summary of television programming by a typical network affiliate on a seasonal and daily basis. A network is responsible for at least 50 percent of an affiliate's schedule.

Major Network Programming Distribution

	ABC		CBS		NBC	
	# of shows per season	Hours per show	# of shows per season	Hours per show	# of shows per season	Hours per show
Dramas	9	9	14	14	10	10
Sitcoms	10	5	6	3	13	6.5
Feature Films	1	2	2	4	2	4
News-magazines	2	2	0	0	0	0
Anthologies	1	1	0	0	1	.5
Sports Events	1	2	0	0	0	0
Total	24	21	22	21	26	21

TELEVISION PROGRAMMING GENRES. Television programming comprises a diversified menu of shows designed to entertain and inform; the shows are often targeted for specific demographic groups. The table on page 302 shows the genres of television programming and brief summaries of each. Also included are the customary network time slots for these shows, although on independent TV stations many of the shows may be found to run at any hour. In any case, the time slots given are general and exceptions will abound. There are also shows that are hybrids of two or more genres, such as dramas and sitcoms or dramas and anthologies. The following table delineates the genres in pure form only.

Television Genres

Genre	Description	Customary Network Time Slot
Action-adventure	Leading characters defeat their foes or overcome seemingly insurmountable obstacles by daring physical feats and cunning strategies; stunts and special effects integral to plot.	Prime time
Anthology	A series of shows interrelated by concept but which each feature different characters, acting ensembles, situations, and themes.	Prime time
Children	Programs of an education and entertainment mix designed for youngsters up to about twelve years of age.	Early morning, morning
Cop/crime	A category of drama (*see below*) with emphasis on action.	Prime time
Documentary	A motion picture essay with narration reporting on a real-life topic.	Prime time
Drama	Series that emphasize plot, dialogue, human emotions; a broad category that includes shows such as cop/detective series and mysteries.	Prime time

Continued from previous page

Evangelical	Preachers discuss how faith leads to a more en- riching life; viewers in- vited to send in donations.	Early morning, morning
Game	Contestants compete against one another for prizes in games of chance, skill, or knowledge.	Morning, prime-time access
Information	Programs dedicated to providing information on subjects such as business, medicine, and cooking.	Early morning
Magazine-format	A heterogenous mixture of reports on controversial events, human-interest stories, and commentaries.	Prime time
Made-for-TV movie	A dramatic conflict focus- ing on social issue or themes of current interest.	Prime time
Miniseries	Multiple-part dramas often adapted from best-selling books (novels and biographies, particularly) made espe- cially for televison and designed to appeal to spe- cific demographic groups.	Prime time
Miscellaneous	Programs that fit no con- ventional classifications and may not be regularly broadcast (e.g., blooper shows, exercise classes, telethons).	Prime time

Continued on next page

Continued from previous page

Genre	Description	Customary Network Time Slot
Movie of the week	Television broadcasts of motion pictures made for theatrical release.	Prime time
Music video	A potpourri of concept videos of various musical genres.	Late night
News	Daily telecasts of world, national, and local news with sports and weather; network programs feature only world and national news.	Early evening, prime-time access
Public affairs	Shows devoted to community affairs or commentaries.	Morning
Religious	Masses, sermons performed by clergymen or discussions of a religious nature.	Early morning
Science fiction	Dramas with supernatural or extraordinary settings and developments.	Prime time, late night
Sitcom	Innocuous plots highlighted by jokes, double-entendres, blunderings, and pratfalls.	Prime time

Continued on next page

Soap opera (or daytime serial episodes)	Emotional interactions between characters as they face distressing problems and try to resolve personal conflicts between themselves (e.g., affairs, out-of-wedlock pregnancies, miscarriages, abortions, incest, blackmail).	Afternoon, prime time
Special	A show of distinctive nature not broadcast weekly by a network or station that preempts regular programming; examples of specials are award ceremonies, beauty pageants, holiday animated and variety shows, news stories of significance or widespread interest, and hour-long reprises of old series.	Prime time
Sports	Championship games and other important sporting events; some sports such as wrestling and golf are regularly telecast.	Afternoon, prime time
Talk	A host interviews celebrity guests and others.	Early morning, morning, afternoon, late night
Variety	A mix of musical, comedy, and acrobatic entertainment.	Prime time

TELEVISION SEASON. A television season is any of the individual seasons that constitute a TV year, or the entire period from when the new TV year begins till reruns start. Traditionally, there were only two television seasons—the fall season and mid-season—but with new shows now debuting and time schedules changing year-round, the seasons have become less distinct.

However, because seasons are a convenient method to distinguish between some elements of programming, the terms *fall season*, *midseason*, and *summer season* are still used. (See pages 307 and 308.) Moreover, the fall is still the time of year when networks introduce their new high-budget prime-time shows and resume first-run programming from shows carried over to the new season.

The new television year begins with the commencement of the fall season, which ranges from late September to early October, depending upon the schedules of the networks. It runs till May or June (the conclusion of mid-season) when the prime-time shows have concluded their first run. Usually, twenty-two or more shows comprise a prime-time series in a television year.

Following the regular television series is the rerun, or summer, season. This too, in recent years, has broken tradition, with new or experimental programming airing in place of some reruns on the networks. Lineups are also juggled, with shows put into different time slots so they may find new audiences. Different days, different competition, and new lead-ins could significantly alter the composition of a TV program's audience.

TELEVISION STATIONS, FEDERAL REGULATION OF. Under current rules of the **Federal Communications Commission (FCC)**, a corporation may own up to but not more than twelve stations in each of the broadcast services (TV, AM, or FM), except if the license is minority-controled, in which case it can own up to fourteen stations in each service. The total number of TV stations must not reach an aggregate national audience of 25 percent, or, for minority-controled licenses, 30 percent. Furthermore, a broadcasting entity may not operate more than one station of a particular kind

Television Programming

FALL SEASON	MID-SEASON	SUMMER SEASON
New shows debut.	Low rated series are canceled.	Reruns.
Successful and promising shows from last season return.	New series replacements are tested.	Small number of new pilots.
	Shows are moved to different time slots.	
New lineups.	Programming decisions are made for the following fall	

DAILY

Early Morning 5:30A.M.–9A.M.	Morning 9A.M.–12P.M.	Afternoon 12P.M.–5P.M.	Early Evening 5P.M.–7P.M.	Prime-time Lead-In 7P.M.–8P.M.	Prime-Time 8P.M.–11P.M.	Late Night 11P.M.–5:30A.M.
news shows talk shows	talk shows game shows	soap operas talk shows game shows	news shows	news shows game shows	sitcoms action shows dramas made-for-television movies miniseries variety shows newsmagazine shows miscellaneous (e.g., blooper programs, specials, sports events)	news shows talk shows old movies syndicated shows

308

in the same area; one company, for example, may not own two television stations in Detroit.

FCC licenses for television stations are valid for a term of five years. At the end of each term the license must be renewed. Applications for renewal with the FCC must be filed four months prior to expiration. The renewal application requires broadcasters to certify whether they have been subject to legal action by a court or administrative body, and whether they have compiled with FCC rules on employment practices and station ownership, and legal provisions relating to foreign persons and governments. The FCC also requires stations to maintain files, available to the public, including copies of their FCC application, information on station ownership and employment practices, updated lists of public-affairs issues addressed by the station in its broadcasts, and, for commercial stations, written comments from the public for three years following their receipt.

Contrary to popular belief, TV stations are not limited by the FCC regarding the number of commercial minutes they may broadcast in an hour. Stations do not even have to indicate in renewal applications the amount of airtime devoted to advertising.

TIME PERIODS AND SEASONS, TELEVISION AND MOTION PICTURES. Industry lingo comprises various terms used to describe TV programs and films with respect to scheduling, release, and related characteristics. Some of the jargon is defined in the table that begins on page 310.

THRILLER. *See* **Film Genres.**

TIME LINE. *See* **Script Supervisor.**

TITLE ARTIST. A title artist draws the artwork that appears in the credits of a film or television show. Although titles are sometimes generated by computer, they are also done by hand.

Scheduling Terms

Term	Medium	Description
afternoon	television	The period from 12:00 P.M. to 5 P.M. Late afternoon runs from 5 P.M. to 6 P.M.
checkerboarding	television	Running a different show every weekday in the same time slot, such as a different sitcom Monday through Friday in the 7:30 P.M. to 8:00 P.M. time period (*see* "stripping," below).
Christmas season	motion pictures	Running from Thanksgiving to Christmas, a period of generally voluminous box-office activity due to the holiday season.
episode	television	A single show from a series.
fall season	television	A period when networks readjust their lineups, introducing new shows and new schedules; begins year in late September or early October.
feature	motion pictures	A film that costs about $10 million or more to make.

Continued on next page

Continued from previous page

late night	television	The period from 11:30 P.M. to 5:30 A.M.
lead-in	television	A show that precedes another, usually a popular one whose audience might stay tuned to the same station and watch the later show.
low-budget	motion pictures	A film that costs up to a few million dollars to make.
mid-season	television	A period when the networks make further adjustments in their schedules; begins in January.
morning	television	The period from 5:30 A.M. to 12 P.M.; the time slot from 5:30 A.M. to 9 A.M. is commonly referred to as "early morning."
off-network	television	A rerun of a previous or currently running network show.
pilot	television	An introductory episode of a planned TV series that may or may not get aired.
premiere	television	The first episode of a new series.

Continued on next page

Continued from previous page

Term	Medium	Description
prequel	motion pictures	A film in which the story line precedes that of a previously released movie and which stars an actor playing the same character.
prime time	television	The period from 8 P.M. to 11 P.M. Monday through Saturday and 7:00 P.M. to 11 P.M. Sunday.
prime-time access	television	The hour preceding prime time.
reissue	motion pictures	Any theatrical distribution of a film subsequent to its initial release; some classics are reissued regularly through the years.
remake	motion pictures	A new version of an old movie.
rerun	television	A broadcast of a show previously aired
revival	television	A one- or two-hour special of an old television series, using the same actors or those who are alive.

Continued on next page

Continued from previous page

sequel	motion pictures	A film produced subsequent to a previous one, having the same leading character/actor.
series	television	The shows that collectively form a programming unit.
special	television	A one-time program of particular content that replaces a regularly scheduled show.
stripping	television	Airing episodes of a syndicated series Monday through Friday; "stripping" is running one show on five different nights, as opposed to "checkerboarding," which is airing five different shows on five different nights.
summer season	motion pictures	Running from Memorial Day to Labor Day weekend, a period of increased box-office activity due primarily to school vacations.
summer season	television	A period marked by reruns of prime-time network shows.

TITLES OF MOVIES AND TV PROGRAMS. The copyright law does not extend protection to titles, whether they be titles of motion pictures, television programs, plays, songs, books, or other works. Copyright protection extends to the expression of ideas, but not to ideas themselves, or unsubstantial amounts of original authorship, and a title would ordinarily be considered to lack a substantial amount of original authorship.

Protection for a title, however, may subsist under the laws of unfair competition. The gauge for this is for a title to have acquired a "secondary meaning." This happens when a title becomes so well known through the years that it becomes associated in the public's mind with a particular work. Some examples of movies and television programs whose titles might qualify for protection under the laws of unfair competition are *Gone With the Wind, The Ten Commandments, "Star Trek,"* and *The Flinstones."*

TITLES, PUTTING ON FILM. Titles, or screen credits, are put on a film by an optical-effects company. After the company is hired by the producer (and a price is settled on), the process is generally as follows: The editor or assistant editor brings a workprint (a positive print of the finished film) to the optical-effects company, with a list of the negatives that will be coming from the negative matcher. The optical-effects technician runs through the workprint, which is spliced together with Mylar tape and has grease markings on it, and is in effect a blueprint.

When the negative arrives from the negative matcher, the optical-effects technician makes a registration interpositive (a fine-grain positive image) which is sent for processing. When the interpositive returns, it is matched against the workprint, which has edge numbers on it.

Projections, or blow-ups, are prepared for the title scenes. These are eight-by-ten enlargements of the scenes that are used to show the producer or editor what the titles will look like in the actual scene so that they can move them around and choose their exact location. A typeface will also be selected (there are libraries of typefaces). The artwork that has been created is then photographed and combined with the interpositive to make a finished optical negative. If this is approved by the producer or editor, it is sent to the negative matcher, who cuts it back into the original negative, which in turn is sent to a film laboratory to make an answer print.

Commonly, changes will be made later in the titles. In the rush to meet deadlines, credits may be misspelled or omitted. Or, because final contracts for some of the participants may not have been signed at that point, only temporary titles will have been used. Also, other work may not have been done or completed yet, such as the scoring, for example, and so the composer's name may not be known. In such cases, the optical-effects technician can either leave blank spaces for these credits or use fabricated names and change them later on.

TRADE PUBLICATIONS. Motion picture and television industry news is covered by professional trade publications. *Variety* and *The Hollywood Reporter* are the two most important publications. *Variety* is published weekly and covers the motion picture, television, home-video, radio, music, and theater industries. Among its features are weekend box-office reports, film grosses at theaters in major U.S. cities, the top-grossing pictures (based on a sampling of theaters), film and television reviews, and statistical data. Published under the same corporate banner is *Daily Variety*.

The Hollywood Reporter, published daily, contains up-to-the-minute news, detailed reports of job changes and hirings, production information, domestic and foreign box-office charts, television and film reviews, and special weekly reports on international show business. *The Hollywood Reporter* also annually publishes the *Studio Blu-Book Directory*, a classified directory of the film and television industries in Los Angeles. Included are professional listings in more than two hundred categories, including production companies, celebrity contacts, camera equipment, lighting equipment, television distribution companies, casting agencies, film laboratories, props, stunt services, and talent agencies. Other trades and journals include *American Cinematographer, Broadcasting, Screen International, Television/Radio Age, Advertising Age, Adweek,*

American Cinemeditor, Video Forecaster, Broadcast Management/ Engineering, Millimeter, Ross Reports, Television Broadcast, Cable Communications, Cable Television Business, Communications Technology, FCC Week, Media and Values, Multichannel News, Television Digest, TV World, Videography, and *View.* Unions, guilds, and trade and professional organizations also regularly publish magazines and newsletters.

TRANSPORTATION COORDINATOR/CAPTAIN. The ground transportation operations of a feature or television film production fall under the responsibility of the transportation department and its operations. Both on-camera and behind the scenes operations are supervised by the transportation coordinator. The first of this department to be hired, the transportation coordinator breaks down the script in preproduction to determine the transportation needs and the most economical way of fulfilling them. He or she pays close attention to such areas as location shooting, stunt work, and day versus night work. The transportation coordinator is responsible for securing vehicles that will appear on screen and be used as conveyances off-camera in production and post-production, as well as the hiring and supervising of the drivers of these vehicles. In preparing a budget the transportation coordinator takes into consideration the transportation needs of the production, which might include conventional cars, racing cars, antique cars, Jeeps, motorcycles, armored tanks, or other special vehicles, and the moving of cast members to different sites.

The transportation coordinator has input in the selection of locations for shooting. He or she will canvass potential sites and render advice from the transportation perspective. For example, the location manager or director may favor a particular site, but the transportation coordinator must assess it in terms of the department's operations. How feasible will it be for the movement, parking, and accessibility of the vehicles? Off-screen vehicles typically include a production van carrying the electrical and grip equipment, a semitrailer towed by a tractor carrying two 1,000 amp generators to supply power for the film crew, a camera sound truck, a truck carrying the props and special effects, trucks carrying the construction and set dressing equipment and crews, a 65-foot truck and trailer (called a *honeywagon*) with several dressing rooms and bathrooms for the stars and crew, a wardrobe trailer, and a makeup and hairdressing trailer towed by two crew-cab pick-up trucks, a catering truck with all of the meals for the day for the entire cast and crew, and cars and buses to transport the dozens of crew members during production. The locations must be evaluated in terms of handling the quantity, weight, and size of these vehicles, which can include 18-wheelers and five-ton trucks.

The transportation coordinator must be knowledgeable about all areas of transportation, including applicable laws at the federal, state, and local levels. Prior to production, he or she will meet with any of the various law enforcement and municipal agencies in the locations where filming is to take place. These may include the police, members of city and public works departments, and local teamsters unions to ensure compliance with ordinances, laws, and regulations. He or she will deal with city film and television offices to rent city-owned vehicles such as subway cars, street-cleaning equipment, fire trucks, police cars, and garbage trucks when necessary. The transportation coordinator also makes sure the drivers in the transportation department meet the various legal requirements, such as having the particular class of license for the vehicles that will be driven and a valid medical certificate with certification of having been drug-tested. Records of activities are kept in log books by the drivers who submit them after completing a work day.

The *right-hand person* of the transportation coordinator is the transportation captain, also called the gang boss. This person is the first of the transportation department to arrive on the set each day in order to supervise the unit's work. The gang boss guides the production vehicles to parking locations that will be out of view of the camera during shooting, and makes sure that the vehicles needed for shooting are on the set. During production, the gang boss oversees the transportation of cast, crew, equipment, and props. Drivers are assigned to fulfill any transportation needs of the work shift and crews are safely transported at the end of the day to their hotels or

317

to the studio. The gang boss submits calls for the next work day to each of the drivers.

TREATMENT. A treatment is a synopsis of a concept for a movie that is written in narrative form and eventually may be converted into a screenplay. Treatments usually run several pages, may include some dialogue, and are usually written in the third person. They are used to interest story editors, producers, and directors in commissioning a writer of a screenplay. A treatment is a selling device and should successfully convey action, mood, character, and setting.

A producer may request a treatment before hiring a writer for the screenplay in order to make sure they have the same concept in mind. If a producer is displeased with one writer's treatment, others are hired until a satisfactory concept is generated.

TURNAROUND DEAL. A turnaround deal is an arrangement in which rights to a screenwriter's work revert to the writer if it is not produced within a certain time period, usually on the provision that an amount is paid to the producer equal to what was received for the property. Screenwriters who have scripts under option to producers often negotiate turnaround deals. It is common for the writer to be paid for a property under option to be developed, even if the project is never made into a film. A writer who receives the rights to a script back is free to sell it elsewhere.

UNIONS. Trade unions in the entertainment industry are organizations that protect the rights of industry employees by negotiating for minimum wages and working conditions with employers through collective bargaining. They include the Screen Actors Guild (SAG), the American Federation of Television and Radio Artists (AFTRA), the International Alliance of Theatrical Stage Employees and Moving Picture Machine Operators of the United States and Canada (IATSE), the National Association of Broadcast Employees and Technicians (NABET), and the International Brotherhood of Electrical Workers (IBEW). The **Associated Actors and Artistes of America (Four A's)** controls the jurisdictional charters of several performance unions (including AFTRA and SAG), and reciprocal agreements between Four A's affiliates allow members in good standing of one union to join a sister union at reduced rates. Because entertainment industry unions have separate jurisdictions, union members often must join more than one union to work in multiple mediums.

Producers sometimes try to minimize the expenses of film and television production by employing workers whose wages and benefits are the least costly. There are often problems in the motion picture and television industries regarding the hiring of members of one union over another union, or using non-union workers instead of union members. Using one IATSE local over another, for example, may be cheaper. The disparity between IATSE and NABET scales and perks may be substantial enough to induce an employer to hire NABET workers over IATSE. The use of non-union workers saves money normally spent on fringe benefits. Often workers from both IATSE and NABET may be used to solve the problem.

The tables that begin on page 320 list the unions and guilds representing entertainment professionals.

UNIT. A unit is a filming crew. There are often multiple units in a motion picture production referred to numerically. The first unit is the crew that films the principal photography. The other units are engaged for particular shots. For example, the first unit may cover

Unions and Guilds

Actors' Equity Association	Equity
American Federation of Musicians	AFM
American Federation of Television and Radio Artists	AFTRA
American Guild of Variety Artists	AGVA
Directors Guild of America Inc.	DGA
International Alliance of Theatrical Stage Employees and Moving Picture Machine Operators of the United States and Canada	IATSE
International Brotherhood of Electrical Workers	IBEW
National Association of Broadcast Employees and Technicians	NABET
Screen Actors Guild	SAG
Screen Extras Guild	SEG
Writers Guild of America	WGA

Trade or Profession	Union or Guild
actor: daytime TV, live programs, videotape	AFTRA
actor: theater	Equity
actor: motion pictures and filmed television programs and commercials	SAG
animator	IATSE locals

Continued on next page

Continued from previous page

announcer: live TV, videotape, commercials, radio	AFTRA
arranger	AFM
art director	IATSE locals, NABET locals
best boy	IATSE locals, NABET locals
boom operator	IATSE locals, NABET locals
camera assistant	IATSE locals, NABET locals
camera operator	IATSE locals, NABET locals
cartoonist	IATSE locals
comedian: banquets, cabarets, nightclubs, fairs, resorts	AGVA
commercial coordinator	IATSE locals
construction coordinator	NABET locals
costume designer	IATSE locals, NABET locals
dancer: ballet, grand opera	AGVA
dancer: banquets, caberets, fairs, nightclubs, resorts	AGVA
dancer: legitimate theater	Equity
director	DGA

Continued on next page

321

Continued from previous page

Trade or Profession	Union or Guild
director, first assistant	DGA
director, second assistant	DGA
director of photography	IATSE locals, NABET locals
editor: film or electronic	IATSE locals, NABET locals
electric lighting technician	IATSE locals
electrician	IBEW locals
electronic editor	NABET locals
electronic video cameraman	NABET locals
extra (nationwide except N.Y.)	SEG
extra (N.Y. only)	SAG
film editor	IATSE locals, NABET locals
film loader	IATSE locals, NABET locals
gaffer	IATSE locals, NABET locals
graphic designer	IASTE locals
grip	IATSE locals, NABET locals
grip, motion picture studio	IATSE locals

Continued on next page

Continued from previous page

hairstylist	IATSE lcoals, NABET locals
illustrator	IATSE locals, NABET locals
instrumentalist, solo: ballet, grand opera	AGVA
key grip	IATSE locals, NABET locals
laboratory technician	IATSE locals, NABET locals
lighting technician: video	IATSE locals, NABET locals
magician: banquets, fairs, nightclubs, resorts, vaudeville	AGVA
makeup artist	IATSE locals, NABET locals
matte artist	IATSE locals, NABET locals
miniature builder	IATSE locals, NABET locals
mixer/recordist	IATSE locals, NABET locals
model maker	IATSE locals, NABET locals
motion picture editor	IATSE locals, NABET locals
music editor	IATSE locals, NABET locals
musician: recordings, film, TV videotape, videocassettes, Broadway, symphonies, clubs	AFM

Continued on next page

Continued from previous page

Trade or Profession	Union or Guild
narrator: concert, grand opera oratorio, recital	AGMA
narrator: live TV, videotape, recordings, radio	AFTRA
newsperson: live TV, video-tape, radio	AFTRA
news writer: TV	NABET locals
orchestrator	AFM
painter	IATSE locals, NABET locals
production accountant	IATSE locals
production manager	DGA
production office coordinator	IATSE locals
projectionist	IATSE locals, NABET locals
prop maker	IATSE locals, NABET locals
property master	IATSE locals, NABET locals
publicist	IATSE locals, NABET locals
recordist/boom operator	IATSE locals, NABET locals
scenic artist	IATSE locals, NABET locals

Continued on next page

Continued from previous page

script supervisor	IATSE locals, NABET locals
scriptwriter	WGA
set builder	IATSE locals, NABET locals
set designer	IATSE locals, NABET locals
set dresser	IATSE locals, NABET locals
set painter: motion picture	IATSE locals, NABET locals
shop craftsman	IATSE locals, NABET locals
singer: legitimate theater	Equity
singer: motion pictures, television, film	SAG
singer: television videotape, commercials, recordings	AFTRA
sound-effects artist: live TV, videotape, commercials, recordings	AFTRA
sound technician	IATSE locals, NABET locals
sound track editor	IATSE locals, NABET locals
special-effects person	IATSE locals, NABET locals
sportscaster: live TV, videotape	AFTRA

Continued on next page

Continued from previous page

Trade or Profession	Union or Guild
still photographer	NABET locals
story analyst	IATSE locals
stuntman	SAG
swing-gang person	IATSE locals, NABET locals
technical coordinator	DGA, NABET locals
ticket seller, movie theaters	IATSE locals
title artist	IATSE locals
transportation driver, studio (L.A.)	IATSE locals
TV maintenance engineer	NABET locals
TV recording engineer	IBEW locals
unit production manager	DGA
video illustrator	IATSE locals, NABET locals
video monitor person	IATSE locals, NABET locals
video utility person	IATSE locals, NABET locals
wardrobe attendant	IATSE locals, NABET locals
wrangler	IATSE locals

dramatic scenes, the second, action scenes, a third, miniature or special-effects shots, and a fourth, aerial sequences. In films extra units are also used for minor scenes filmed while the director is working with the leading actors. Having other units makes it possible for the main director to concentrate on the major areas of production while assistant directors cover the less complex scenes. Ultimately this practice saves both time and money.

UNIT PRODUCTION MANAGER. The unit production manager or production manager, coordinates and supervises the business affairs of a film or television production. Duties include preparing a budget, hiring personnel, setting up a production office, overseeing the movement of equipment and supplies, monitoring the budget, and taking care of location arrangements. The unit production manager reports to the producer.

The basic agreement of the **Directors Guild of America (DGA)** outlines the duties to be assigned to unit production managers.

Development Duties

- Does a **script breakdown**. The unit production manager breaks down the script into its basic components for each scene: the principal actors, major equipment, location, and shooting time. A more estensive breakdown will be done later by the assistant director.
- Prepares a **stripboard** (with the director or assistant director).
- Prepares a **budget**. The unit production manager may not be privy to the deals the producer makes with the director and the stars. The unit production manager is responsible primarily for the below-the-line budget and the above-the-line budget with numbers supplied by the producer.
- Oversees the search for locations and handles related business arrangements. Along with the **location manager**, the unit production manager may personally canvass potential location sites called for by the script.

- Prepares a "day out of days" chart that shows what days the leading actors work. This enables the unit production manager to plan the shooting in an economical way. Since SAG rules provide for day players to be paid on a consecutive-day basis, the unit production manager tries to arrange the schedule so that the days when they are not working are minimized.

Preproduction Duties

- Sets up a production office and hires a **production accountant, production coordinator**, and other production personnel.
- Hires crew members. Through years of building relationships and contacts, unit production managers have a pool of key crew people to draw upon.
- Oversees the securing of permits and clearances obtained by the location manager and communicates with local agencies regarding use of public streets or facilities.
- Updates the stripboard after locations have been scouted and selected.

By the time principal photography commences, the unit production manager should have a crew, a shooting schedule, locations, and the necessary permits.

Production Duties

- Approves **call sheets** submitted by the assistant director.
- Makes decisions relating to the budget.
- Approves purchases.
- Supervises transportation for cast and crew as well as accommodations for them when on location.
- Reviews the **production report** that is prepared each day and submitted to the studio, production company, and completion guarantor.

• Closes down the production when shooting has been completed and bills have been paid.

The unit production manager's responsibilities in television are basically the same as they are in motion pictures, although, with the smaller budgets of TV, a television unit production manager's duties may be broader in scope, including the scouting and selection of locations.

VARIETY SHOW. *See* Television Programming Genres.

VIDEO. *See* Home Video.

VOICE-OVER. *See* Dubbing.

WARDROBE SUPERVISOR. A wardrobe supervisor is responsible for costume maintenance and alteration, and for monitoring the actors' wardrobes on the sets during shooting for continuity. Over the course of one film or television day, the actors' costumes often must be steamed, cleaned, and pressed several times because the shooting of that one film day might actually span over a period of a week or longer. When the actors come in each morning, they put on costumes that have been laundered.

The wardrobe supervisor's responsibilities include:

- Breaking down the script to determine where days begin and end, and where costume changes occur.
- Laying out costumes for the principal actors.
- Supervising the upkeep of costumes.
- Making sure the actors wear the correct costumes.
- Logging the actors' costumes daily.
- Selecting outfits from a costume house with the costume designer.
- Preparing costumes as called for by the script.
- Returning costumes to the costume house at the end of production.

The wardrobe supervisor may be hired by the costume designer or the production company. Wardrobe personnel must be union members. There is no formal training available for those who seek employment as a wardrobe supervisor, although the wardrobe unions sometimes sponsor lectures, which novices might find instructional. The education comes from experience, which is gained by serving an apprenticeship. One can also break in by working in theater and then crossing over to television or film.

WESTERN. *See* **Film Genres.**

WHODUNIT MOVIE. *See* **Film Genres.**

WILD TRACK. *See* **Sound Recording, Production.**

WINNER. *See* **Hit Movie.**

WIRELESS MICROPHONE. *See* **Sound Recording, Production.**

WORK-FOR-HIRE.. In the motion picture and television industries, many works are created under *work-for-hire* or *employee-for-hire* agreements, whereby creative people are given assignments and paid salaries or fees to do whatever work the producer requests. A salaried writer, for example, might be on staff to write teleplays for a sitcom series. Or a composer might be hired to write the score to a movie.

The concept of work-for-hire is an important one because of copyright considerations. Under a work-for-hire agreement, the copyright for the original work belongs not to the author, but to the employer (usually the producer). In certain cases, renowned authors are able to retain ownership rights through negotiation.

Under the copyright law, a work made for hire is defined as: "1) a work prepared by an employee within the scope of his or her employment; or 2) a work specially ordered or commissioned for use as a contribution to a collective work, and part of a motion picture or other audiovisual work, as a translation, as a supplementary work . . . if the parties expressly agree in a written instrument signed by them that the work shall be considered a work made for hire."

The duration of copyright protection of work made for hire is seventy-five years from the date of first publication, or a term of one hundred years from the year of its creation, whichever ends first.

WRANGLER. A wrangler is an animal trainer who specializes in horses or large farm animals such as bulls, cows, and steer. On a motion picture or television set, the wrangler is in charge of the horse stock or other large farm animals. It is difficult to break into the entertainment industry as a wrangler, as there is a limited amount of work available, and often it is the same group of trainers who are hired to work in new productions. Wranglers do not have agents.

WRITERS GUILD OF AMERICA (WGA). WGA is a union representing U.S. scriptwriters in the entertainment industry. The Guild has collective bargaining agreements in several areas, including theatrical films, television films, documentaries, live television shows, and taped television shows, providing minimum compensation and terms of employment for its members in these areas.

To comply with the business statutes of California and New York, the Writers Guild comprises two separate corporations: Writers Guild of America West, and Writers Guild of America East. Writers who live west of the Mississippi River become members of WGA West; those residing east of the Mississippi join WGA East. However, the Guild is considered a single national association and members benefit from the privileges of both branches.

The Writers Guild provides services for its members that include a manuscript registration service that writers can use to register a completion date for a work (this does not satisfy the copyright law's requirement of registration, however, which is a prerequisite to commencing an infringement suit). Membership in the Writers Guild is available to anyone who has sold a script for film, television, or radio. Members pay an initiation fee and annual dues, as well as a small percentage of their annual professional earnings to the Guild.

Appendix:
Directory of TV and Movie
Organizations and Businesses

ABC
4151 Prospect Avenue
Los Angeles, CA 90027

77 West 66th Street
New York, NY 10023

Academy of Canadian Cinema
and Television
653 Yonge Street
Toronto, Ontario M4Y 1Z9

1600 Avenue De Lorimier
Montreal, P.Q. H2K 3W5

5211 Blowers Street
Halifax, Nova Scotia B35 252

Academy of Motion Pictures
Arts and Sciences
8949 Wilshire Boulevard
Beverly Hills, CA 90211-1972

Academy of Television Arts and
Sciences
3500 West Olive Avenue
Burbank, CA 91505-4628

Actors' Equity Association
165 West 46th Street
New York, NY 10036

6430 Sunset Boulevard
Los Angeles, CA 90028

Actors' Fund of America
1501 Broadway
New York, NY 10036

Alliance of Motion Picture and
Television Producers
14144 Ventura Boulevard
Sherman Oaks, CA 91423

American Cinema Editors Inc.
4416½ Finley Avenue
Los Angeles, CA 90024

American Federation of
Musicians
1501 Broadway
New York, NY 10036

American Federation of
Television and Radio Artists
260 Madison Avenue
New York, NY 10016

American Film Institute
The John F. Kennedy Center for
the Performing Arts
Washington, D.C. 20566

2021 N. Western Avenue
Los Angeles, CA 90027

American Guild of Musical Artists
12650 Riverside Drive
North Hollywood, CA 91607

1727 Broadway
New York, NY 10019

American Guild of Variety Artists
4741 Laurel Canyon Boulevard
North Hollywood, CA 91607

184 Fifth Avenue
New York, NY 10017

American Humane Association
14144 Ventura Boulevard
Sherman Oaks, CA 91423

American Marketing Association
250 South Wacker Drive
Chicago, IL 60606-5819

American Museum of the Moving Image
34-12 36th Street
Astoria, NY 11106

American Society of Cinematographers
1782 North Orange Drive
Los Angeles, CA 90028

American Society of Composers, Authors and Publishers (ASCAP)
One Lincoln Plaza
New York, NY 10023

6430 Sunset Boulevard
Hollywood, CA 90028

Arbitron
142 West 57th Street
New York, NY 10019

3333 Wilshire Boulevard
Los Angeles, CA 90010

Associated Actors and Artistes of America
165 West 46th Street
New York, NY 10036

Association of Independent Television Stations Inc.
1200 Eighteenth St., N.W.
Washington, D.C. 20036

Association of Independent Video and Filmmakers Inc.
625 Broadway
New York, N.Y. 10012

Association of Talent Agents
9255 Sunset Boulevard
Los Angeles, CA 90069

Broadcast Music Inc. (BMI)
320 West 57th Street
New York, NY 10019

6255 Sunset Boulevard
Hollywood, CA 90028

Casting Society of America
311 West 43rd Street
New York, NY 10036

6565 Sunset Boulevard
Los Angeles, CA 90028

CBS
7800 Beverly Boulevard
Los Angeles, CA 90036

51 West 52nd Street
New York, NY 10019

Canadian Radio-Television and Telecommunications Commission
Ottawa, Ontario K1A ON2

Cinema Audio Society
P.O. Box 1390
Hollywood, CA 90033

Copyright Office
Library of Congress
Washington, D.C. 20559

Directors Guild of America Inc.
7950 Sunset Boulevard
Los Angeles, CA 90046

110 West 57th Street
New York, NY 10019

Dramatists Guild
234 West 44th Street
New York, NY 10036

Federal Communications Commission
1919 M Street, W.W.
Washington, D.C. 20554

Federal Trade Commission
6th Street and Pennsylvania Avenue, N.W.
Washington, D.C. 20554

Fox Broadcasting Company
1021 West Pico Boulevard
Los Angeles, CA 90035

Harry Fox Agency
205 East 42nd Street
New York, NY 10017

Hollywood Foreign Press Association
292 South La Cienega Boulevard
Beverly Hills, CA 90211

International Alliance of Theatrical Stage Employees and Moving Picture Machine Operators of the United States and Canada
1515 Broadway
New York, NY 10036

14724 Ventura Boulevard
Sherman Oaks, CA 91403

Los Angeles Area Locals:

Local 44, Propmakers
11500 Burbank Boulevard
North Hollywood, CA 91601

Local 80, Grips
6926 Melrose Avenue
Hollywood, CA 90038

Local 659, Cameramen
7715 Sunset Boulevard
Hollywood, CA 90046

Local 695, Sound Technicians
P.O. Box 1726
Studio City, CA 91614

Local 705, Costumers
1427 North La Brea Avenue
Hollywood, CA 90046

Local 706, Make-Up and Hair
Stylists
11519 Chandler Boulevard
North Hollywood, CA 91601

Local 727, Crafts Service
14629 Nordhoff Street
Panorama City, CA 91402

Local 728, Studio Electrical
Technicians
14629 Nordhoff Street
Panorama City, CA 91401

Local 729, Motion Picture Set
Painters
11365 Ventura Boulevard
Studio City, CA 91604-3138

Local 776, Film Editors
7715 Sunset Boulevard
Hollywood, CA 90046

Local 790, Illustrators and Matte
Artists
14724 Ventura Boulevard
Sherman Oaks, CA 91403

Local 816, Scenic and Title
Artists
6180 Laurel Canyon Boulevard
North Hollywood, CA 91606

Local 818, Publicists
14724 Ventura Boulevard
Sherman Oaks, CA 91403

Local 847, Set Designers
14724 Ventura Boulevard
Sherman Oaks, CA 91403

Local 854, Story Analysts
14724 Ventura Boulevard
Sherman Oaks, CA 91403

Local 871, Script Supervisors
7061-B Hayvenhurst Avenue
Van Nuys, CA 91406

Local 876, Art Directors
14724 Ventura Boulevard
Sherman Oaks, CA 91403

Local 892, Costume Designers
Guild
14724 Ventura Boulevard
Sherman Oaks, CA 91403

Local 52, Grips, Gaffers, Sound
Effects Technicians
326 West 48th Street
New York, NY 10036

Local 161, Script Supervisors,
Production Office Coordinators
1697 Broadway
New York, NY 10019

Local 644, Camera Operators
505 Eighth Avenue
New York, NY 10018

Local 764, Wardrobe
Supervisors, Dressers, Assistants
and Star Dressers
1501 Broadway
New York, NY 10036

Local 771, Film and Videotape
Editors
353 West 48th Street
New York, NY 10036

Local 798, Makeup and Hair
Personnel
31 West 21st Street
New York, NY 10010

**International Radio and
Television Society Inc.**
420 Lexington Avenue
New York, NY 10017

International Tape Association
505 Eighth Avenue
New York, NY 10018

**Licensing Industry
Merchandisers' Association**
350 Fifth Avenue
New York, NY 10118

**Motion Picture Association of
America Inc.**
1600 Eye Street, N.W.
Washington, D.C. 20006

14144 Ventura Boulevard
Sherman Oaks, CA 91423

1133 Avenue of the Americas
New York, NY 10036

**Motion Picture Export
Association of America Inc.**
1133 Avenue of the Americas
New York, NY 10036

Museum of Broadcasting
1 East 53rd Street
New York, NY 10022

**National Academy of Television
Arts and Sciences**
National Headquarters
111 West 57th Street
New York, NY 10019

New York Chapter
1560 Broadway
New York, NY 10036

**National Association of
Broadcast Employees and
Technicians**
NABET Local 15
322 Eighth Avenue
New York, NY 10001

Local 531
2501 W. Burbank Boulevard
Burbank, CA 91505

**National Association of
Broadcasters**
1771 N Street, N.W.
Washington, D.C. 20036

**National Association of Public
Television Stations**
1818 N Street, N.W.
Washington, D.C. 20036

**National Association of
Television Program Executives**
10100 Santa Monica Boulevard
Los Angeles, CA 90067

National Cable Television Association
1724 Massachusetts Avenue, N.W.
Washington, D.C. 20036

National Captioning Institute Inc.
5203 Leesburg Pike
Falls Church, VA 22041

National Conference of Personal Managers
20411 Chapter Drive
Woodland Hills, CA 91364

National Labor Relations Board
1717 Pennsylvania Avenue, NW.
Washington, D.C. 20554

NBC
30 Rockefeller Plaza
New York, NY 10020

3000 West Alameda Boulevard
Burbank, CA 91523

A. C. Nielsen Company
Nielsen Plaza
North Brook, IL 60062

1290 Avenue of the Americas
New York, NY 10104

6255 Sunset Boulevard
Los Angeles, CA 90028

Screen Actors Guild
7065 Hollywood Boulevard
Hollywood, CA 90028-7594

1515 Broadway
New York, NY 10036

Screen Extras Guild
3629 Cahvenga Boulevard, West
Hollywood, CA 90068

SESAC Inc.
156 West 56th Street
New York, NY 10019

55 Music Square East
Nashville, TN 37203

Society of Broadcast Engineers Inc.
P.O. Box 50844
Indianapolis, IN 46250

Society of Motion Picture and Television Engineers
595 West Hartsdale Avenue
White Plains, NY 10607-1824

Studio Transportation Drivers
Local Union Number 399
4747 Vineland Avenue
North Hollywood, CA 91602

Television Bureau of Advertising
477 Madison Avenue
New York, NY 10022

Appendix: Directory of TV and Movie Organizations and Businesses

Television Information Office
745 Fifth Avenue
New York, NY 10151

Theatre Authority Inc.
16 East 42nd Street
New York, NY 10017-6907

Video Software Dealers Association
3 Eves Drive
Marlton, NJ 08053

Writers Guild of America, East
555 West 57th Street
New York, NY 10019

Writers Guild of America, West
8955 Beverly Boulevard
Los Angeles, CA 90048

ACKNOWLEDGMENTS

I am first and foremost grateful to Michael Pietsch, my editor at Harmony, who signed up this book and nurtured it from idea through publication. I wish also to thank Alec M. Foege and Margaret Drislane, the book's copy editors.

For the most part, the entries in this book are based on personal interviews with top professionals in their respective fields. Interviews, as opposed to other forms of research, enable the information to be most up-to-date and practical. Many generously gave hours of their time, and to all I am extremely grateful.

To Ray daSilva, I would like to express my utmost appreciation for his assistance with the entry on animation. Ray persevered through several interviews and rounds of proofreading, always patient and kind. A gem of a fellow!

I am very grateful to Mike Connolly, organizer and business agent of the Studio Transportation Drivers Local Union Number 399 and to Bette L. Smith of The Completion Bond Company, Inc. The entries on Transportation Coordinator/Captain and Completion Guarantor are based on information they generously provided.

I would also like to express special gratitude to the following persons for the entries they assisted with: George Hively and Jim Blakely, Film Editing; Sol Negrin, Director of Photography; Deac Rossel of the Directors Guild of America, West; Sherrill Patten, Production Auditor; Cindy Weston, Merchandise Licensing; David Phillips, Film Stocks; Samantha Dean, Public Relations; Patrizia von Brandenstein, Production Designer; Bob Schulman, Grip; Renee H. Bodner, Script Supervisor; Jim Mullaney, Financing a Film; Clement Fowler, Actor; Gustave Mortensen, Sound Recording; Joseph Musso, Illustrator entries; Michael S. Weiser, Syndication; David Ross, Story Editor; Monica D. Gilbert, Story Editor; Stanley Ackerman, Director; Cabot McMullen, Art Director; Edgard Mourino, Stuntman; Tom Wright, Property Master; Jacob Conrad, Location Manager; Robert Colloff, Local and National

Acknowledgments

Spot Advertising; Lu Ann Horstman Person, No-Budget Film; James Kelly Durgin, Script Supervisor; Mike Maddi, Special-Effects Makeup; Kenneth Haber, Location Manager.

While I wish I could list the contributions and affiliations of each of the following, there's just not enough room. But I am very indebted to them all. They are: William Fouch, Buzz Mathesius, Francis X. Hanley, Jane Carter, Mike Marden, Al Cerullo, Colleen Callaghan, Fern Buchner, Herman Buchner, Howard J. Smit, Jane Trapnell, Kevin Haney, Steve Stockage, Carolyn Zatz, Lee Haas, Candy Kugel, Henry Alford, Howard Berk, Marty Appel, Gerry Clark, George Cain, Betty Fishman, Edward J. Welsh, Walter Edel, James Gaffney, Dan O'Grady, Albert Griswold, Ed Swanson, Jim Hagerman, Larry Osborne, Ken Goss, Red Burke, Hans Dudelheim, Carey Broslovsky, Dan Wright, Eric Albertson, Steve Bobek, Arthur W. Scott, Jr., Nancy Neubauer, Bill Dunlap, Mark Davies, Donna Lerner, Alann Heldfond, Barbara Lewis Marco, Fifi Oscard, Frederick O'Neill, Jenny Shore, Dan Pinsky, Jack Spellman, Doros Evangelides, Paul Westerfer, Robert Udell, George Detitta, Nancy Casey, Beth Lynn Hand, Marjo Bernay, Andy Samet, Anna Mark, Roann L. Rubin, Jerry Moriarty, Bernice Zigas, Paul Menaguale, Jim Ryan, Victor Irving, Joanne LaVerde-Curcio, Adele Irving, Dean Spotts, Felicita Campbell-Duke, Shelton Leigh Palmer, Jonathan Angier, Ann-Marie Vitello, Moses Weitzman, Bob Bolds, Dick Swanek, Beverly Chase, Richard Dollinger, Stephen Devita, Jim Crispi, Jerry Pantzer, Konstantin Kalser, Ginny Frey, Debbie Reid, Bob Waters, Carmelita Pope, Betty Denny Smith, Steve Wagner, Paul Adler, Gary Roth, Jerry Forway, Jeanne Chrzanowski, Judy Henderson, Joseph Sangilli, Ken Golden, Norm Hess, Ron Inman, Don Thieme, Dawn Steinberg, Carole Strasser, Walter W. Wurfel, Fredda Briant, Kenneth Yount, John Leverance, Scott Hersh, Patrick Stockstill, John F. Vorisek, Victor Nerone, Joe Wachter, John Kasarda, Dana Kornbluth.

I am immensely grateful to Henry Bloomstein and Hal Dresner, whose special insights into the motion picture and television industries were most helpful. And to Bonnie Schachter for being the agent of introduction here.

Acknowledgments

Among the many professional organizations I would like to thank are the following: Stuntman's Association, Actors' Fund of America, ASCAP, BMI, SESAC, Harry Fox Agency, IATSE, Television Information Office, NABET Local 15, Academy of Canadian Cinema and Television, and Theatre Authority.

Among the publications used for research were *Variety*, *The Hollywood Reporter*, *Broadcasting/Cablecasting Yearbook*, NBC's 1985 and 1986 Annual Reports, "The Voluntary Movie Rating System" by Jack Valenti of MPAA, and "The MPAA and MPEAA," "The Story of the Screen Actors Guild," the Directors Guild of America Basic Agreement, and various materials of the Federal Communications Commission.

I am very grateful to the literary agent, Martha Millard.

I am most indebted to my typist, Margaret Dyke, who was available at all hours of the day, every day, and who always cheerfully accepted my pages of chicken scratch. Paulette Kloepfer also handled typing chores.

Finally, loving thanks to my wife, Marla, who patiently endured long periods of separation from me during the research and writing of this book.

Research Assistant: Craig Rachlin